Praise for *The Red Years*

"Gavin Walker's extraordinary collection of essays on the long Japanese '68 is a path-breaking contribution to a history capable of theorizing the present. Singly, each brilliant chapter illuminates new facets of the decade's energetic politics of global insurrection. Together, they clarify how the political problem of '68 continues to constrain the left. So long as defeat appears as liberation, even victorious struggles will reinforce what they aim to overthrow."

Jodi Dean, author of *Comrade*

"This invaluable collection redraws the political and philosophical maps that continue to frame our understanding of the last great challenge, on a world scale, to the dominant order of things. Walker's *The Red Years* testifies to the exceptionally inventive and far-reaching scope of the rebellions that shaped Japan all through the 1960s and early '70s, and it shows how their unended history, like that of other apparently defeated or 'failed' revolutions, continues to inspire principled defiance to this day."

Peter Hallward, author of *The Will of the People and the Struggle for Mass Sovereignty*

"*The Red Years* is an exciting collection that brings to life the original *theoretical* developments surrounding the Japanese 1968, which are not merely of historical interest but instead offer revolutionary potential for our political situation today."

Michael Hardt, coauthor (with Antonio Negri) of *Empire*

"*The Red Years*, edited by Gavin Walker, brings together a number of perceptive essays that seek to chart the convergence when, in the decade of the 1960s, Japan both broke out of a slumbered spell of isolation imposed by America's long postwar domination, marking what writer and thinker Takeuchi Yoshimi proclaimed as the beginning of the Japanese Revolution, and encountered the epochal world historical conjuncture of May '68 and a triumphalist Third World struggle against colonialism. If the former provided a release from an American-induced seclusion to turn Japanese society toward engaging the wider world, the latter sparked the production of new worldly thought that promised to realize the conjuncture's revolutionary awakening. While May '68 was a revolution that failed to happen, the globally driven perspectives of the essays in Walker's *The Red Years* masterfully show the inscription of an energetic intellectual afterlife in the working-through of a mission to rescue the memory of rebellion's ruins and reanimate its vanquished possibilities for a different historical time, and, as Gramsci might have advised, armed with the appropriate political vocation."

Harry Harootunian, author of *Marx after Marx*

The Red Years

Theory, Politics, and Aesthetics in the Japanese '68

Edited by Gavin Walker

VERSO
London • New York

First published by Verso 2020

1 3 5 7 9 10 8 6 4 2

Verso
UK: 6 Meard Street, London W1F 0EG
US: 20 Jay Street, Suite 1010, Brooklyn, NY 11201
versobooks.com

Verso is the imprint of New Left Books

ISBN-13: 978-1-78863-722-2
ISBN-13: 978-1-78873-163-8 (LIBRARY)
ISBN-13: 978-1-78663-724-6 (US EBK)
ISBN-13: 978-1-78663-723-9 (UK EBK)

British Library Cataloguing in Publication Data
A catalogue record for this book is available from the British Library

Library of Congress Cataloging-in-Publication Data
A catalog record for this book is available from the Library of Congress
LCNN: 2020944759

Typeset in Minion Pro by Hewer Text UK Ltd, Edinburgh
Printed and bound by CPI Group (UK) Ltd, Croydon CR0 4YY

For Anne, who “won’t give up”

Contents

Acknowledgments

The present volume is in every way a collective product, a product of discussions, encounters, and shared problematics. In particular, I would like to single out the discussions I have had with Yutaka Nagahara over the last fifteen years, discussions that have shaped my grasp of the moment of 1968, but especially of the question of how we are to continue in the wake of '68, not only for those who lived this moment, but also those of us who inherited it as both a beacon and a burden of politics and thought. My deep gratitude and appreciation goes to Yutaka, for our theoretical-political discussions over many years, for his concrete work in making sure the present volume could be realized, and for his friendship and support.

I owe thanks to many colleagues and friends for discussions and suggestions over the years. Beyond the present contributors, I would mention in particular Sandeep Banerjee, Tani Barlow, Subho Basu, Bruno Bosteels, Nathan Brown, Luca Caminati, Eric Cazdyn, Brett de Bary, Kanishka Goonewardena, Ken Kawashima, J. Victor Koschmann, Asad Haider, Harry Harootunian, Katsuya Hirano, Rebecca Karl, Jonathan Martineau, Junichiro Matsumoto, Sandro Mezzadra, Salar Mohandesi, Benjamin Noys, Kenta Ohji, Kosuke Oki, Jason Opal, William Clare Roberts, Naoki Sakai, Masha Salazkina, Hasana Sharp, Jason Smith, Robert Stolz, Daviken Studnicki-Gizbert, Mark Winchester, and Yves Winter. I discussed this project a number of times with Jarrett Rudy, who tragically left us in April 2020. I would like to remember him here. Guy Yasko provided initial translations of three of the texts. His own work on the history of the Japanese '68 is essential reading. Felix Fuchs provided editorial and research assistance. The research project in recent years directed by Yoshihiko Ichida and Kenta Ohji on thought and politics after '68 at Kyoto University's Institute for Research in the Humanities has been a source of inspiration and theoretical orientation. Sebastian Budgen expressed a strong interest in this project a number of years ago and has long supported me in making it a concrete reality. His friendship, support, encouragement, patience, and persistence have been absolutely crucial, along with that of the Verso staff, particularly Rosie Warren and Cian McCourt. I owe many thanks in innumberable ways to John Frederick Walker and Elin McCoy for their love and support. Rachel Sandwell is always the first interlocutor: our shared love, life, and politics inform everything herein. Anne Walker is the spontaneously "ultraleft adventurist" conduit of goodness, joy, thought, and love that makes it all worthwhile. She insists that she "will never give up" and I believe her.

For support in the creation of this volume, I owe thanks to the Institute for the Public Life of Arts and Ideas at McGill University, where I was a Faculty Fellow from 2016–18, the Social Sciences and Humanities Research Council of Canada for an Insight Grant, the McGill Faculty of Arts for an internal SSHRC grant, and Kyoto University's Institute for Research in the Humanities, where I was a visiting researcher in 2019.

Note on the Text

Throughout this book, Japanese language is transliterated according to the modified Hepburn system, with the macron indicating a long vowel—for example, *kaikyū tōsō*.

Japanese names referenced in the text—with the exception of the contributors to the present volume—are given in Japanese order (surname first and given name second) except in cases where the person in question is known under the Western order (given name first and surname second).

1

Revolution and Retrospection

Gavin Walker

Hegel once famously wrote that "what is well known, precisely because it is *well* known, is not known at all."[1] This line sums up, in effect, our "knowledge" of the global 1960s—we know the story around the world so well, too well in fact, but it is this "little knowledge" that leads us continually into error, that tells us that this period and chain of events is just another period, with a timeline, with principal actors, with an easily summed up "moral of the story." Like so many historical moments when revolution was on the agenda, the moment we enter this retrospective knowledge into our general encyclopedia of a closed and achieved history, we have lost all the contingency, openness, and possibility of the era. But history has a way of surprising us, not with novelty in its immediacy, but with the novelty of what has never yet been properly entered into the seemingly immovable structure of the existing knowledge. In this sense, this volume of critical and theoretical reflections on the "red years," the Japan of the long '68—and we might call it the longest '68 on earth, stretching from 1960–73, or even polemically from 1955–73—aims to unsettle what little knowledge already exists in English and other European languages dealing with this phenomenon. Above all, this volume and its contents refuse the dominant mode of approaching such "facts," refusing first and foremost to relegate the "non-European" '68s to mere "data sets" of political upheavals that still locate their "thought"

1 G. W. Hegel, *Phenomenology of Spirit*, trans. Terry Pinkard, New York: Cambridge University Press, 2017, 20. Translation modified.

in French-, German-, and English-language documents, instead choosing actively to see this moment and its terms as itself an instance of thought, of another emancipatory universal, a chain of signification as relevant conceptually and politically for North America and Western Europe as it was for Japan.

Rather than a year as such, we ought to think of 1968 in Japan as a period of nearly thirteen years, from the experience of the first mass movement against the renewal of the United States–Japan Joint Security Treaty (Anpō, in its Japanese abbreviation) in 1960 through to the bloody and grim end of the United Red Army in the mountains of Nagano Prefecture in 1972. The following volume of critical reflections and essays on the experience, thought, and political legacy of the Japanese 1968 appears over a half-century after this pivotal global moment. In the ensuing years, the geopolitical order has transformed in ways that could never have been foreseen from its vantage point, and the global level of technical development has been revolutionized. In numerous ways, the thought and concepts of 1968 predicted in part the transformations of our world, while in others, they remain linked to a world that no longer exists, especially since the epochal moments of 1989–91.

In the final analysis today, the historical process situates us further from the global 1968 than ever; in fact, we ought to remember that 1968 is now closer to the epochal moment of 1917 and the global impact of the October Revolution than we currently are to the changes brought about by '68 and its political culture. Do we then need to speak of an "end of 1968"? The present volume follows a different logic. In Kristin Ross's crucial *May '68 and Its Afterlives,* she calls instead for a reflexive doubling of this question, a call, in a sense, for "an end to . . . the end of May."[2] Like the French May, the notion of the Japanese '68—or the longer Japanese 1960s—has been the product of innumerable endings: the bloody end of its utopian character, with the descent into internal terrorism of certain armed-struggle organizations, its end in the Japanese '70s, conditioned by the international oil crisis and growing speculative bubble economy, an end to radical thought as much of the former left settles into old-age liberalism. But perhaps what we need the most is an end to these endings, an end to the melancholic treatment of the radical postwar Japanese years,

2 Kristin Ross, *May '68 and Its Afterlives*, Chicago: University of Chicago Press, 2002, 215.

whereby they are remembered, but only in the style of commemoration. To commemorate is also to entomb. In a moment of global crisis, an end to the end of the Japanese "red years" would provide us with a powerful body of thought, knowledge, struggle, organization, the exercise of power, the reflection on the tasks of politics, and the spirit of rebellion.

The present volume of essays and investigations does not purport to be a comprehensive history; it cannot be. The events of the long 1968 in Japan are too manifold and made up of too many interdependent storylines to be told as one. And if anything, what we have too much of today is a type of history-as-trivia of 1968. There is no shortage of conceptually impoverished writing on 1968 across the world, more or less simply recounting a timeline of supposed "events" in narrative form, as if chronology would give us access to *what happened*. The majority of "'68 histories" today have done nothing but overwhelm us with the trivia of another time, in that sense functioning only to neatly seal off '68 into the entombed past, where it safely and comfortably buttresses our weary, nostalgic disavowal. As a historical object, 1968 is subtly erased by the positivist "history" done around it, its danger eliminated by its melancholy relegation to a long list of "failed experiments." If we are to try to imagine what was—and *what is*—this uncanny thing called 1968, we must take it as a problem of the present, as *our* problem. In essence, what we lack around 1968—with a few notable exceptions—is *thought*.

It is in this sense that Ross also powerfully characterizes what she calls the two "confiscations" of the Parisian May '68: on one hand, the tendency toward biography or personalization of this period; on the other, the reduction to the merely sociological or empirical. Perhaps Ross, more than any other contemporary thinker on the aftermath and afterlife of '68, is the one who has attempted to restore to us exactly this element: the possibility of '68 as thought in the present, and, in a sense, her work serves as a kind of lodestar that a new generation of thinkers, inspired by '68 but living through its ambivalent aftermath, has used to orient itself (ourselves). It is this project that the present volume attempts to assist, a project of rethinking the actuality of '68 rather than buttressing its status as a mere "fact" of the past. Yet we must wager on a flirtation with the empirical, if only to emphasize that we have not yet gained a global grasp of '68, because our world and its globalization remains a globalization of capital and of institutions, not a globalization of resistance or a globalization of forms of thought. Even fifty years after the simultaneous world revolutions of the long '68, the left remains fragmented and parceled into linguistic enclosures that hinder a consciousness of the common historical actuality of our struggles.

The analysis of May '68 in Paris, the impact of the Prague Spring, and the mobilizations in West Germany have been widely disseminated in the fields of intellectual and social history, social theory, and political thought. May '68—both its actuality and its mythology, as the conceptually iconic or metonymic year of the 1960s—is by now a canonical moment of modern European history or, perhaps, the history of "the West." But 1968 is not only a year that conjures up images of Paris, Frankfurt, or Berkeley: it is also, in some sense, the pivotal year for a new anticolonial and anticapitalist politics to erupt across the Third World, a crucial and central moment in the history, thought, and politics of Asia, Africa, the Middle East, and Latin America.

Today, over fifty years after 1968, this broader global legacy of "the other '68" is crucial for us to rediscover, in thought, in histories, and in the memory and actuality of another combative left that asserted itself in the wake of decolonization and the great Third World uprisings (the Chinese revolution of 1949, the Cuban revolution of 1959, and the connections and links of both Bandung nonalignment and new proletarian internationalisms).

The Japanese case is perhaps the least known—outside of Japan, at any rate—but one of the most expansive and important moments of the global insurrection that goes under the name of 1968. After the end of World War II, the Japanese Communist Party (JCP) returned to the forefront of Japanese society, bolstered by the sacrifice and legitimacy of its main leaders, Tokuda Kyūichi (imprisoned for eighteen years under the fascist government) and Nosaka Sanzō, who had spent the bulk of the war years in clandestine operations for the Comintern, and with the Chinese Communist Party in Yenan and the liberated base areas, fighting his own country's imperialist expansion on the front lines. Hailed as uncorrupted by the war years, the JCP and the Japanese Socialist Party undertook a concerted electoral effort in 1946 and '47. Alarmed at the wide favor these parties enjoyed, MacArthur and the Supreme Command of the Allied Powers (SCAP) made a pivotal decision: what came to be known among historians as the "reverse course," changing strategy to prevent the spread of socialism rather than principally attempt to rid the Japanese state of fascism. Thus, the so-called "red purges" of the late 1940s attempted to destroy the sudden resurgence of the prewar Japanese communist tradition, once the strongest in Asia (in the 1920s and '30s), and the source of major theoretical work in Marxist thought. This drove the JCP underground and led to a short period (late '40s to 1955) of emphasis on armed struggle, underground clandestine work, and a renewed proximity to the Chinese line. In 1955, however, at the Sixth Congress of the postwar JCP, this line of armed struggle in the countryside was repudiated, its supporters expelled, and a new "historic compromise" (along the lines of the Italian Communist Party) was installed, paving the way for the JCP's full transition to reformism and participation in government.

But as the 1950s drew to a close, a new social mass of students, intellectuals, workers, peasants, and the popular classes was once again rising, in particular around the 1960 renewal of the Anpō treaty. The inaugural mass demonstrations of the 1960s around this issue mobilized immense numbers: a single one of the three major general strikes called by the unions brought 6.2 million onto the streets in June 1960. With this intense level of mobilization, a new combative left had formed, heralding a new social arrangement: no longer beholden to the JCP, who were by now regarded by many on the left to have betrayed their politics, this New Left in Japan came to produce one of the most intense decades of political organization, political thought, and political aesthetics in the global twentieth century.

However, in recent years, the retrospective evaluation of 1968 in Japan has become something of a "sad passion" in the Spinozist sense. The outright enemies of 1968 are no longer the problem: the key problem is the "decent" academic, democratic liberal, for whom '68 remains important but who is now resigned to a sad, melancholic nostalgia for "engagement" and "participation"—or, even worse, for the possibilities of "civil society." This "sad passion" inhabits such a wide array of figures and discourses in contemporary Japan that it is almost ubiquitous, culminating in the phone-book sized text of Oguma Eiji, titled simply *1968*.[3] This text, which can be internationally compared to the interventions of Todd Gitlin and others, is an exhausting/exhaustive bibliographic summary of 1968 as trivia, in a double sense. On the one hand, it is literally a *trivial* book, full of trivial ideas, liberal platitudes, and pre-critical conceptions of politics. On the other hand, it is also a book devoted to flattening an irreducible concept-period into the realm of pure trivia, a collection of somewhat interrelated facts, events, testimonies, and archival texts, to

3 Oguma Eiji, *1968*, 2 vols., Tokyo: Shin'yōsha, 2009.

produce an utterly meaningless whole, eviscerated of any conceptual problems. The reduction to trivia is a gesture within history, a historical act to eliminate the *historicity* of 1968, the fact that it remains *present to us* as a challenge of thought.

The present volume intervenes against such readings. It is not a question of upholding 1968 as some fetishistic object against its betrayers and apostates, but a question of *refusing to give up on its potential.* To refuse to give up on '68 is not to treat it uncritically, nor is it to simply worship at its feet, as if the period had not been one of extraordinary heterogeneity and intense contestations. Nor is it to posit a unitary, univocal '68, one in which the very term "'68" would come to deliver a clear and obvious meaning. Having said that, there is also here an important and critical lesson in the discipline of history. So much recent social history of the radical politics of the twentieth century has found itself reduced to a rather sad and generalized liberalism, constantly emphasizing that the work of history is to "complicate" and "make ambiguous" the supposedly simple dialectic of reaction and resistance. Such social history—now more or less hegemonic in "empire studies" or histories of the global 1960s—has replaced the older political commitments with a new kind of bureaucratic or administrative project: making sure to render political clarity into motivational "complexity" or "ambiguity." For instance, should we take seriously the primacy of politics for the FLN in Algeria? The contemporary social historian will reply: yes, but we ought to also know what the militants ate, the clothes they wore, the sexual relations between them, the social dramas of their internal culture, and the style of their aesthetic life. Importantly, however, this turn toward the everyday has not been one firmly situated within a *political* concept of everydayness—like that deployed in Ross' important and pivotal *May '68 and Its Afterlives,* a notable exception. Over the past thirty years, but particularly in the most recent decades, the historical profession has seen a dramatic new turn toward the social sciences: virtually all of the currently dominant trends within the discipline—the new social history, new urban histories, new forms of political history, historical demography, and historical sociology—all take a point of departure in their "return to the archive," so to speak, emphasizing a new materiality of the past beyond an exclusive focus on institutions and achieved situations. This "return" has yielded extraordinary new histories of global projects, of political belonging, of social upheaval, and so forth. In a sense, it has revolutionized the work of the professional historian to a remarkable degree—often nearly singularizing it as a discipline proximate to the other "archival" social sciences. But history in particular has a remarkably multivalent status as a discipline of knowledge.

From classical thought through the canonical figures of the Western philosophical tradition—say, through Hegel or Vico—history and its writing remained generally understood as a division within the broad field of rhetoric. That is, historiography—a contested and slippery term, to be sure, but let us use it here to signify history *writing*—was understood first and foremost as a form of knowledge conditioned *principally* by its written character. In such a sense, history exhibited an entirely different proximity: rather than to social-scientific inquiry, the natural or expected proximity exhibited here was instead to literature and especially to literary forms. Hayden White often quoted Jacques Barzun to the effect that history, strictly speaking, does not exist—cannot exist—in any way without being written. Such an emphasis, while seemingly obvious (and certainly Barzun's original point served simply to differentiate history from myth, from ideology, from sentiment, from sheer knowledge), nevertheless contains a crucial point: that historiographical writing exists *under the condition of writing as such*. To exist under the condition of writing opens up a space of infinite regress: the condition of writing implies the specific history of writing systems, it implies structural features of a grammar, the conceptual features of sentences, the position of subjects, objects, verbs, but also narrative structures: metaphor, metonymy, allegory, analogy, and so on. Benedetto Croce famously argued that history was the product of the combination of philology and philosophy, and only through this combination could what lay in the archive (which he termed the "certain") be converted into the "true," the task of historiography itself, and our task in the present collection.

The texts in this volume consist of reflections on the legacy, thought, and social, historical, and political context of this era, all of which take seriously the *thought* of '68 as a problem *for us*. In 1969, Hiroshi Nagasaki wrote one of the most important theoretical texts not just "on" the movement, but *of* the movement, in the form of his *Hanranron* or "Theory of Rebellion." Developing at length a powerful reflection on the category of rebellion itself, Nagasaki's piece here is a new intervention, commissioned solely for this volume. Providing a formidable overview of the historical development of the Zenkyōtō movement, in which he himself was a major figure, Nagasaki gives the entire volume a structuring historical grasp that culminates in his call to create for ourselves a new inheritance of '68—to enact it again, a powerful call to arms from one of the most important thinkers of this moment. Yoshihiko Ichida likewise takes up Nagasaki's work, on the questions of the party and the "agitator," a subjective disposition that is powerfully cross-read with European developments in the same period, in figures such as Mario Tronti and Louis Althusser. Drawing our attention back from the philosophical to the historical register, William Marotti extends his own wide-ranging work on the Japanese '60s to give us an intense history of the struggles—both on the street and immediately mediatized—of the "Japanese" '68 and also to insist that there is no specific "particularity" or "Japaneseness" to this global moment, but a local inflection of a broader world process. Marotti takes influence from—like Nagasaki—Rancière's "dissensus," a conception of the political that militates at all times against an obvious, given, immediate experience of politics solely delimited to "what appears political." This leads Marotti to touch on the arts—his specialization—an analysis that is echoed in the piece by his collaborator, Yoshiko Shimada. Shimada, in her own right an important figure of post-'60s art and its feminist inflection, analyzes the role played by radical publishing company Gendai Shichōsha on the aesthetic front, providing avenues and spaces of intervention for the organizations of the left in the wake of the 1969 occupation of the University of Tokyo. Taken together, Marotti and Shimada also provide a crucial roadmap for the "afterlives" of the Japanese '68 and the pathways by which its thought, concepts, and forms of movement permeated into post-'68 publishing, the arts, and activist circles.

Setsu Shigematsu, known for her important work on the women's liberation movement in 1960s Japan, offers to this volume a crucial overview of both of the radical feminist currents that emerged at this moment, but also a powerful corrective to the frequent tendency in the history of radical politics in Japan (and everywhere, frankly) to minimize the contributions of nonhegemonic groups and leaders. Shigematsu reminds us of the long, complex, and still-resonant critiques that radical feminism of the '60s made of its liberal counterparts. "Women's liberation" was the battle cry, a demand that has today been eclipsed by new liberalisms of the "lean-in" variety. Complementing Shigematsu's synthetic grasp of feminism in these "red years" is the text of Chelsea Szendi Schieder, whose recent work has given us a crucial historical analysis of the category of the female student in the 1960s New Left. To say that the global New Left was unable to avoid the broader social determinations of the moment, including an often radical rhetoric of feminism and women's liberation coupled to regressive gender politics at the organizational level (male cadre theorizing, female cadre cleaning up), is to simply state the obvious. Any historical rethinking of the experience of the global '60s must reckon with the gendered organizational legacies that this moment often produced.

Hidemi Suga, one of the most prolific writers of the radical left on the legacy of 1968 and a former participant in the movement himself, here provides a synthetic analysis of the development of '68 and its place within postwar Japanese history, a history in which certain institutions—chief among them the "Emperor system"—remain fixtures of the political landscape. Suga's analysis takes in both an organizational grasp of the 1968 movements and their political party formations as well as an intellectual historical analysis linked to major figures of postwar Japanese history, such as Maruyama Masao. He locates one of the most crucial political-intellectual crossroads of '68 thought in the encounter between the Zenkyōtō movement and Yukio Mishima, probably the best-known postwar Japanese writer on a global scale, important figure of the Japanese literary tradition, and self-made intellectual of the radical right wing. Mishima's legacy, however, is quite a bit more complicated than to simply relegate him to the status of a banal fascist counterpart to the movements of the left. As Suga demonstrates incisively, Mishima's theoretical grasp of the place of the emperor-system in the postwar era touched on a blind spot of much analysis of the time and, in a sense, was more probing of the social foundations of postwar democracy than many aspects of the movement.

Yoshiyuki Koizumi contributes here a remarkable and important reflection on a quite understudied question: the thought, internal culture, and political shifts of the Japanese Communist Party in relation to 1968. In a way, the story of the JCP has been often simply told in such a way as to sound familiar globally: the official communist parties around the world largely held the 1960s rebellions in disdain, considering them "petty bourgeois" in character, "adventurist" in political terms, and even "antiworker" in rather blinkered Stalinist terms. Like the French and Italian parties in the postwar European context, the JCP has long had a genuinely mass base with an extremely large membership, in comparison to other OECD countries. And aspects of the JCP have also retained insurrectionist elements, even if its mainstream discourse tended toward social democracy and parliamentary participation.

Koizumi's original, striking, and powerful discussion also provides an important analysis of the ways in which the JCP position through the years of the "long '68" also provided a point of departure for us to understand how it is that the JCP could last so long as an organization when its comparable Eurocommunist parties have long since collapsed into relative obscurity.

Yutaka Nagahara and Alberto Toscano, both in their own ways, chart out our own inheritances of these "red years" as thought. Nagahara's extraordinary piece—both personal in its important generational analysis and analytically powerful in its theoretical conclusions—begins with a reminder that '68 was not a year, but a period. Treating head-on the bloody end of this moment (although the post-'68 armed-struggle organizations would continue almost into the 1980s) in the United Red Army's standoff at Mt. Asama Lodge, and the subsequent grim discovery of their internal killings, Nagahara reminds us that such moments did not come from the fringes exclusively—anyone who had taken seriously the call of rebellion on the streets could have found themselves on a pathway to the armed struggle. Nagahara's theoretical summation of the experience of these "red years" also considers the question of persistence: how to go on after defeat. Rather than simply treat '68 with melancholy, Nagahara exhorts us to *inherit* '68 after its events, but precisely in order to remake them as a precursor to another departure for revolution in our time. Toscano extends his important work on the category of "fanaticism" in relation to the Japanese '68, a crucial theoretical task for us, as it is the primary "mainstream" mechanism through which the most radical sections of the Japanese experience of the global 1960s are understood. In particular, Toscano's analysis adds a crucial look at the centrality of film—and a specific type of radical filmmaking—to the Japanese '68. Treating in particular Oshima Nagisa and Wakamatsu Koji, Toscano broadens his reflection into an important, reflexive unfolding of the glimpses of the Japanese '68 that have appeared in contemporary European thought, only in order to remind us that the appearance of these figures of fanaticism, the trauma (and its return) of "late fascism," provides points of theoretical connectivity between the radical years and its global modernity, never simply sealed into signifiers of national uniqueness.

What all of these contributions share is an attempt not simply to recount "what happened" but to *think with* the Japanese '68. To think with '68 is to restore it to history, to take it away from the field of memory, where it is sealed into the museum, the memorial, and the testament. To restore the historicity of '68 is also to insist that its problems—inflected differently, of course—remain our own, that nothing about it has been solved, only left behind. To paraphrase Nagahara's text, included in this volume, we have to conjure up '68 not to mourn it post-eventally, but to restore from this defeat a new pre-evental politics in our own time.

2

On the Japanese '68

Hiroshi Nagasaki

Once There Was a Japanese '68 . . .

The Japanese 1968 can be seen as represented, above all, by the Zenkyōtō movement—the "All-Campus Joint Struggle League." At the national institution of the University of Tokyo (*tōdai*, in its Japanese abbreviation), for instance, the struggle against student penalties in the Department of Medicine began in January 1968. Independently, however, at the private Nihon University, protest actions by students demanding autonomy took place in May, following revelations of irregular accounting practices on the part of the administration. This was the first experience of the student movement at Nihon University.

Each of these mobilizations, in the early period of '68, began around points of contestation specific to their individual educational settings. However, news of the simultaneous, multiply occurring rebellions, such as the university struggles in the United States and the Parisian May, reached Japan and exerted an influence on its own '68 movements, developing a qualitative similarity that came to be known among dissidents around the world. In other words, *in Japan there was a 1968*. In order for us to understand its specificity and commonality, we must contribute to an elucidation of the historical turning point that Immanuel Wallerstein has termed "the world revolution of 1968."

The Zenkyōtō movement was organized around the All-Campus Joint Struggle League—the name adopted by the militant group that emerged from the 1968 movements in struggle at various universities.

The league objected to the university administrations and professors; the movement stood out for its characteristic strikes (abandonment of classes) in addition to its occupations of university buildings. The Zenkyōtō movement began at the University of Tokyo and Nihon University, respectively, and expanded rapidly to the other major universities over the subsequent three years, until roughly 1970. Among four-year universities across the country, 127 universities (or 24 percent nationally) experienced strikes or occupations in 1968, and in 1969 this rose to 153 universities (41 percent). There was also a Zenkyōtō movement in the high schools. Due to its scale and relatively homogeneous quality across the country, the Zenkyōtō movement is seen as the archetypal or representative movement of the Japanese '68.

However, we ought to state clearly in advance that there is a prehistory to the 1968 Zenkyōtō movement. There were, for example, student movements in 1965 at Keio University and in 1966 at Waseda University against the raising of tuition fees. In occupying these institutions and declaring the presence of the commune, these movements clearly possessed a set of characteristics that heralded the coming of the Zenkyōtō movement. Moreover, it was the second half of the 1960s that saw an intensification of the American war on Vietnam. The resistance movements against the Vietnam War were also forerunners, in this sense, of the development of the Zenkyōtō. From 1968 onward, in addition to the Zenkyōtō movement in the universities, there were the parallel anti-war struggles in the streets, organized by the political parties (or sects) of the New Left, and the movements mutually upheld each other. The struggles in the streets saw the participation not only of students but also of workers, although this participation by workers was not organized within the labor unions or mainstream parties. This was, rather, the Youth Anti-War Committee [Hansen seinen i'inkai], an anti-war organization of young workers that shared fundamental characteristics with the Zenkyōtō.

In the broad sense, then, we can say that given the scale and characteristics of the movement itself, the Japanese '68 in general found its representative expression in the Zenkyōtō movement. Turning specifically to the University of Tokyo struggle, I want to recall somewhat the *concrete* history of the Japanese '68.

The Zenkyōtō Movement

The University of Tokyo All-Student Joint Struggle Committee [Tōdai tōsō zengaku kyōtō kaigi] (the Tōdai Zenkyōtō) was formed on July 5, 1968. The graduate students' all-student struggle union (Zentōren in abbreviation) and the joint-struggle committee of university assistants were also included within the Tōdai Zenkyōtō in its broad sense. Officially recognized student councils existed within all ten of the university's departments, but these were also largely held by the Japanese Communist Party's youth wing, the Democratic Youth League of Japan, known colloquially as Minsei (an abbreviation of Minshushugi seinen dōmei). Independent of these councils, the Zenkyōtō formed as a university-wide mechanism comprised of the struggle committees from each department. Up to this point, mobilizing in the student movement meant conforming to the rules of the student council and constituting a clear majority within it. The Zenkyōtō, however, was formed in a voluntarist manner—or *directly democratically*, so to speak—through the conditions of struggle by those who were themselves struggling, as an extralegal organization operating outside the rules (and unrecognized by the university administration) that consciously opposed the existing type of conformism. The Zenkyōtō had no rules. Neither membership nor leadership were governed by rules or protocols, but rather were entrusted to each individual's autonomy, it might be said. Political sects along with a multitude of nonpartisan small groups participated in the movement, but these organizations fought under the banner of each specific university in the Zenkyōtō. From the moment of its formation, the Zenkyōtō spread to universities across the entirety of Japan, something never before seen in the postwar Japanese student movement, marking the specific character of 1968. On the other hand, due to its overthrowing of the democratic institution of the student councils and the long-standing political wisdom accumulated through them, the Zenkyōtō as an organization overburdened itself from the outset with political difficulties peculiar to the practice of direct democracy, difficulties that actualized themselves alongside the movement's development.

The Tōdai Zenkyōtō put forward seven demands to the university administration as strategic objectives of the movement. These began with the demand for the "total retraction of unjust punishments in the Department of Medicine," and ended with the following call: "The above six demands must be committed to in writing within a public negotiation, and the responsible parties must take responsibility by resigning." The term "public negotiation" [*taishū danko*] here indicates a form of negotiation derived originally from the opposition between the trade unions and management. The Zenkyōtō, unrecognized as an official entity, took the stance that it would accept the results of demands put forward through the site of direct exchange —the public or mass negotiation—with the administration.

In examining the aims of the Tōdai Zenkyōtō through these seven points, the movement's overall demand was for individual, concrete rights. In this sense, it posed a *possible* issue: given the history of Japanese student movements, it was what had come to be referred to traditionally as a "school-specific struggle" [*kobetsu gakuen tōsō*], in contrast to a nationwide political struggle, and as such, ought to be resolved independently by the university itself. The movement posed demands for rights concerning tuition fees, the curriculum, and student self-governance—what Minsei referred to as "democratization of the schools." What came to be the ultimate form of school struggle, though, was the boycotting of classes—in other words, the strike. While the Zenkyōtō movement began outside of the institutional framework of democracy, its tasks and tactics were either adopted or rejected by majority decision making in the officially recognized student assembly. Moreover, the point that characterized the University of Tokyo struggle was that the resolution to strike (and its eventual abandonment) depended until the end on the decisions of the student assembly, and there the students of the Zenkyōtō faction not only participated in the assembly but worked to form a majority. That struggle was also characterized by the fact that the strike began in the medical school, and it was the engineering students and graduate students who reacted most sensitively to this action. In other words, the struggle began from the department that, even within the Tōdai educational structure, most retained the characteristics of the guild system (which was the most backward in terms of democratization). We can see here, then, one reason that the medical faculty association's structure aggravated the problem of punishments within the department.

The Zenkyōtō movement quickly transformed from demanding rights based on democratic legal forms into a phase that I call the student insurrection or rebellion [*gakusei hanran*], which burst through the limits of the individual school struggles. In June, the Zenkyōtō occupied the clock tower, the central symbol of Tōdai's Hongo campus, and maintained the occupation until January of the following year, after the incursion of riot police. Then, on June 11, the Zenkyōtō of Nihon University began its blockade of the school buildings using barricades. This was a form of struggle not previously seen within the Japanese student movement. Of course, it goes without saying that an awareness of the days of insurrection and rebellion in the Parisian May had also been widely circulated in Japan. The blockades and occupations were independent actions, undertaken without the approval of the official student councils or assemblies. Typically, the radicals who blockaded administration buildings with barricades ended up defeated and isolated, not only due to the intervention of the riot police but also because they were besieged by the "regular" students. Minsei, the JCP youth league, counted on this being the case, but, contrary to expectations, official resolutions by the student assemblies for an indefinite strike that presupposed occupations and blockades spread to all universities. Additionally, the opening of the indefinite strike on July 3 by the College of General Education (at the Komaba campus), which accounted for more than half of the total student body, gave an enormous impetus to the whole movement. At Komaba, with its large number of students, the students' assembly consisted of representatives, but the resolution to strike was taken through a university-wide vote. The result: out of 4,870 possible votes, 2,632 were in favor and 1,904 were against, with 333 abstentions. The total enrollment at the time was 7,119, so nearly 70 percent of the student body participated in the vote. The indefinite strike persisted until the following year. With the participation of the Department of Law beginning on October 12, all ten major departments had joined the strike and constituted a formidable lineup, and what tied together the indefinite strike in each department with the broader school occupations was the Tōdai Zenkyōtō. This was an extremely rare occurrence in the history of the postwar student movement. How did this happen? Such a situation could not have come to pass solely on the basis of empathy for the expelled medical students, nor simply on the basis of the demand for greater student rights ("school democratization"). Something else was at stake.

As strikes objecting to the administration massified and spread throughout the Japanese university system, new watchwords, different from the "demand for rights," began to spread through the Zenkyōtō itself. These new watchwords—the "establishment of subjectivity" [*shutaisei no kakuritsu*], "questioning one's way of life," "what is scholarship or research?"—emerged as the representative slogans, along with "self-negation" (the contradictory view of the self as potential elite).

Despite the pressure and force exerted by the indefinite strikes, university administrations were not inclined to respond to the students' demands. In such a situation, the student movement questioned the stance of their teachers, who were involved in education and research, and at the same time, urged a new introspection into the subjects of the movement themselves. "Self-negation" as a term emerged from the graduate students and young lecturers influenced by their professors who had participated in earlier struggles, but as a phrase it came to be generalized in a loose, moral manner to mean something like "question how you live" and, as such, permeated the movement, even reaching high school students in their early teens. In classrooms and public forums, teachers and professors were pressed and questioned, not on the pros and cons of university management policy, but on how they themselves ought to act. Even among friends and colleagues, the question of how you yourself would go on living, what you will decide to do, and so forth was relentlessly debated in mutual accusations and demands for decisions. The Zenkyōtō movement seemed to have entered the same phase as the student insurrection itself.

In close proximity to the documentation of this deluge of words, there arose an excessively moralistic evaluation of the Zenkyōtō movement. This can be seen in Oguma Eiji's notion that following the university-wide Zenkyōtō strikes, the Tōdai struggle ceased to be a *political* struggle and ended up simply as a "self-affirmation of youth," similar to the idea that the '68 movement was nothing but a "search for the self." But it was at precisely the moment that the subjects of the movement tried to question their own ethical stance that the Zenkyōtō movement became—for better or worse—something befitting the Japanese '68. It was following this period, too, that there emerged the consensus that the Tōdai Zenkyōtō had clearly, in everyone's eyes, created a political movement within the university. To stipulate that a political movement means demanding rights solely through legal forms is to remain trapped within a preliminary ideal; we must not overlook the fact that a political movement could simultaneously be a mutual ethical elevation between subjects: '68 transformed the *style* of politics.

Thus, while the Zenkyōtō movement was entering the same phase as the student insurrection as a whole, the reaction of the Tōdai administration rapidly began to take political form. It did not put into question how the university (or the students) ought to be, or how they ought to live, but instead took up a politics that grasped the problem as one of negotiation between groups internal to the university. On November 1, the president, Ōuchi Kazuo, a liberal since the prewar period, resigned. All trustees and deans of the different faculties also resigned, and it was determined that the medical students' expulsions would be withdrawn. We could say that, basically, all of the seven demands put forward by the Zenkyōtō movement were met. Thus, a new executive branch of the university, represented by Katō Ichirō, the dean of the law faculty, appeared before the students. "You're barking up the wrong tree with all this self-negation stuff and the agony of youth, just settle it among yourselves, once and for all." Katō's straightforward attitude, so different from the equivocation of the Ōuchi administration, was almost refreshing in its directness. "The point is for us to negotiate." If the Zenkyōtō sought a yes or no answer to its list of seven demands, Katō's reply came straight back to them: "From among the demands made by you gentlemen, we have accepted those things we feel to be just, but are unable to accept those things that we consider unjust."

As the autumn deepened that year, pressure from the Ministry of Education and the problem of how to implement the following year's entrance exams came to weigh heavily on the Tōdai administration. This necessitated the rapid development of negotiations "to rationally resolve the University of Tokyo crisis." The university appealed to the students themselves, arguing that if things kept going this way, graduation and educational progress for the student body would be put into question. There existed within the university and among the students an opposition to the Zenkyōtō—for instance, figures like Machimura Nobutaka (who would later become minister of education and foreign affairs) and the Minsei front group Shichi-gakubu daihyōdan [Seven-Faculty Representative Group]. The opposition between the Zenkyōtō and Minsei had long since gone beyond the merely rhetorical level to forms of violent confrontation. Consequently, on January 10, 1969, the Tōdai administration officially exchanged notes of confirmation for the resolution of the struggle with these "representative groups." The direct result of this was the end of the occupation of the Tōdai clock tower on January 18–19 after a major intervention by riot police. Yet, on January 20, the Japanese government announced the suspension of the Tōdai entrance exams for the following year. The administration could not, in the end, declare "victory" in the Tōdai struggle.

It goes without saying that the aforementioned situation and its tendencies forced a difficult politics onto the Zenkyōtō movement. As the movement tried to strengthen its insurrectionary phase, it had already become impossible for the Zenkyōtō to return to a politics of negotiation with the university administration. The focal point was no longer the pros and cons of the list of seven demands. To wrest hegemony over the negotiations on the student side from Minsei and the "representative groups" was one possible strategy, but it was abandoned along with negotiation itself. There existed no nationwide organization of the Zenkyōtō. Moreover, within the politics of the Japanese New Left at the time, there was no consistent and systematic backing of the Tōdai Zenkyōtō by the different political factions. Even further, unlike the situation of the Zengakuren during the 1960 Anpō struggle, the Zenkyōtō movement had exerted no direct influence on public opinion or the political process and had no expectation of doing so. Above all else, the insurrection of the Zenkyōtō movement obsessively aimed at a politics of completely resetting the established and given political order. Thus, the Tōdai Zenkyōtō were physically eliminated from any space outside of the university when the riot police entered campus.

Compared to the Tōdai struggle, the Zenkyōtō at Nihon University (Nichidai) began in a form that attempted to thwart this outcome, but under inferior conditions of internal university autonomy. It is clear that the struggle began with demands for student rights—but as soon as the barricades went up on campus, it quickly switched over to a phase of student insurrection.

The Zenkyōtō movement, which spread in waves from the experiences of Tōdai and Nichidai, developed from demands for the democratization of education into strikes and occupations of schools and research offices, but it became a pattern of the movement that all of this would end each time with the expulsion of the Zenkyōtō from the university by the administration and the riot police. And throughout this time, although communication between the Zenkyōtō at various universities was frequent, there existed no nationwide Zenkyōtō leadership or even a national council. The Japanese '68, even seen domestically, took place not as "one" thing, but as a series of similar, simultaneous, repeated insurrections.

'68 in Postwar History

The Japanese '68 cannot be adequately understood without a grasp of the 1960 movement against the renewal of the US–Japan Joint Security

Treaty (the 1960 Anpō Struggle), and this, in turn, leads us to view '68 within the history of Japan following its defeat in World War II. In 1956, a government white paper declared that "it is no longer the postwar." This was the period during which Japanese industry began to emerge from under the damage of the war, and when the Japanese state entered into its long-lasting period of high economic growth. Until 1973, the average growth rate exceeded 10 percent; during the same period, many Western countries experienced similar effects.

The political process, too, bore traces of the unique and peculiar character of the years 1956 to 1960. Prior to this moment, the situation was far from stable: under the occupation of the Allied forces and the general disorder of the postwar years, labor disputes occurred repeatedly while political parties allied and ruptured over and over again. We might call it the "chaotic period" of the "postwar revolution." This chaotic cycle of politics broke in 1955, with the consolidation of a system of two major conservative and progressive parties, the Liberal Democratic Party (LDP) and the Socialist Party of Japan. This system, typically dubbed "the '55 system," continued largely until the end of the Cold War. However, stabilizing the '55 system necessitated its own political process, the pinnacle of which was the 1960 Anpō struggle. Throughout this period, the "national assembly," formed with the National Center of Labor Unions (Sōhyō) (itself under the influence of the Socialist Party), created a style of mass mobilization that corresponded to parliamentarian politics. This was the sort of "citizens' movement" [*kokumin undō*] that advocated peace, democracy, and the postwar constitution, the medium through which the thought and style of the postwar reform movement—later viciously criticized by the Zenkyōtō movement, under the name "postwar democracy"—was originally formed. The citizens' movement continually undertook "joint actions" according to a strict schedule, each time organizing protest demonstrations and delivering petitions to the National Diet within the Tokyo metropolitan area. By linking its established practice of annual labor struggles in the springtime (the "spring struggles," [*shuntō*]) to these joint actions, Sōhyō aimed to—and, in fact, was able to—improve working conditions in ways that went beyond the framework of demands on single corporations. Through heightened confrontation in the National Diet with the LDP, the Socialist Party could respond to the calls of joint actions.

On the other hand, the LDP, the party in government throughout this period, was led by politicians from the prewar era. The quintessential figure was Prime Minister Kishi Nobusuke (1956–60), a former defendant in the Tokyo Tribunal accused of Class A war crimes. The Japanese Constitution, written under occupation, took as its basis a form of constitutional democracy, distinguished by its Article 9, which prohibited the maintenance of a national armed force and renounced war. The Kishi government hoped to revise the article on the renunciation of war, rearm the Japanese state, and enhance the self-reliance of an independent Japan by reforming the security treaties and guarantees that enabled unilateral American control into a new bilateral agreement. This "reverse course" of overbearing political management invited a strong response from the side of reform. Each time this took place, a citizens' movement was organized. Although it may seem paradoxical at first glance, it was the conservatives who aimed at autonomy from the United States and the establishment of a new, self-reliant military force, while the reformers opposed them, seeking to protect the peace constitution (the defense of postwar democracy). Against the backdrop of high economic growth, the period following 1956 saw the formation of a specific postwar political process characterized by the aforementioned elements. The focal point of contestation in the composition of this antagonism was, above all, the 1960 Anpō struggle—in other words, the protest actions that began with the formation of a Citizens' Council to Stop the Revision of the United States–Japan Security Treaty [Nichibei anpō jōyaku kaitei soshi kokumin kaigi] in March 1956.

The Anpō struggle consisted of nineteen repeated "joint actions" and, in its heyday, saw the participation of 5.8 million people. The citizens' movement's character and the aims of its leadership became significantly radicalized in this context, producing a general situation of rebellion in the area around the National Diet. "This is a revolution!," cried a segment of LDP politicians. In the end, the Kishi cabinet was forced to resign. US President Eisenhower, whose support prolonged the life of the Kishi cabinet, suspended his visit to Japan, while news of the "Tokyo Rebellion" was widely broadcast in the United States. In terms of the scale of the mass movement and its successful defeat of the cabinet, the Anpō struggle was the first and probably last of its kind in modern Japanese political history. In the wake of this moment, the prewar politicians, symbolized by Kishi Nobusuke, exited the stage, and in their place was established the fundamental character of the new administration, one based on the drafting and implementation of plans for economic growth. Both the government and the LDP studiously avoided any talk of constitutional reform. Successful economic growth would stabilize the LDP as the eternal governing party, while, on the other side, the reformers would be cast out as perpetually in opposition. The "citizens" [*kokumin*] who achieved victory in the citizens' movements thus chose to take the path of moving on from the experience of war—economic growth guaranteed and assured them lifetime employment and consumption. It is not that the main thematics of the Anpō struggle, peace and democracy, faded out following its end; rather, postwar democracy became entrenched even in the citizens' unconscious. In the wake of this moment, any attempt to encroach upon the postwar constitutional system immediately occasioned a counterattack by intellectuals and the media. As an unconscious expression of the citizenry, constitutional reform became a complete taboo, a repudiation of postwar democracy, even among LDP politicians. And, on the other side of the equation, the model of mass mobilization taken by the citizens' movements rapidly disintegrated after the Anpō struggle.

Thus, the 1960 Anpō struggle came to occupy the historical position of a citizens' revolution for Japan. Through the victory of the citizenry and intellectuals in this national revolution, Japan saw the completion of its 100 years of modernization since the Meiji Restoration. It was as if the Anpō struggle had opened the floodgates for the arrival of a society of high economic growth and high-level mass consumption. The citizenry treated the victory of the Anpō struggle as a rite of passage and cheerfully accepted the advent of mass consumer society. With the television as its point of departure, the middle of the 1960s saw a notable high in the diffusion of durable consumer goods.

The national citizens' movements that culminated in the 1960 Anpō struggle did not take the nonpartisan citizenry (the masses) as the subject of the movement. The social composition of the Citizens' Council to Stop the Treaty Revisions was formed from various hierarchies and groups, including the trade unions and their National Center [Sōhyō], the student councils and their national organization (Zengakuren), and so on—at its peak, 1,633 different groups participated in the Citizens' Council (and the JCP had "observer" status). With the Socialist Party as its center, the progressive and reform-oriented parties represented the Council in the National Diet. This is also to say that postwar Japanese society was formed hierarchically, and those individuals and residents who did not belong to these hierarchies were deemed nonexistent. To be a worker meant belonging to a trade union; to be a peasant meant holding membership in an agricultural cooperative [*nōkyō*]; to be a student meant being a member of a student council.

The history of the postwar is essentially a history of the citizenry's formation and composition into these sociopolitical groups. The simple public [*shimin*], residents or consumers, essentially did not exist. Political parties like the LDP and the Socialist Party furnished the popular will through the medium of these hierarchical groupings.

Nevertheless, while the Anpō struggle was won as a unified struggle of postwar reform-oriented class strata, it was paradoxically also the beginning of the self-dissolution of these hierarchical groups themselves. The trade unions and the Zengakuren abruptly lost their militant edge, and the form of mass mobilization that had been the model of the postwar political process suddenly disappeared. Progressive and rapid urbanization contributed to the deterioration of the influence of agricultural cooperatives, the intellectual class became an obsolete term, and the citizen [*shimin*] became simply a resident. Politicians no longer mediated various class fractions but simply had to appeal to each resident individually for one vote apiece, like regional grains of sand.

This was the society in which the young postwar baby boomer generation was raised: what they confronted in '68 was the absurdity of this society formed by their parents. As a result, although the Zenkyōtō movement began with students as a specific social stratum, within it there was a rapid acceleration of the dissolution of this group identity "student" as a form of social belonging. In the years to follow, a movement of students as a social stratum unto itself would not be revived. Thus, in comparison with the prior generation that made up the Anpō Zengakuren, the Zenkyōtō generation was far more pluralistic or perhaps had a much messier subjective composition. This is one reason that, thereafter, the Japanese '68 would be referred to not as a "student" movement but as a rebellion of the "youth." When compared to the employment of the 1960 generation in the elite workplaces of the high-growth era—corporations, government agencies, universities—the prospects and post-graduation career paths of the Zenkyōtō generation were also much messier and unclear. Even today, while stories and legends of those involved are retold, they provide no universal historical depiction of the Japanese '68. We might say that the Zenkyōtō itself promoted a certain suspicion of any such "universal history"—and it is precisely this dilemma of the Zenkyōtō generation that problematized its ability to pass on the lessons of the Japanese '68 to the generations that followed.

Organization and Movement in the New Left

The Japanese '68 owes its origins to the revolutionary faction in the 1960 Anpō struggle; this is why we must treat the radical movements of the 1960s as one historically linked sequence. The Zengakuren (All-Japan Federation of Students' Self-Governing Associations, formed in 1948) was a united organization, joined together through resolutions passed by each individual university's student council, and in 1960 it encompassed the majority of national and private universities. All new entering students were automatically registered as part of the student council; student council fees were routinely collected alongside the initial entrance and matriculation fee. Just as Japanese trade unions were largely single-company unions, so too the student councils served as a type of student version of the union shop system located within each university, and in this sense the councils were an organization of students as a specific class stratum. Unlike the situation of Western Europe, in Japan these councils never grew into "student unions" as such. On the other hand, as organizations recognized by the university authorities, they were required to follow strictly their own officially recognized council protocols. The decision-making process of the councils had to be based on the resolutions passed in the student assembly of each department, and the student assemblies formed quorum by a fixed proportion of students relative to the total (in the national universities, typically this would be one-third to one-fourth of the student body). If the assembly could not make quorum, resolutions were invalidated, and if this resulted in the breaking of university prohibitions, those responsible would be punished. Thus, the student councils in each department were effectively unified with the university itself and in turn joined to the Zengakuren as a whole. The Zengakuren participated in the Citizens' Council during the 1960 Anpō struggle, thereby representing the movement of students as a specific class fraction.

In the '60 Anpō struggle, the Zengakuren were at the leading edge of the use of joint actions as a tactic, and their radicalism was the subject of criticism from the JCP as well as from the other groups participating in the Citizens' Council. Nevertheless, it was widely recognized that it was the student movement that pushed the momentum of the '60 Anpō struggle into a genuine "revolution" of the national citizenry. When the decision was taken to hold a "national funeral" for the female student at the University of Tokyo who had died at the peak of the struggle (June

15, 1960), political parties (including the JCP), trade unions, and people from the worlds of education, culture, and religion all put forward the names of their representatives to serve as members of the funeral service. In a sense, the Anpō struggle was given a national burial. And with the victory of the citizenry in this struggle, the period of the "golden '60s" opened.

From its inception, the Zengakuren was under the leadership of the JCP. However, as the student movement became increasingly radicalized within the national movement as a whole, the opposition between student party members and the party leadership began to deepen. Then, in 1958, with these student party members as its core, the Communist League (the Bund) was formed as a split from the JCP, upholding the slogan of "A New Vanguard Party." This was the year that the Soviet revelations and critique of Stalin had become publicly known, followed by the occurrence of the Hungarian rebellion against the Soviets and against the Communist Party. Besides the Bund, around the same time, numerous Trotskyist organizations were forming outside of the JCP, represented above all by the Kakukyōdō or Revolutionary Communist League [Kakumeiteki kyōsanshugisha dōmei]. Thereafter, both the Bund and Kakukyōdō would go through numerous splits, giving rise to the numerous party formations (sects) that were collectively referred to as the New Left in the 1960s. The dogmatic slogan "one vanguard party in each nation" had de facto imploded.

In effect, the leadership of the Zengakuren in the 1960 Anpō struggle was run by the student organization of the Bund. The Bund constituted the internal opposition within the Zengakuren to the student organization linked to the JCP (Minsei), and it became the political organization most representative of the radical faction of the Anpō struggle. The program of the Bund, which opposed the JCP while upholding the line of "a new vanguard party," rested on a revival of the orthodoxy of Marxist revolution and the Leninist vanguard party-form. Beginning with the Soviet Union, they saw the communist parties of the world as betrayers of this orthodoxy, and themselves as the legitimate "left opposition" to this betrayal. The two pillars of its program were the seizure of state power by means of class struggle on the part of the working class and leadership of this struggle by a strong and stable party-community.

However, no matter how intense this "national revolution" that sprang from the mass movement of 1960, it was only superficially similar to the program of revolution upheld by the Bund. Following the Leninist theory of the vanguard party, the party should lead particular, discrete mass movements as only one means of progressing toward the ultimate, final revolution in the future. By utilizing its accomplishments in specific struggles, the party organization must preserve and strengthen itself toward the future. The Bund proclaimed, "Will Anpō be crushed or will the Bund be crushed?," wagering its organization on the mass movement by hoping to rally to it the student activists of the Zengakuren. Saddled with intense internal splits yet at the forefront of this national revolution—with its minimal similarity to their party program—the league members of the Bund had no choice but to keep running at the head of this insurrectionary situation that they themselves had created. In the end, they contributed to opening the floodgates of the high-consumption society of the 1960s. When this became clear, there was no way to avoid the internal opposition that had riven the Bund, while at the same time the Anpō struggle had also reached its end. The Bund was split and finally liquidated under the force of the opposition between the faction that upheld and defended the ideology of the vanguard party, and the faction that advocated direct action [*kōdōshugi*]. The vanguardist side chose to unify with Kakukyōdō, while the other side formed the so-called "Second Bund" (Dainiji bunto) during the '60s. The latter comprised many seasoned veterans of the Anpō struggle but generally had a younger composition in comparison to the membership at the time of the foundation of the first Bund. Importantly, the majority of members no longer had the experience of passing through the Communist Party—they were youth who had grown up in the midst of the insurrectionary circumstances of the "golden period" of the Anpō struggle and became the bearers of the legacy of that mass rebellion, ensuring its continuity into 1968.

Nonetheless, this in no way meant that the internal contradiction between vanguardism and "mass movementism" disappeared; unquestionably, the political party-sects of 1968 also inherited this contradiction. Regardless of "sect" or "non-sect," the problem of vanguardism constituted the essential experience of the Japanese '68. Beyond Kakukyōdō and the Bund, there existed within the Zenkyōtō movement the youth organization of the Socialist Party, the various organizations that upheld "structural reform" [*kōzō kaikaku-ha*] and that had been expelled from the JCP, and various other sects that were active side-by-side with the movement. Throughout the '68 period, these various sects were unable to form a national coordination council to enact a unified strategy of action, while the Zenkyōtō movement was in organizational conflict at every single university. During the University of Tokyo struggle, regular meetings were held between representatives of the Zenkyōtō and the sects, and the movement was formed out of the individual departmental Zenkyōtō, but even these departmental Zenkyōtō were themselves constituted by multiple groupings.

The political sects would come to be called the "New Left," but unlike the situation that had existed until the 1960 Anpō struggle, in fact, they had ceased to be a left opposition against the old left. The model of a national movement had expired and, within the boundaries of that same movement, no longer played the role of an oppositional faction criticizing the JCP from the left. At most universities, occasional violent disputes between the sects and Minsei, the youth section of the JCP, had long since become normal and routine. For the Zenkyōtō sects, the Communist Party was no longer an organization that represented anything more than simply one part of the system, the mainstream. What is, in fact, the original or unique organizational character of the New Left sects? Sect or non-sect, this was one major problem bequeathed to us in the aftermath of the Japanese '68.

Revolution and Rebellion

If we consider the Zenkyōtō as the model of the Japanese '68, this form of organization (the joint struggle committee) shared important qualitative characteristics with the first revolutionary groups that emerged on the historical level—that is, the form of the council [*Räte* or *soviet*]. The council must be positioned as a mechanism for mass rebellion independent of the Leninist conception of revolution, defined as "the problem of the seizure of state power." Mass rebellion has been the first event of a revolutionary sequence; it has also been the last. This was mass insurrection and its organization was the council; '68 was a council movement of mass insurrection. For precisely this reason, the '68 movement diverged from and opposed, at the level of style, the prior forms, in a double sense. The prior style of movement was, on the one hand, a constitutionalism that foregrounded the liberal right of opposition and, on the other hand, the Marxist-Leninist view of revolution. The quintessential expression of the former was the citizens' movement for postwar democracy; the archetypal form of the latter was the theory of revolution of the New Left sects. The striking characteristic of '68 was precisely to have liberated the concept of rebellion [*hanran*] from this double-layered framework.

If we examine the case of the Tōdai Zenkyōtō movement discussed earlier, there the Zenkyōtō confronted power by occupying the "point of production," this space of knowledge-production that we call the university. It obviously recalls for us the syndicalist understanding of worker-led factory occupations. While the university-wide Zenkyōtō's base was comprised of the individual Zenkyōtō organizations of each department, it also included activists from the Marxist-Leninist sects, numerous activists of the so-called "non-sect radicals," and various small, relatively loose groupings. These were encompassed within the movement as part of the council-form known as the All-Campus Joint Struggle League. As its membership was not fixed or set, it experienced intense volatility and fluctuation in terms of individual comings and goings. Within each university, alongside the Zenkyōtō radicals existed their opposition, Minsei (the JCP youth organization), as well as numerous organizations of the general student population who were unilaterally opposed to the struggle itself. At Tōdai, for instance, these organizations joined with the general student population at university assemblies to determine individual department policies. In such sites, violence was taboo, so decision making was supposed to remain at the level of a discursive war. The student assemblies in each department would incessantly and endlessly repeat again and again these discursive struggles, often lasting until the next morning. Far exceeding in numbers the necessary quorum to fulfill protocol, these assemblies became in reality open to the participation of the entire student body. For the Zenkyōtō movement, this intricate and complex war of discourse was an experience that bore close resemblance to what Arendt famously called "the emergence of political space."

The Zenkyōtō movement was a student rebellion that broke from the prior style of postwar Japanese political movements. But it was not only this. The liberation of the concept of rebellion [*hanran*] from the theoretical framework of revolution was also a fundamental paradigm shift from the traditions of the revolutionary movement. The various party formations of the Japanese New Left generally saw themselves theoretically as vanguard parties, inheritors and successors of the Marxist tradition; that is, they saw themselves as *the* Marxist-Leninist party. This is the source of the sectarian literary style, beginning with the party program. Within the movement, too, each individual struggle [*ein Kampf*] must be positioned as merely one means in a connected chain leading to the final, ultimate revolution [*der Kampf*], the movement-form aimed at by the entire national political struggle. Here, the vanguard party is understood as the "headquarters," the order-giving division, of the mass movement, which must independently be a steadfast and strong community of revolutionaries. This is the logic of vanguardism. Yet, at the time, the "new vanguard parties" were tiny in comparison to the working class or even to the Communist Party, so they resorted to another self-determination: the Marxist-Leninist "left opposition." These characteristic "revolutionary parties" were an extension of the 1960 Anpō struggle, and when they encountered the Zenkyōtō movement, they quickly became influential members and organizers. The composition of the Zenkyōtō as a group was an amalgamation of the masses in rebellion and the various sectarian formations. This produced a constant flux within the Zenkyōtō movement, the sects, and the masses from vanguardism to mass-movementism and vice versa. The revolutionary parties had now experienced a mass rebellion, a moment of insurrection.

However, in Japan, this term "rebellion" [*hanran*] brings up, rather, associations with the rebellion of nationalists in the military, as in the famous 2–26 Incident of 1936.[1] For Marxist-Leninists, it recalls perhaps the "counter-revolutionary" Kronstadt rebellion. In short, it is not exactly a positive term for political movements of the left. What Japanese revolutionaries experienced in '68 compelled them to fundamentally reconsider the history and theory of prior revolutionary movements. Precisely through this experience, Marxism itself was subject to close scrutiny. Since the Japanese '68, mass political movements have largely disappeared, and since the 1990s and the implosion of the socialist system, the interest in Marx or Marxism-Leninism has also largely been lost. There are scarcely any traces of the New Left sects of '68. Yet what cannot be destroyed, eliminated, or forgotten from our actual moment is the fact that this concept of rebellion was liberated from the tradition of revolutionary politics, this concept that exerted such a force on the theoretical experience of 1968. It transformed the style, the grammar, of revolution.

1 [Trans]. The 2–26 Incident or February 26 Incident of 1936 was an influential attempted coup d'état by young officers of the Kōdōha [Imperial Way Faction] who believed that the Japanese state had lost its spiritual and national force. Unsuccessful and resulting in the execution of its main figures, the incident has made a lasting impresion on political and social memory. In Nagasaki's distinctive use of the concept *hanran* [rebellion], we should keep in mind that the main government charge against the plotters of the 2–26 Incident was the "crime of rebellion" [*hanran-zai*].

Democracy as Struggle

Postwar Japanese discourse in general was strikingly influenced by Marxism. Marxist theoretical research in Japan was considered "peerless in the world," and it was within the realm of this influence that left-wing intellectuals were raised. Such intellectuals were not only distributed throughout the space of public discourse, but also in the political administration of education and educational policy. Marxism was linked to the experience of postwar democracy, putting forward figureheads of the liberal left who eventually became widely recognized opinion leaders in postwar Japan. On the other hand, the wholesale damage caused by the nationalism and militarism of the World War II period had become a type of trauma, and conservatives along with right-wing liberals from the prewar period were almost completely excluded and eradicated from the fields of education and public discourse. Following the victory of the citizens' revolution of 1960, even LDP politicians could not be openly conservative. The LDP considers itself essentially a type of universal national party, and it is in this sense that what was practically a one-party system could exist in Japan for so long. From time to time, LDP politicians would let slip the wry, self-deprecating remark that "in fact, Japan is a more socialist country than the Soviet Union or China."

This is how the postwar Japanese left came to establish itself, particularly since within education and public discourse those referred to as left-wing "persons of culture" [*bunkajin*] had become—and remain even today—the mainstream of Japanese cultural power and authority. We might say as well that it was this cultural power of the left that allowed the Zenkyōtō movement to make such deep inroads in its confrontations with the university. From the outset, the Zenkyōtō made heavy use of a certain Marxist vocabulary, speaking, for instance, of its opposition to the "imperialist reorganization" of education and medical care. Throughout the 1960s, the rate of students' advancement into higher education experienced a rapid rise in tandem with high economic growth: including the junior colleges, the rate in 1960 was 10 percent, but it had risen to 19 percent by 1968 and to 24 percent by 1970. The education system could barely keep pace with this growth; nevertheless, a number of private universities, such as Nihon University, prepared to welcome a huge number of incoming students, leading the Zenkyōtō to declare itself against the "harmful effects of creating mammoth universities." The Zengakuren-era students represented the elite, but it was thought that the Zenkyōtō students no longer fit this profile, with the claim instead that students constituted a form of the industrial reserve army. Thus, there were grounds for the students' demand for rights, summed up by the JCP's youth section Minsei, which upheld the "democratization of education."

Yet, as seen in the case of Tōdai, the Zenkyōtō movement rapidly deviated from a struggle for rights claims to a student rebellion that upheld self-negation and the dismantling of the university as such. This spread immediately to universities across the nation. At precisely the same moment that research in the university and the positionality of professors was subject to intense critique, this form of critique also became internal to the student population. Students themselves were asked to manifest their self-critique in the same way that they had demanded of their professors. Certainly, in contrast to those who were persecuted in the name of "self-negation," there was the motivation of indicting the elite social status of Tōdai students. Yet, this slogan quickly spread to the broader Zenkyōtō movement across the country. Breaking with one's social determination (the class stratum of worker or student) in rebellion is part of what defines the rebellious subject, but it gradually became a kind of ethical self-expression of the excess of rebellion, in a form missing even from this definition. Once again, the Zenkyōtō fundamentally transformed the *style* of politics. It replaced the emphasis on the "we," sustained by Marxism's scientific analysis, with the entrance of the "I" as the grammatical subject of the political text. Even when put forward with the grammatical subject "we," in truth, it was the self-expression of multiple individual "I"s. To say that rebellion was liberated from revolution is also to say that another political style and grammar was liberated from the prior style of the political text. This was the actualization of the themes of rebellion and politics, which, at the same time, destroyed the consensus that education was a sort of cooperative enterprise between teachers and students in the university as a site.

Education is a system composed of teachers and students, one premised on their inequality or asymmetry. But this inequality is meant to function precisely in order to eliminate the inequality itself. The pupil is brought up to the level of the teacher. The teacher's capability for specialization, however, negates the self within the pupil, and so, paradoxically, one must be particularly strict in self-awareness with respect to one's own professionalism. This is the originary self-contradiction of what it means to educate, but sometimes the contradiction loses its substance and is transformed into a type of relation between teacher and pupil, resulting in the systematization of inequality. So long as education consists of the teacher bringing the pupil to a higher level, there can be no equality. To be a professor at Tōdai is to be a figure of authority, a leader. These leaders take their own authority to be stable, as a function of being leftist intellectuals, and self-deceivingly hide the fact that they themselves are precisely the figures of cultural power in the postwar era. Is this not exactly the form of the university today, a mere shadow of its former self from the days of postwar democracy? The Zenkyōtō students wanted nothing less than to bring down teachers and the university to this point of origin that is the contradiction of education. What seems to be an excessively ethical fixation on the self and other could be interpreted as an attempt to persevere toward this point of origin. The students self-negated the position of pupil, but this could never begin without the teachers' self-renouncement of their own privileged position. And as this was intolerable for the teachers themselves, it could only function as an absurd demand. Perhaps, deep down, the professors were simply disgusted by the idea that some student with the bearing of a teenager could have the temerity to try to grasp their specialized research—but since declaring openly that students were incapable of understanding would make the professors fearful of how they were perceived, so what if this asymmetry between teacher and pupil remained fast in place as a formality? If we return back to the originary sense of democracy as equality, what emerges, in this case, is what Rancière referred to as "dissensus." The Zenkyōtō critique of university education and academic research had already unconciously moved far from a place where it could be settled by slogans like "the democratization of education" or "reform of the educational curriculum." Paradoxically, it was a movement that attempted to reset education all the way back to an originary democracy.

Having said that, the very word "democracy" is seductive. "Democratization of education" was certainly a slogan of the anti-Zenkyōtō factions and, by contrast, the Zenkyōtō itself tended toward a complete negation of postwar democracy as such. Today, virtually everyone upholds democracy and critiques its opponents, protecting their own position by means of the name "democracy." The more this goes on, the greater the proliferation of individual definitions of democracy, all with the same result: that in the end it comes to mean nothing at all. And yet this seems to make no difference, never stopping claims in the name of democracy from persistently appearing. Further, today, in the wake of the collapse of the socialist system and the fall from grace of the Marxist-Leninist theory of revolution, all the convenient slogans have been lost, and no matter how radical the movement, everyone upholds the pretense of democracy. From the viewpoint of this contemporary inflation of the concept of democracy, we can consider the unconscious of the Zenkyōtō to have been a demand for "democracy" in education. Not any sort of organized "democratization," but an attempt to restore the dimension of struggle to the ideal of equality at the foundation of the emergence of democratic systems by means of dissensus.

The Zenkyōtō generation was raised in the system of democratic education of postwar Japan. The right of opposition is, of course, included within democracy, but only when internal to the limits of liberal politics and the legal system. Through the personification of resistance as struggle and as rebellion, the movement experienced its estrangement from liberal democracy. So, where, outside of liberal democracy, can one discover the style and grammar of struggle and rebellion Japan's accumulated knowledge? Such a search would open our eyes to the excavation of minor knowledges beyond the traditional authoritarian literature, but which are subordinated and concealed by it. Once this might have been the emperorist rebellions of the military, and at the time of the long '68, it might have been the rise to rebellion of the writer Yukio Mishima and his comrades. Both examples were held back from becoming events that might disclose forms of knowledge suppressed by postwar democracy. The rebellion of 1968 would thereafter be inherited as a rebellion of knowledge.

The Critique of Modern Rationalism

Among the main theoretical arguments of the Zenkyōtō movement was what its members referred to as the "critique of modern rationalism." This clearly expresses the powerful influence of students and researchers in the sciences within the movement—and it is no accident, considering the degree to which postwar Japan intensively promoted the advancement and development of the sciences and technology. In the war that had passed, Japan had lost to American science and scientific thought. In this sense, to be scientific became a sort of national mantra for postwar reconstruction and modernization. Scientific education was heavily emphasized, and with the industrial reconstruction of the country came the introduction of advanced American scientific technologies. One of the major reasons that postwar reconstruction led to the period of high economic growth was precisely this relentless promotion of science. But, with the end of the 1960s, which had been the main motor-force for the modernization of society and the development of mass consumption, the demand for science also transformed from a national slogan into a simple convenience. A certain part of the American way of life had permeated into the household. Perhaps to be scientific was a form of life that had been acquired over a long period of time in the context of Western modernity, but, in Japan, the advent of scientific technology that aimed at convenience was a sudden, immediate transformation. This type of adaptation had perhaps been the special ability of the Japanese nation since antiquity. Regardless, the Zenkyōtō generation was born and raised within a culture that accepted this demand for convenience. Since they felt that such a society was underpinned by a fundamental irrationality, and the university constituted the Mecca of scientificity, it is no surprise that the Zenkyōtō movement essentially turned against and developed a critique of science and technology as the ideology of modernity.

It has to be said that, in an originary sense, Japan had no tradition of modern rationality. With the advent of the postwar era, scientific thought, jumbled together with a certain Americanism, was heralded as the future. In addition, there was the major influence of Marxism on the intellectual class, a certain scientific Marxism: "The economic base appears as the necessity of the laws of history." The all-out flourishing of scientific technology would take place only when it was liberated from the limits of capital in a socialist society. In this sense, to be a Marxist was to be scientific. Consequently, the critique of science undertaken by the Zenkyōtō movement was also necessary in the sense that it saw the limits of Marxism as a worldview linked to a specific modernity. Thus, another key implication of this critique of "modern rationalism" was that it was fundamentally a critique of so-called "scientific Marxism." And, again on this point, there had been the experience of the thought of the '60s following the 1960 Anpō struggle.

In postwar Japan, alternatives to orthodox Marxism generally took two divergent paths. The first was the genealogy of thought broadly known as the materialism of subjectivity [*shutaisei yuibutsuron*]. From this perspective, it was crucial that Marxism reacquire a sense of the significance of the subject of practice [*jissen shutai*]. What spurred this on was unquestionably the excavation and rediscovery of the theory of alienated labor in the young Marx. In this optic, alienated labor within capitalism had its homeland in a conception of original, practical labor. Labor indicates a practice of self-transformation that naturally externalizes itself, thus re-recovering a humanized nature. Here, the finality and rationality of human activity are posited, and we become practically able to ascribe significance to the development of science as something disclosing the causal laws of nature, a point that gave rise to the philosophy of technology. The theory of technology was first raised by physicists and exerted a major influence on the theoretical composition of the postwar theories of subjective materialism. Technology indicates, in essence, the correct application of science, but the specific utility of this theory of technology lay in its emphasis on the conscious use of the objective and causal character of these laws within the practice of production (labor). Based on this concept of nonalienating technology, it undertook a critique of scientific technology distorted under capitalism. The protagonists of this theory were quite unaware of it, but it was an extremely intellectualist determination of technology by way of Bacon and originating in Plato. Technology differs fundamentally from technical skill. It was necessary to theoretically demonstrate not only that technology is useful, but why it should be so.

For the Zenkyōtō movement's critique of modern rationalism, these theoretical attempts within postwar Japanese Marxism were paradoxical. Although they functioned as critiques of orthodox Marxism, the trends of subjective materialism and the theory of technology also served as skillful theorizations of a certain scientific Marxism. Thus, did they not precisely function to ground the postwar national slogan of "scientific development"? Rather than a critique of modern rationalism, this discourse became instead its vanguard. The reason is that, when we examine it epistemologically, the Zenkyōtō attempted to comprehend and rectify the naïve theory of reflection, from which followed the intelligibility of the objective law-like character of nature. This law-like character is consciously utilized in the practice of production, substantializing science and technology. But is this not precisely the self-understanding of scientific modernity? "Capitalism" here is converted and expanded into the concept "modernity."

From the theoretical experience of the 1960s, we see here the sudden influence of phenomenology. At the outset, there was obviously a critical view of the simplistic epistemology of reflection theory within Marxism. However, in Japan, rather than deepening epistemology within its own terms for Marxism, the influence of phenomenology occasioned a sudden turn to ontology. For Husserl, Galileo was a genius of discovery and, at the same time, a genius of concealment. For Heidegger, the essence of materialism lies within a metaphysics for which all beings appear as the raw materials of labor, and this is in turn hidden within the essence of technology. At the level of the critique of modern rationalism, the influence of these master oracles was enormous. In the making of the modern world-picture, it was possible to have this planetary view from above.

On the other hand, Marx's earlier theory of labor alienation, rediscovered by postwar subjective materialism, came to be frequently employed as a simple "theory of alienation," with the concept "labor" dropping out, over the course of the 1960s. The sociopolitical reality of the 1960s, together with the contemporary situation of the socialist system, was indicted for its "human alienation." A way of being non-alienating to the human (Marx's humanism as naturalism) was assumed, in this context, as a desire, and referred to often as the "alienation theory of revolution" [*sogai kakumeiron*]. From the side of philosophy, this theory of human alienation was critically dismissed as non-theoretical or irrational, yet it became what most aptly expressed the mood and style of the broad social movement that culminated in the Zenkyōtō. Still today, the "alienation theory of revolution" could be called the dominant thought of mass rebellion.

There is one further implication of the Zenkyōtō's critique of modern rationalism; it concerns the transformation of the understanding of Marxian political economy that occurred through the 1960s. In the orthodox conception, *Capital* was simply a work of political economy, but one that provided proof of the necessity of proletarian revolution. In opposition to this, and from the side of rather academic Marxian political economy, emerged the thought of Uno Kōzō, concentrated in his *Keizai genron* [Principles of Political Economy], an attempt to logically purify *Capital* as a type of science. According to Uno, *Capital* was a text that must be read as an irrefutable science, not at all as a text theoretically proving that there was any necessity for capitalism's downfall or the inevitability of revolution. Instead, he attempted to reconstruct *Capital* as a science unto itself, at what he referred to as the level of principle, or the theory of pure capitalism [*genriron*]. For example, the orthodox Marxist theory of revolution tends to be one that locates the roots of revolution in economic crisis and the concomitant advent of a more general social crisis, but Uno's theory of principle instead considers crisis as that which actually enhances the functioning, sophistication, and intensification of the capitalist system. Thus, revolution, rather than being something derived from the science of political economy, is taken to be, above all, a task for practice, no matter how much it is an application of science. Revolution is thereby expelled to the margins of Marx's *Capital*.

The influence of Uno's political economy on the thought of the New Left was immense. On the one hand, as a method of political economy for disclosing the objective crises of capitalism anew, it provided powerful and independent thematics of economic analysis. It emphasized the need to write a new theory of imperialism. On the other hand, Uno's theory of principle, by locating the motor-force of revolution outside the text of *Capital*, provided a conception of "freedom" to practice. It was the opportunity in thought that allowed for the liberation of "rebellion" from the Marxist theory of revolution. Rebellion was, therefore, not based in the necessity of capitalism but was precisely an antimodernity for modern society, an attempt to overcome modernity. There was only a short distance from there to the Zenkyōtō movement of '68. Long before the implosion of official socialism in 1990, the Zenkyōtō movement was a moment of liberation from Marxism. Yet this event was simultaneously left to subsequent generations as the conceptual equivalent to posing the question: is revolution possible, or impossible?

The year 1968 was the beginning of the second half of the 100 years since the October Revolution of 1917 in Russia. The first fifty years saw, for everyone, the development of "Revolution" in capital letters, but in the fifty years since 1968, the Revolution has been actively forgotten as just another historical event. This period of forgetting has now been longer than the initial fifty years since its occurrence. Today, after the 2018 bicentennial of Marx's birth, we have no choice but to think, even unconsciously, of the destruction of the rebellions of 1968, of the ruins of this demolished form of thought. Only a thought and practice that rises and emerges from these ruins can become the present we need in order to inherit and follow 1968 today.

Translated by Gavin Walker

3

The Ethics of the Agitator: On Hiroshi Nagasaki's *The Phenomenology of Politics*

Yoshihiko Ichida

> We too have considered in the first place capitalist development, and only afterward workers' struggles. This is an error. It is necessary to invert the problem, change the sign, and begin again: and the beginning is the struggle of the working class.
>
> Mario Tronti, *Operai e capitale*, 1966

> For reformism, classes exist prior to class struggle, a little bit like two rugby teams each exist on their own before the game . . . In contrast, for revolutionaries, one must begin from class struggle to understand class distinctions, to understand the existence and nature of classes.
>
> Louis Althusser, *Réponse à John Lewis*, 1973

> For *me*, 'class' is just a name for the political group which *we* have built ourselves during a long, antagonistic struggle . . . To cut a long story short, the working class or labor unions have in this respect no relation to the proletariat as a class.
>
> Nagasaki Hiroshi, *The Phenomenology of Politics*, 1977

Inversion: The Fate of Autonomy

The problematics of the writers of these three epigraphs do not make "1968" a direct theoretical object. Tronti's text was written in 1966 and it would have been simply impossible for him to take up the subject of

1968 before the events occurred. From the standpoint of a "revolutionary," Althusser dismissed the May 1968 student uprising as a "petit bourgeois rebellion." In other words, for him, 1968 was not an object of analysis because it could not serve as an example of theoretical rectitude. Though it was written as part of a general inquiry, only Nagasaki Hiroshi's analysis could be said to be a "1968" theory in its proper sense. Since it was written as an extension of his *Hanranron*, it could even be given the status of a privileged object or example.[1] The object of Nagasaki's study is, in the end, the politics of the experience (or pilgrimage) of the self as agitator that develops through rebellion. Of course, 1968, to say nothing of the Russian revolution, is but one historical example of a rebellion. Nagasaki thus treats 1968 as an example of the same type of movement as the Meiji period's Chichibu Konmintō movement. All three of the above formulations are consonant with the historical fact of 1968. Straddling its prehistory until the "post-'68" period, the relationships that prepared the ground for '68, those that were extracted from '68, and those that amplified the event from within '68 all came to be more and more widely examined in the interval of '68 itself. And as time passed, this tendency only became stronger. By passing through 1968, these three formulations became formulations *about* 1968. Tronti's workerism was a slogan to take the workers' struggle out of the factory, the locus of capitalist development, and onto the streets. Althusser's formulation was welcomed by the 1968 activists themselves—even if Althusser was politically opposed to 1968. (According to his student, Jacques Rancière, Althusser was playing a long game to draw students closer to the Communist Party.)[2] In 1968 and its aftermath, Tronti's figure of the worker, Althusser's theory of class struggle, and Nagasaki's conceptions of rebellion and the agitator each developed into more than merely an ideal, and as the years have gone by, all have come to operate as catalysts to push 1968 itself into the position of an *idea*. To borrow Nagasaki's expression, these three formulations go far beyond their strict theoretical meanings to show what we might call a "realism of idealism" (about which more later) in their relation to 1968 as a historical event. Today, these three formulations have become, in their own countries—and even internationally—elements of the idealization of 1968.

But have these three formulations each independently become formulations *proper* to 1968? Not at all. From the perspective of 1968,

1 See Nagasaki Hiroshi, *Hanranron*, Tokyo: Sairyūsha, 1991.

2 See Jacques Rancière, *La Leçon d'Althusser*, Paris: La Fabrique, 2011.

each formulation expresses a kind of "inversion" [*tentō*] or "reversal," but from the perspective of 1968 as an event that was itself full of inversions and reversals, it would be better to say that 1968 *captured* these formulations in order to express itself. It was a revolution that went beyond the Russian revolution in resisting *Das Kapital.* Continuously, if hesitantly, debated then and now as to its status under the name "revolution" and transformed into an ideal with a year attached, "1968" could be said to have reversed the formulae "base = economy" and "superstructure = politics."[3] The fact that, during a period without economic crisis in the country, students, who were not workers, led the movement, and workers and their unions followed, tends to reverse the materialist relationship of determination. The autonomy of politics from economics? Tronti obviously called for taking the workers' struggle out of the factory, Althusser certainly wanted to liberate class struggle from class existence and essence, and Nagasaki Hiroshi clearly made the "self as agitator" autonomous from its social attributes and class organizations.[4] All three liberated "politics" from the determinant force of the economic "base" and found, along with a new dynamism of its own, a power to transform that base. However, through wrapping things up in this manner, "1968" as an idea abandoned a whole set of meanings developed out of the long history of post-nineteenth-century Marxism. This is because politics exercised a unique "instance"; not only does politics exceed the economic as determinant in the last instance, but, as we have seen from this historical point of departure, the political even produces side effects within the economy. In the history of Marxism, the political is always relative—in other words, in its relation to the base, it is autonomous and self-regulating. The autonomy of politics by means of this inversion transforms this relativity into an absolute. In Nagasaki's language, the political group bearing the name "proletariat" had "in this instance, absolutely no connection to the working class."[5] But what ended up happening to this "base" that had lost its connection to "politics"? According to Althusser, the base would toll the final bell,

3 According to Suga Hidemi, 1968 was a victorious struggle for hegemony over the transformation of capitalism; see *68-nen*, Tokyo: Chikuma Shobō, 2006. According to Luc Boltanski and Eve Chiapello, 1968 became the new spirit of capitalism; see Luc Boltanski and Eve Chiapello, *Le nouvel esprit du capitalisme*, Paris: Gallimard, 1999. These are texts that confirm this reversal in that they argue that transformation of the economic base was promoted by a political events.

4 Nagasaki, *Seiji no genshōgaku aruiha ajiteta no henrekishi* [The Phenomenology of Politics, or, the Pilgrimage of the Agitator], Tokyo: Tabata Shoten, 1977, 14.

5 Ibid., 278.

but when would that be? Until that final instance, what is to be done and where? How does Tronti's street as "social factory" relate to materialist production? That is, how does it relate to people's conditions of existence?

Politics is not only self-regulating at the level of the superstructure, but with its autonomy, it can descend to the level of the base. The question then arises as to what relation it forms with a "base" that no longer functions *as* a base? Is this relation economic? Social? Is it a class relationship? Whatever name you give it, whatever theoretical credential you award it, it will not disappear, and this fact makes one thing clear. A politics that has become absolute "encounters" what occupied the space prior to the inversion as a parallel existence. Politics "discovers" it. The site of "encounter" or "discovery"—these are the keywords that run through Nagasaki's *The Phenomenology of Politics*—becomes the location of the base's retransformation into a thesis.

The site of the encounter becomes a place where things "which have absolutely no connection" to each other begin to renew their dialectical relationship and reappear on the stage of "theory." This is not the problem of the self-regulation of politics, where Tronti thought he was drawing from Kant.[6] Nor is it a political problem like Althusser's final surrender to "contingency"—as it is often received—under the name of the "materialism of the encounter."[7] This is likely a rather more classic problem: to what degree are "mind" and "body," which seem to be thoroughly and mutually heterogeneous, integrated in the self? Gaining autonomy through inversion moves the problematic from the nineteenth back to the seventeenth century. In fact, above "politics" is a historical period's social organizing principle or "spirit," and the base could be considered its material form. The individual in a society that has been liberated from hierarchical relations through inversion must return to the position of a human freed from the control of a God on high.

Nevertheless, this method does not deal with the problem directly—it strays from 1968 in Japan. Here we have to look at one manifestation of the problem, or its traces, and to do this, let us examine Nagasaki Hiroshi's *The Phenomenology of Politics.*

---

6 See Mario Tronti, *La politique au crépuscule*, Paris: Éditions de l'Éclat, 2000.

7 See Louis Althusser, "Le courant souterrain du matérialisme de la rencontre," in *Écrits philosophiques et politiques*, ed. François Matheron, Paris: Stock/IMEC, 1994, 1: 539–79.

"The I as we and we as I": The General Will of the Agitator

Nagasaki's phenomenological narrative begins with a close examination of the scenes of the Spanish Revolution (1937), the Chichibu Incident (1884), and the Nihon University struggle (1968–9) as examples of "rebellion" [*hanran*]. The political, as experienced by an arbitrary *I*—who is not yet an agitator—begins in rebellion. Following the method of Hegelian phenomenology, Nagasaki attempts to trace the origin of the political, which manifests itself as the experience of an *I* who is both nobody and anybody. But why within rebellion? As a negative action, rebellion attempts to negate, for example, the government in power, individual policies, or the iniquity of individual politicians. Leaving aside the presupposition of various forms of political existence, rebellion would seem to be an inappropriate place to trace the essential form of the political back to zero. Recall that in order to establish the social contract that enabled the continued existence of his politics, Rousseau posited the "primitive." For Rousseau, the origin of politics—or, rather, what came before the origin—was a state of nature in which individuals had no relation to each other and where no one was anyone. In this state of nature, everyone is in themselves [*an sich*] and categorical (I = we). The state of nature is a world dominated by the species-necessity of the human being. It is clear that as long as humans are in a state of nature, there can be no politics. The *I* who is anyone and no one is also the *I* who encounters almost no one. This *I* does not have sufficient motivation or the external ground to engage in group activities, which are the beginning of politics. However, when Rousseau put man in a state of nature at what he imagined to be the origin of politics, he accidentally returned to the true origin of politics. Through repeated chance encounters, individuals begin to fight among each other and the peculiar social form of a state of war is produced (society is the politics of continuing a state of war; there is no necessity in this), and a social contract is entered as a means for all to return completely to the state of nature. The result is Rousseau's politics. Once all are bound by the social contract, politics' unique necessity is born. In other words, it is in fact possible to see Rousseau's politics as born out of rebellion. Politics begins out of a rebellion against a political situation—which is a social situation produced by an accidental accumulation of results. Or, at least, this is the manner in which Hegel saw Rousseau, and what he learned from the French Revolution as completion of the social contract. Politics does not begin out of an absence of politics, but as an attempt to nullify politics. The first experience in the actual existence of the *I* who can be anyone or no one is the denial or the forgetting of the existence of some other *I* in rebellion. When the political—which makes the *I* into somebody—is denied, the self becomes something that precedes any sort of politics and earns the license to generate the political.

Hegel feared the paradox that the construction of the state at the beginning of the political was equivalent to destruction and terror. For this reason, he tried to sublate it with the history [*Geschichte*] of the national spirit.[8] In other words, the negation of a certain politics [*la politique quelconque*] was one step away from a runaway process that would negate politics [*la politique*] completely (Hegel's politics were the politics of terror). This is why Hegel gave the *I* existential status as a member of an ethnos. The ethnos does not make the *I* into somebody. No matter what social status or attributes the self may have, the *I* who has been defined by the national spirit has all of these markers erased and becomes "German" or "French." Within the ethnos, the political has already disappeared. This is because the *I* who is no one and who should be present at the origin of the political is not present (it is instead "the German" or "the French" who are present). The political is replaced by the history of interethnic struggle. According to Nagasaki, Hegel's goal, to put politics on a shelf after it has been sublated, threatens a return to Rousseau's paradoxical process of the *I* who is both nobody and anyone, where the political arises once again. It is safe to say that the unique problem in Nagasaki's *The Phenomenology of Politics* is at this point clear: What happens to a phenomenology when "spirit" is not taken into account? As long as *The Phenomenology of Politics* is a phenomenology of politics—that is, as long as it asserts that it does not become a phenomenology of spirit—will it somewhere collide with phenomenology?

"In the midst of the rebellion, 'I am now trying to trespass in the city' [*shichū e ranyu*]. And the I that is attempting to trespass *just happens to see from the corner of my eye* another taking the same action as myself."[9] Meeting some unknown other by chance in the midst of the rebellion transforms the *I* into nobody and anyone. This differs subtly yet definitively from what Rousseau's primitive

8 The argument here borrows from Étienne Balibar's "Ich, das Wir, und Wir, das Ich ist: Le mot de l'esprit" in *Citoyen sujet et autres essais d'anthropologie philosophique*, Paris : PUF, 2011.

9 Nagasaki, *Seiji no genshōgaku,* 13; emphasis added. This phrase is taken from the original documents of the Chichibu Incident.

experiences when encountering the other in the forest. The primitive discovers a similar other just by encountering the other. At the mere sight of the other, primitives understand the other is like themselves. However, in the rebellion, the *I* encounters others who "are taking the same action." Because they are doing the same thing, they can exchange actions.[10] Through this exchange, the *I* receives from the other the status of the self who is at once nobody and anyone. As one can see from the use of Marx's quote, what Nagasaki is using as a model is not Rousseau discussing the primitive's encounter with the other in the forest, but Marx, who, in the beginning of *Capital*, is tracing the origins of money from the encounter between exchangers of commodities. In *The Phenomenology of Politics*, the primitive is rediscovered/repositioned in the "equivalent form" of the individual. In other words, the experience of rebellion is none other than the latent dissociation of the human being as "relative value form," "equivalent form," "use value," and "exchange value." What Hegel saw in the French Revolution as the true fruit of the social contract was the contradiction between a given existing political order and a politics starting from zero. Just before this point, Nagasaki discovers the "contradiction" that the *I* is derived from the *we*. However, is this, strictly speaking, a true contradiction? Is this a case of A being in contradiction with B as not-A? And in this case, is not-A the other that I encounter and share actions with during the rebellion? A set including both A and not-A is not a contradictory relationship. When *we* is split into *I* and *he* or *she*, and when one is divided into two, a logical contradiction arises from the meanings of the words. However, here the *I* and *he* or *she* are accomplices, acquaintances, and agents of the rebellion who together form a *we*. Thus, if something is presumed to be divided here, it is, rather, the self (which is split between the *I* who is someone and the *I* who is nobody). However, this dual layering of the self is not something that exists before the rebellion. Before the rebellion, the self does not know the distinction between the *I* who is part of the *we* and the self as a discrete, embodied someone. It does not experience it. The experience of the rebellion makes a *we* out of the *I* and *him* or *her*—the experience of the rebellion lets us know "I was not alone!"—and finally, it creates, in a latent form, the *I* that is not in the equivalent form (the *I* in its relative value form).[11] Here "latent" means that these

10 Marx—quoted by Nagasaki on page 14.

11 Nagasaki, *Seiji no genshōgaku*, 17.

two selves have yet to discover their conflict. The possibility of division or splitting—and therefore carrying the possibility of contradiction—is created just at that moment through the "exchange of action." In other words, in the midst of the rebellion, *we* and *I* are not split, and they are in fact created simultaneously and directly connected. That is the "exchange of actions" between the self and the other in rebellion, and this exchange forces a mutual exchange of the *I* for the *we*.

Hegel, too, noticed this exchange. In the *Phenomenology of Spirit*, he provided the formula "Ich, das Wir, und Wir, das Ich ist" [the we as I, the I as we].[12] However, as we have already seen, Hegel saw this as an opportunity to introduce *spirit*. In other words, for Hegel, the *I* and the *we* are already split and awaiting sublation [*Aufheben*]. Hegel saw Rousseau's individual will and general will in a similar manner, and he substituted spirit for general will. In contrast, in Nagasaki's *The Phenomenology of Politics*, the general will is formed first in the midst of rebellion, so to speak—and experienced without a contract. Only later does individual consciousness become aware of itself as a shared part of the general will ("I was not alone!"). The pilgrimage of the *I*—which does not end in the sublation of the self—begins at this point.

The first step in the pilgrimage is becoming an "agitator." This newly formed agitator is not yet the leader of a group. The agitator is the self as viewed from the eyes of the other, with whom the self exchanges actions. In the midst of the rebellion, the *I* sees his or her own exchange value form in the other. In other words, the self sees in the other his or her own equivalent value form. From the perspective of the *I*, the other just happens to be a person with whom the self shares an action. However, the same thing happens from the perspective of the other: I am the equivalent value form of the other. In other words, I make the other, with whom I just happen to have shared an activity, into an equivalent form of myself. When seen from the perspective of the other who does the same to me, the *I* is the equivalent form of *he* or *she*. The agitator is none other than the self who has come to this realization. Agitators intuitively understand that they express and represent the other. When the self realizes that its equivalent form is not only a single other, but that all others with whom it shares activity in the midst of the rebellion are also in this equivalent form, the self becomes a true agitator. The *I* becomes aware of this:

12 Compare this to Balibar's article, discussed above.

> Through my actions as an individual, as a flesh and blood human being, and by expressing the meaning of the style of our action in concentrated form and through the mediation of my action, others can mutually transact as equals. Through the medium of the self which functions just like money, others carry out a mutual exchange of actions.[13]

In other words, there are many of these selves. Each one is an equivalent form of the many, which amounts to being an agitator. The state in which each individual rebel takes the form of the general value-form C (general equivalence) in Marx's argument in the chapter on value in *Capital* is, according to Nagasaki, the self's first step in its pilgrimage. One could say that Nagasaki's version of Rousseau's general will is formed by every rebel becoming an agitator. To repeat, in contrast to the usual interpretation of the word, here the concept of "rebellion" is overflowing with agitators. Rather than every rebel group having a single agitator, each rebel group is internally full of agitators. Every member is an agitator. Within these groups, being an agitator has nothing to do with a member's personality or charisma. Each agitator is precisely equivalent in the sense that each is simply a member of the group.

A Parallel Theory of Ideals and Action: The *Conatus* of the Rebel Group

Can such a group persist? If a voice of the group—the members, at least ostensibly, are equally representative of the group—calls for action, is it possible to sustain the action of the group as something more than a momentary riot? Furthermore, is it possible to connect the formation of a group to the beginnings of its political experience? Nagasaki replies yes, it is possible. It is similar to the problem of bridging the gap between the general equivalent form and money in Marx's account of the "Genesis of Money" (his theory of the value-form). Why, when all commodities can become the general equivalent form of value, is one of them, namely money, selected as the universal equivalent? Why do the general equivalent forms not destroy market relations before the figure of money is chosen from among them to become every commodity's slave or master? Nagasaki writes: "So long as the group is the set of

13 Nagasaki, *Seiji no genshōgaku*, 24.

every act of integration of each member . . . it cannot possibly evolve into a Group-for-Itself transcending each member."[14] As is well known, Marx resolved this issue by resorting to actual facts or the realm of history; in other words, Marx saw no rationality within the value-form that would resolve the problem. However, Nagasaki's resolution differs: he strays from both Hegel's master-slave dialectic and Marx's theory of value. Nagasaki believes neither that the group is constituted through competition—on the basis of winners and losers, in which someone is chosen and someone is cast out from the group—nor that in the long history of exchange, a materially appropriate thing is finally chosen as the general equivalent form of value.

According to Nagasaki, what sustains a group in which every member is an agitator in their own right, and what keeps the group from dismantling itself, is the "style" of their actions and gestures:

> Where does the existence of the group come from? It is certainly not the essence of the agitator's existence, nor in the agitator's individual existence. It arises from the social style the agitator embodies and from the agitator's words . . . For the agitator, that style and those words are what is essential.[15]

What does this mean?

> My gestures, together with the words I yell, "To fall behind is cowardice! Forward! Forward!" and the words (of the voluntary others) "Viva!" . . . can be read as something exchanged among all the members of the group, or as a style effecting a meaning of assent.[16]

This exchange occurs as long as "the homogeneity of action is preserved."[17] Moreover, "no matter how varied this style is, it tends to express a certain meaning and provides a real foundation for the continuity of shared action." But can one say that the homogeneity of action and the realization of exchange are necessary and sufficient conditions? And can the content of exchange, put schematically, be divided into 1) the formation of style/symbolization developed out of the exchange/

14 Ibid., 30.
15 Ibid., 31.
16 Ibid., 32.
17 Ibid.

contrast of gestures and words; and 2) the exchange as the dissemination of style? It is certainly not a question of which one of these exchanges precedes the other. Even if the meaning-carrying symbol develops first and only then is transmitted after its meaning is developed—or, alternatively, if a shared meaning comes first—the question of which gesture or word corresponds to which meaning is not settled. Consequently, 1) and 2) should be seen as arising simultaneously. On this point, Nagasaki's theory can be seen as analogous to the basics of Saussurean linguistics. Aspects 1) and 2) carry out a process of exchange—and for this reason, they are represented by the same word, "exchange." As this process is unfolding, it preserves the homogeneity of action. Similarly, while the homogeneity of action is maintained, 1) and 2) continue to arise simultaneously. It is possible to understand the relationship between the agitation of the agitator (the sum of the agitator's gestures and words) and the continuity of the group. If this is true, then the relationship between agitators and their agitation reproduces Spinoza's famous parallelism—"the order and connections between ideas is the same as the order and connections between things"—on two levels.[18] First, within individual actions (invading a space, for instance), the order and connection between words are the same as the order and connections between physical gestures. Next, within a series of actions by many (a succession of rebellious acts, for example), the order and connections of their style is the same as the order and connections between the acts themselves. It is for this reason that Nagasaki's concept of exchange can be understood as Spinoza's "order and connections." Because the locus of the meaning of style as symbol is paraphrased as a "communal ideal," the homology with Spinoza's parallelism gains even more legitimacy. The communal ideal as "order and connection" of ideas is the same as the continuity of the group in its "order and connections" between actions. But can the unique place of the "agitator," who provides a solution to the problem of the foundation of the "group as group" that is neither dialectical nor actual-historical, be established through such a reading?

It goes without saying that the theory of parallelism was a Spinozian solution to the so-called mind-body problem passed down by Descartes: how to conceive of the unity between mind and body. Spinoza was never satisfied with his solution—he wrote in a footnote to Proposition 7: "At this point I cannot explain this problem with any greater clarity,"

18 Spinoza, *Ethics*, Harmondsworth: Penguin, 2005, 2.7.

but it is well known that through this provisional explanation, he moved the problem of the individuality of humans and groups and the parallel problem of mind and body in one set to the question of their continuity and reintroduced the idea of *conatus*. In *The Phenomenology of Politics*, Nagasaki momentarily takes leave of his thought of the agitator when he writes, after providing a provisional resolution to the questions of the continuity and origin of the "group as group," that "in contrast to their appearance, leaders are originally nameless," and moves his gaze to a kind—and only a kind—of *conatus* within the parallel processes encompassing style and action.[19] First, this appears as the tendency toward hypertrophy and fanaticism that accompanies the communal ideal. According to Nagasaki, this comes from the tendency of "our communal ideals to greatly exceed the scope of existing organizations and expand to the realm of the ideal world," and this is mirrored or paralleled by its other side, "the strength of the internal ligaments of the group's shared existence."[20]

This does not mean that Nagasaki gave communal ideals themselves the power to form and maintain groups. The process is still a parallel one. The group itself, in other words, the body of the group, "bears within itself the destiny to transform, unavoidably, into something different."[21] At the origin of this destiny is the group's "internal contradiction," and this contradiction is based in the agitator's "original anonymity."[22] In a group that is actually unified by the fact that all members are agitators, one can read a legitimate standing contradiction between the agitator and the masses, who are also made up of all the members of the group. On this point, Nagasaki is loyal to Hegel to a fault. The growing ideals are expressions of actually existing contradictions—that is, expressions of a contradictory relationship, not items in contradiction. However, Nagasaki states that these contradictions "fatigue" the dialectic.[23] This is quite a distance from the Hegelian "sublation" [*Aufheben*]. The contradiction between the agitator and the masses is not resolved, but remains to the end, confronting the group directly and bringing about its death in the form of "fatigue." What does bring new energy to the weary group is the "out-of-scale expansion" of the communal ideal, which not only preserves the group's homogeneity

19 Nagasaki, *Seiji no genshōgaku*, 33.
20 Ibid., 39.
21 Ibid., 65.
22 Ibid., 52.
23 Ibid., 52.

but also pushes the group out of its status quo through the introduction of "violence."[24] The expression of this contradiction causes a new contradiction between the expression and the object of expression—the group as standing contradiction—and promotes a change in the object. By exceeding (itself) and becoming "something else," the group changes form and tries to survive. This shows us the *conatus* of Nagasaki's *The Phenomenology of Politics*, a process whose initiative is seized by the figure of the agitator as the persistence of a style. Here, the *I* (as agitator) replenishes the group with energy—but also with political contradictions and illogic. However, as the motor-force pushing the group's experiences further and further, the self gradually comes to the realization that the group's internal contradictions are on full display.[25] From this point begins the agitator's "pilgrimage" in the literal sense of the term, the *I* is in a state of confusion that is not yet an "apprenticeship" [*apprentissage*]. Contradictions remain unresolved and are merely transferred and renewed. The self does not know whether this makes the group larger—as if keeping pace with the expansion of ideals—or whether it tears it apart, with the expanded ideals taking leave of reality and leading to the group's self-destruction.[26] In other words, within this process, nothing is determined. Nagasaki says that any vector can create "a scene of common-place rebellion."[27] Motivated by internal contradiction, the agitator's ideal and corporeal initiative is nothing less than what Althusser called a "*fuite en avant*," a "flight forward" or "headlong retreat," and is most certainly not a mechanism for guaranteeing the continuity of the group. This is the staging of the autonomy of politics that can be extracted from Nagasaki's *Phenomenology*.

What must be emphasized is that by means of this autonomy of politics, the world is split into two. Through internal contradiction, the communal ideal, which has a built-in tendency to expand, reaches the point where it creates an "exclusionary cosmos."[28] In the rebellion, Nagasaki finds the origins of the "mythological world" that Cassirer analyzed and looks to Sorel's "myth of revolution" and conception of "utopia" as typical examples (Chapter II-3). However, what Nagasaki regards here as significant for the history of political experience is that there is no desire for self-continuity in this "exclusionary cosmos": "In

24 Ibid., 71, 72.
25 Ibid. 73.
26 Ibid., 88.
27 Ibid.
28 Ibid., 74.

the structure of space-time in the world of the rebellion, there is no logic of self-continuity or expansion."[29] What gives birth to communal ideals and feeds their growth is the group's *conatus*. However, the ideal that develops is unaware of the reasons for its birth, and even ignores its circumstances. Following Nagasaki's terminology, the ideal is "absolutely subjectified."[30] The utopian character of the ideal is not a meaningless aspect of it: rather, it is precisely because the communal ideal is utopian that it is able to function with practical effect. This is a kind of "realism of idealism" and Nagasaki recognizes in the communal ideal of rebellion the paradox that in separating from the object rather than unifying with it, the communal ideal has power over the object. In any case, the communal political ideal has an "original receptivity," but the "world of rebellion" created by the ideal within itself is "perfectly self-sufficient."[31] If it is not self-sufficient—that is, if it is not itself the cause of its own existence—it cannot be said to be a product of the cause that gave birth to that world. Does the world of the rebellion close its eyes and merely endure reality? No, its eyes are not closed. This is because, through its freedom as self-sufficiency, a "different world" is born again before its eyes. "Speaking of political pilgrimages, we have of course no choice but to pass through historical space-time, but to live in the world of rebellion basically means to live outside this space and time. For precisely this reason, the historical world and the world of another dimension appear hostile and penetrate into me."[32] Through contact with the "other world" brought by its invasion, "I discover the self that has no choice but to grow and reproduce itself."[33] These two worlds are posited as mutually unrelated due to this aspect of "self-sufficiency." Or we might put it as follows: through the contraction of a portion of a world that is one, the world, when seen from the portion that has contracted, divides into two worlds in an antagonistic relationship. The "autonomy of politics" simultaneously carries out the nullification and reconstruction of the relationship.

29 Ibid., 105.
30 Ibid., 74.
31 Ibid., 106.
32 Ibid., 105.
33 Ibid.

Two Parallel Splits and the Technology of the Party

A politics that is phenomenologically established (and self-sufficient) is split in terms of necessity and contingency. On its interior it holds to a cosmic necessity, while it assigns the name of contingency to its relation with the "external world." "In and amongst the days of the ecstasy of rebellion, one day, taking them by surprise from the side, the external world will appear on the scene, in a slight gap in the consciousness of the agitator."[34] Mutually excluded, thereby a relation of necessity and contingency emerges. This again is what Spinoza referred to as the characteristic of man as "individuum." "The mind has not an adequate but only a confused knowledge of itself, its own body, and of external bodies, whenever it perceives things after the common order of nature; that is, whenever it is determined from without, namely, by the fortuitous play of circumstance, to regard this or that" (*Ethics* II, Prop 29.scol). Of course, for the rebel group, it is not a question of whether its recognition of the enemy is "confused" or "impaired." Bluntly speaking, the only problem is whether or not this is an *external* enemy, and a "true awareness" of the world as a whole, encompassing both the world of rebellion and the other world, is beyond its scope. For this reason, the division between necessity and contingency has an unpredicted effect on the world of rebellion, including it under a new necessity. "The rediscovery of the external enemy by the rebel world, precisely as something that develops the group into something for-itself [*für sich*] out of the communality of the self, is totally new."[35]

Only after rediscovering the exterior world, whose existence it has known only "prereflectively" as the enemy, does the rebel group become a "political group." The group's unique political experience begins from this moment. The phenomenological process up to this point—from the appearance out of the rebellion of the *I* who is both anyone and nobody, by way of the actual formation of the chaotic rebel group, up to the arrival of a world of rebellion that subjectively gives the communal ideal a self-creating position—is, in the end, recorded from the observer's vantage point. The agitator, who is the subject of the "pilgrimage," is not aware of his or her origins or current situation. In the final analysis, the agitator merely responds passively to the actions of others when they occur. There is no moment in the process whereby the agitator,

34 Ibid., 101.

35 Ibid., 112.

who is the subject of the "pilgrimage," can reflectively become a *political* subject. Finally, brought about by the autonomy that accompanies self-causation—and once again, from the exterior—the moment of this subjectification arrives. The first externality is the "him/her" encountered in the midst of the rebellion. It is the encounter with this, then, that makes the *I* an agitator. The next externality encountered is the enemy. The encounter with the enemy makes the others, whom the *I* has met previously, into friends, and the friend-enemy relationship transforms the *I* into a political subject.

If this is the case, can the distinctiveness of politics be reduced to the handling of the friend-enemy relationship? Does a Schmittian politics wait for us after phenomenology ends?[36] It is not so simple. This is because the "outside" that appears twice to the *I* is, in reality, the same. The second "exterior" is discovered when it "invades" the *I*. This invasion of an alien world presents us with a "negative mirror which has forced us to look directly and honestly at our communality" and "*as a result*, it brings the discovery that the enemy is also present within us."[37] The "reflection" that leads to political subjectivity is no more than an individual act on the part of the *I*, but at the same time that it establishes *us* as "friends," it also exposes our relationship to a crisis of dissolution. When it is discovered, the "outside" is already "within" our shared *us*, whom we have previously known as friends. That is, the outside is discovered as the presence of a threat to the continuity of the *I-us-friend* relationship. For the self-sufficient interior, this is likely the only way the outside can be discovered. Because *I* and *we* can both be directly connected as—or reduced to—"friends," the "enemy" that "invades me" occupies a seat next to me—just like the first other whom the *I* discovered. This is similar to the way that our internal organs are exposed to a virus. Before they are exposed, is the virus not already present in the body? Because I am *we*, the external enemy is brought in. The other, who has been discovered as a friend, is rediscovered as an existence that may be the enemy of the *I*. As a result, contingency not only pushes a previously self-sufficient necessity into crisis, but actually dissolves it. There is no longer any self-causation. The cause behind my existence transfers to the totality of the current power relation between friend and enemy. "My" existence is now nothing but the result of all causes arising from both friend and enemy. The reflective establishment of the

36 Ibid., 116.
37 Ibid., 123.

I-we-friend relationship pushes the unique *I* to take leave of the *we* and the friend. In this manner, I am split between the *I* as friend and an *I* who latently turns those who had been friends into enemies. The distrust of the *we*, which is the embodiment of the acknowledgment of the enemy, forms the content of political subjectivity. "Our solidarity splits the group apart, and the world of rebellion breaks into many groups."[38] The unique nature of the political experience lies in the experience of the alienated *I* = *we* and the experience of the *I* = *we*'s handling of the split from the self. This occurs in the midst of the friend-enemy relationship, as the friend = enemy relationship is being dealt with. Here, the decision, which carries a determinate meaning in Schmitt's politics, has next to no meaning in and of itself.

Taking a bird's-eye view of this situation, in other words, if we reintroduce the vantage point of the observer, this situation is equivalent to when the agitators simply jumbled together within the rebel group, when each member is in the equivalent form. Not only is there no privileged currency called "money" to bind together an *us*, but each member is potentially the enemy of all other members. *I* reflect on the split in myself between my "relative value form" and my "equivalent form," and all I have become is a subject taking the split as object. If the "decision" is supposed to be an act that erases the split, this abandonment of subjectivity is nothing other than a return to simply being an agitator. Ideals and actions parallel each other and the split in the interior parallels the split between exterior and interior. These *two parallel divisions* must be continually renewed and preserved *by means of the technologies* of the political subject. For Nagasaki, the example of these technologies are Lenin's "April Theses": "A new and different task now faces us: to effect a split *within* this dictatorship between the proletarian elements . . . and the small-proprietor or petty-bourgeois elements."[39] The task of splitting the Soviet has to be posed, along with the function of the slogan "All Power to the Soviets," which is to bring together "friends" and parallel the enemy. If the external enemy is only thrown out from the interior, the interior will gradually grow smaller and wither away. The enemy within must drive out the external enemy in a process of expanding the interior. This must be carried out in step with a process of developing "organs of power" equivalent to those on the exterior. If the

38 Ibid.

39 Lenin, "Letters on Tactics," *Collected Works of VI Lenin*, vol. 24, Moscow: Progress, 1964, 42–54.

interior cannot do that, there is no alternative but for the political group to return to being a "self-sufficient" rebel group. Whether the group can persist and expand depends solely on whether it can maintain these two parallelisms or renew this dynamic as a problem of the technologies of the parallelism of one power versus another, the problem of "dual power."[40]

In actuality, the later accounts in Nagasaki's *The Phenomenology of Politics* offer a description of this difficult struggle and end with the thesis of the *technological group* as a "unique party": "In order to unite with the masses, one must wish to be with them; rather than scholastic this or that about separation and unification, *for the Party, the revolution is the object*; this points to the unique sense in which the Party's practice always has the character of practice vis-à-vis an object."[41] The revolution that liberates those who are dominated under one power relation from their dominators is the greatest social act of *division* and *separation*. By taking that separation and division *as its object*, the party decisively sets itself off from the rebel group—the party, "like a mass organization, absolutely must create itself with a spirit of discovery." In other words, it has to entrust itself to phenomenological creation. The pilgrimage is over when it becomes a party: "Paradoxically, from the point where the mass organization's pilgrimage ends, the party must set out on the path of rebellion."[42] The party was once something of a mass organization, and the actual self-expression of the party is the agitator. However, the party is the "organized distrust" of the entirety of the agitator's pilgrimage as well as its own past.[43] Operating dialectically, "phenomenology" aims for the final erasure of unification or, in other words, for a parallelism. The party is *other* to the agitator on a pilgrimage. The agitator as *I/we* does not become the party but must *encounter* the party. But if that is the case, has not the party been there since the beginning of the pilgrimage? Perhaps the other encountered by the *I* is itself the party? With what sort of existence has the party engaged with the history of pilgrimage? But we should know this already—as observers of the pilgrimage. There is no place in the history of the pilgrimage for the observer. In the final instance, the pilgrimage is passionately motivated toward an

40 Lenin, "The Dual Power," in ibid., 38–41.

41 Nagasaki, *Seiji no genshōgaku*, 323.

42 Ibid., 345.

43 Ibid., 342.

internal encounter with the observer. Has not the agitator been seeing and pursuing the back of this other as observer all along? Is the other encountered in the midst of rebellion, the other that I transform into a primitive, just the figure of God himself from behind? And did not Moses, the Jewish agitator, see God from behind? Perhaps, in the end, Nagasaki's *The Phenomenology of Politics* was a retelling of the story of Exodus under the name of phenomenology.

Translated by Gavin Walker

4

The Perception of Violence, the Violence of Perception, and the Origins of Japan's 1968

William Marotti

> Whatever qualities at present genuinely anticipate a more human existence are always simultaneously, in the eyes of the existing order, damaged rather than harmonious things.
>
> – Adorno, "Sociology and Psychology—II," 1968

Japan's 1968 commemorated the hundredth anniversary of the Meiji Restoration, the "return" of governance from the Tokugawa shogunate, which inaugurated a modern, centralized state and located a supposedly primordial institutional authority in a "restored" imperial rule. The calendar year opened with an event highlighting a rather different source of transcendent authority, with the imminent arrival of the nuclear-powered (and likely nuclear-armed) *USS Enterprise* to US Fleet Activities Sasebo naval base in Nagasaki Prefecture, en route to Yankee Station in the Tonkin Gulf. Activists assembled from across the country to oppose its arrival, and they faced thousands of massed riot police likewise mobilized from throughout the nation. The visit was years in the making, part of a plan to desensitize the Japanese people to nuclear-powered ships in advance of the anticipated reversion of Okinawa to Japanese sovereignty with American military basing rights intact, as well as continuing Vietnam War missions.[1] This primary, though disavowed, mission

1 The plan was for "conditioning the Japanese to military nuclear matters." Action Memorandum, President's Question about Visit of Nuclear Carrier Enterprise to Sasebo, Japan, Philip J. Farley and Samuel D. Berger to Undersecretary of State Nicholas Katzenbach, January 22, 1968, 2, Secret, DNSA, doc. JU00877. Such ulterior motives were tolerably obvious, given the flimsiness of the official stated need for rest and resupply for a ship merely two weeks out of port.

relied upon the fiction of the Japanese government's "three nuclear principles"—neither to manufacture, nor to possess, nor to permit the introduction [*mochikomi*] of nuclear weapons—which dissimulated the regular transit of nuclear armaments as per the secret agreements appended to the United States–Japan Security Treaty (Anpō) in 1960.[2]

The arrival came in the wake of major protest events at Haneda Airport, where activists seeking to block Prime Minister Satō Eisaku's departure for Saigon forcibly clashed with police on October 9, 1967, the "First Haneda Incident." Again, on November 12, in the "Second Haneda Incident," activists opposed Prime Minister Satō's departure (to the United States to meet with President Lyndon B. Johnson) and were met with massed security police—some 5,000 in the vicinity of the airport alone. While a range of groups protested these trips for their participation in the Vietnam War, press coverage focused on the actions of the Sanpa Zengakuren (Three-Faction Alliance, or *Sanpa*), a recent coalition of three radical student groups within the Zengakuren: the All-Japan Federation of Students' Self-Governing Associations. Sanpa was united in a commitment to direct action against the quiescent majority Minsei Zengakuren, an affiliate of the equally quiescent Japan Communist Party (JCP). The First Haneda Incident inaugurated the new policy of Sanpa members to don helmets and use staves and rocks to fight riot police (who were armed, as per usual, with meter-long truncheons, duralumin shields, visored helmets, tear-gas guns, water cannons, and armored vehicles).

While violence was nothing new in post–World War II protest in Japan, events at Haneda commenced the use of violence in order to prevent the exercise of declared state policy—thereby foregrounding the issue of force and its legitimacy in confrontations between protesters and the state.[3] Mainstream press reaction to both Haneda events was dominated, however, by negative appraisals of student "violence" and

2 As detailed in a declassified 1969 top-secret paper on Japan policy, in a discussion of Okinawa reversion, "Japan now acquiesces in transit by naval vessels armed with nuclear weapons. This right would extend automatically to Okinawa. (This is sensitive and closely held information.)" East Asia Interdepartmental Group, NSSM 5: Japan Policy, undated, 25, attachment to Jeanne W. Davis, NSC Memorandum, April 28, 1969, Top Secret, DNSA, doc. JU01061.

3 The Haneda and Sasebo confrontations, and their implications, are discussed at length in Marotti, "Japan 1968: The Performance of Violence and the Theater of Protest," *American Historical Review* 114: 1, 2009, 97–135. Also present at Haneda was the anti-war youth committee, Hansen seinen i'inkai, composed of young workers; several hundred Japan Socialist Party and Japan Communist Party members, together with 350 Minsei students, conducted more conventional protest gestures. The JCP also conducted a "Red Flag Festival" of protest on October 8, some 35 miles away.

featured few serious attempts to consider the substantive issues involved. Writing underground in the group's newspaper, *Zenshin,* Honda Nobuyoshi, the leader of the Chūkaku sect (one of the three Sanpa groups), complained:

> The organs of the bourgeois press and their official critics . . . obscured [our] focus—"oppose the Vietnam war, obstruct the visit"—with the so-called problem of violence, castigating the Zengakuren struggle as a "violent demonstration" and "armed demonstration," while simultaneously maneuvering to conceal and defend the fundamental problem of state violence . . . On October 8, Zengakuren had its right to demonstrate stripped from it: wasn't it police headquarters and the public safety commission whose suppression through outrageous violence ensured that Zengakuren would be unable to exercise its right even to a one-meter-long march without forcibly breaking through the riot police's obstructing line? And isn't it police headquarters and the public safety commission that for seven years since Anpō have mobilized the well-armed riot police against Zengakuren's unarmed demonstrations, inflicting bloody oppression by blows, kicks, and arrests, causing near-fatal injuries for dozens? For one, the right to be armed and to strike, kick, and arrest; for the other, in order to declare an anti-war intent, the right to be struck, kicked, and arrested—only this is permitted. If this isn't state violence, what is? But on October 8, police headquarters and the public safety commission usurped the right even to be hit, kicked, and arrested.[4]

Delighted by such dismissals of protest actions as irrational, criminal, or worse, the government green-lit an even harsher stance to be taken against demonstrators in advance of the *USS Enterprise*'s arrival in Sasebo. The Japanese and American governments both likewise were sanguine about the perceived success of their program of successive SSN visits since 1964 to routinize such events; both countries had witnessed decreasing protester numbers and press coverage, and they looked forward to a successful visit to take their program of nuclear desensitization to the next level.[5]

4 Honda Nobuyoshi, "Haneda tōsō no igi to tatakai no tenbō," *Zenshin* 337 (October 30, 1967), reprinted in Honda, *Honda Nobuyoshi Chosakusen I*, Tokyo: Zenshinsha, 1975, 341–2. Chūkaku's official name is Nihon kakumeiteki kyōsanshugisha dōmei zenkoku iinkai kakumeiteki marukusushugiha, the Japan Revolutionary Communist League, Revolutionary Marxist Faction.

5 See Marotti, "Japan 1968," 114–16.

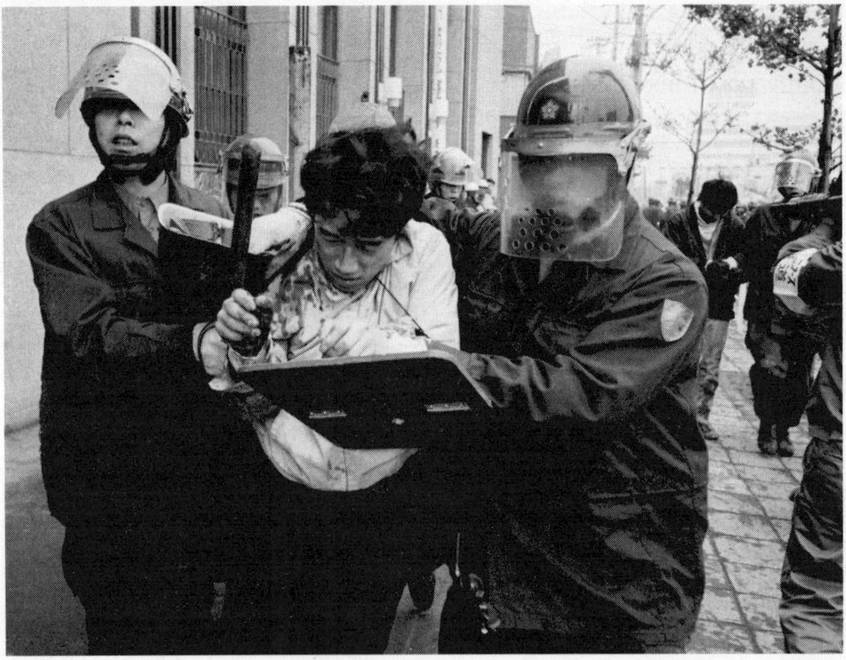

Riot police lead bleeding demonstrator away to waiting wagons, Second Haneda Incident, November 12, 1967. Photo courtesy of Ishiguro Kenji.

The visit, together with the anticipated deployment of state violence against protesters, was thus intended to facilitate closer coordination between the US and Japanese governments in their synchronized strategic posture and support for American cold and hot wars. Likewise, both governments looked ahead to the renewal of the United States–Japan Security Treaty in 1970 and hoped to curtail, overawe, and delegitimize likely sources of protest. Yet all of these plans for an edifying spectacle risked backfiring impressively, particularly in the event of a "fluke," either by a deserter from the ship revealing its actual nuclear armaments or by the accidental creation of a martyr among the protesters.[6]

With such concerns in mind, police paid attention to members of the then-small anti-war "Peace in Vietnam!" Citizens' Committee, Beheiren. The group's pamphlets appealed to American soldiers to consider resistance at all levels, from letter writing and symbolic

6 Telegram 4763, "Enterprise Visit to Sasebo," January 17, 1968, 3, Secret, DNSA, doc. JU00876.

walkouts to filing for conscientious objector status and actual desertion—which they had memorably facilitated in the fall, assisting the departure of the "Intrepid Four" sailors from the *USS Intrepid*, including their escape from service and from Japan through their semi-independent JATEC (Japan Technical Committee for Assistance to Anti-War US Deserters) group.[7] Beheiren had also been frequently visited by seventy-three-year-old Yui Chūnoshin, a longtime peace activist and Esperanto advocate who set himself on fire outside of the prime minister's residence the night before the Second Haneda Incident.

Sanpa mobilized with an eye to Sasebo becoming a "Third Haneda" and possibly finally breaking through to trigger mass opposition to Japan's participation in the Vietnam War.[8] A broad set of other protest groups likewise mobilized, including rightists (estimated by police at around 46,000) in support of the visit, but press attention was overwhelmingly drawn to the "newsworthy" attractiveness of anticipated battles between police and the expected 2,000–3,000 Sanpa members.[9]

As the American embassy recounted, on January 17, two days before the *Enterprise's* arrival,

> as hundreds of reporters and cameramen looked on, about 375 plastic-helmeted, stave-carrying and rock-throwing [Sanpa] students charged about four times as many riot policemen at a bridge directly in front of the US naval base. After taking the first student thrust, the police responded with their own billyclub charge, supported by tear gas and water cannons. The peak of the clash coincided perfectly with the noon television news and millions of television viewers were permitted to see the full force of the police counteroffensive by direct television relay.

Such heroic exercises in symbolic opposition drew rapt press and public attention, with unanticipated results.

---

7 On Beheiren in English, see Simon Andrew Avenell, *Making Japanese Citizens: Civil Society and the Mythology of the Shimin in Postwar Japan*, Berkeley: University of California Press, 2010, 106–47. Beheiren also made appeals to Koreans who were serving in the armed forces and those who were directly engaged in warfare in Vietnam.

8 *Zenshin*, December 25, 1967, 1.

9 The rare exception was press coverage of maneuvers between the Maritime Self-Defense Forces and Beheiren, as the former desperately sought to keep Beheiren's rented water taxi and its pro-desertion banners from approaching the *Enterprise*.

Students battle riot police by Fleet Activities Sasebo as water cannon spray spiked with eye irritant drifts over protesters and observers alike. January 21, 1968, Sasebo, Nagasaki Prefecture. US Navy Archives.

The stunning effect of direct television coverage combined with a popular press thrilled to market such dramatic imagery set the stage for a major reversal in the perceived legitimacy of state force in support of its policies. Hurling concussion grenades and liberally spraying eye-irritant water cannons, the police, over the next several days, enacted something akin to a police riot before the assembled live cameras, reporters, and some 10,000 citizens of Sasebo; officers were captured in acts of indiscriminately dramatic violence. Group beatings of unresisting protesters in hospital courtyards received iconic photographic coverage; likewise, early accounts of citizens and reporters falling victim to unprovoked and coordinated police attacks worked to reverse public perceptions of the legitimacy of such state force—and drew attention to precisely the issues the government had hoped to police with this orchestrated event. The danger of such entanglements was driven further home by the *Enterprise*'s diversion after Sasebo to respond to the January 23 seizure of the vessel *Pueblo* during its naval and NSA surveillance activities off the coast of North Korea—events that threatened the outbreak of a second Korean War involving Japan directly, even as they recalled Japan's colonial legacy and support for the prior war.[10] The January 30 launch of the Tet Offensive added further doubts and concerns, discrediting American claims about the scope and progress of the war and, by extension, the supportive stance of the Japanese government.

The subsequently named "Enterprise Incident" effected a watershed in the possibilities for political subjectivation and action. On the one hand, fearful of a subsequent incident of repression igniting precisely the kinds of conflagration dreamed of by Sanpa and the like, the government reversed its prior repressive stance and directed the riot police to a new and severely restrained posture.[11] On the other, new attention now converged on the meaning of these confrontations. After years of waning public interest—and occasional summary state violence in the absence of that interest—the media now excitedly covered each subsequent protest in hopes of catching similar spectacular confrontations. Public polls, media discussions, and US embassy assessments alike confirmed new attention to strategic and security treaty issues, as well as to their connections to both state actions and daily life in Japan. But even more broadly, the transformation in perception by which protester concerns became reasonable, and police action (and the state policies it supported) violent and illegitimate, in turn prompted a wave of political subjectivations. Illegitimate violence at home echoed not-so-distant illegitimate violence, especially the Vietnam War—and attentiveness disclosed abundant direct connections between the two.

Moved by such concerns, so-called "ordinary people," "typical students," "citizens," the "nonpolitical" all found cause to engage in activism and sought new forms adequate to their understandings of the moment. They particularly swelled the ranks of antihierarchical organizations such as Beheiren, which offered a flexible, horizontal coalition (any group could call itself Beheiren if it adopted the three principles of peace in Vietnam, Vietnam for the Vietnamese, and opposition to

10 Discussed explicitly in Airgram A-1098, "The Enterprise Visit," February 23, 1968, 15, Secret, in *Confidential US State Department Central Files: Japan 1967–1969*, reel 3, 0318-0334. President Nixon in fact concluded that "the whole matter was tied in to Vietnam. They want to keep [South] Korea from sending in that other division of troops to Vietnam." "Notes of the President's Meeting with Senator Dirksen and Congressman Ford," January 30, 1968, Top Secret, LBJ Library, Austin, TX.

11 Airgram A-309, "The Japanese Student Protest Movement," American Embassy Tokyo to Department of State, April 10, 1969, 19, Limited Official Use, CF 1967–1969, Def 7 Japan-US, 3, Confidential, in *Confidential Files: Japan*, reel 10, 0248-0278.

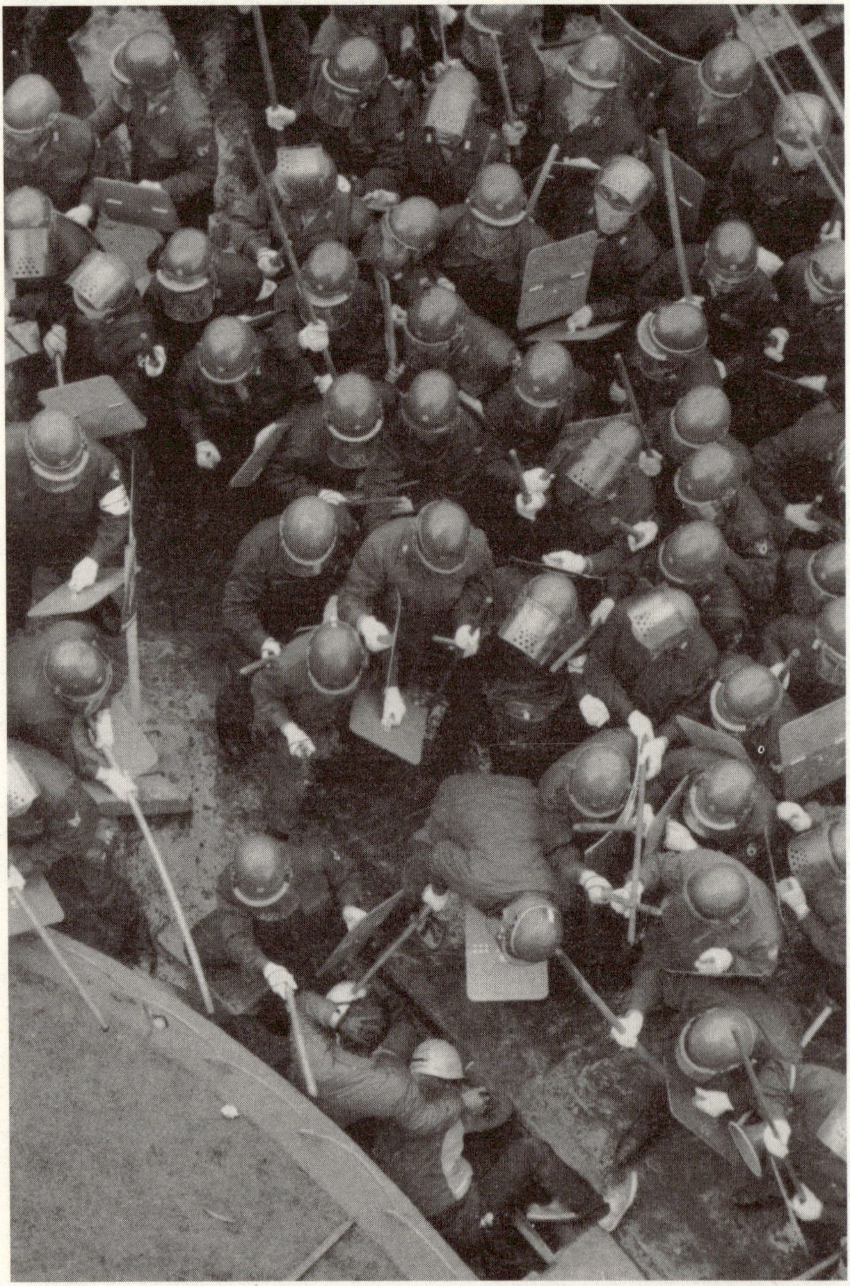

Massed riot police beating fallen demonstrators, January 17, 1968, Sasebo, Nagasaki Prefecture. Photo courtesy of the Asahi Shimbun.

the Japanese government's complicity in the Vietnam War), with each group responsible for its own policies and for communicating across this network. Ordinary people also formed the basis for the explosive spread of the nonsectarian All-Campus Joint Struggle League, or Zenkyōtō. These latter groups, emerging mid-1968 from the developing University of Tokyo and Nihon University conflicts, proliferated across hundreds of university campuses to create more than sixty-seven campus seizures or lockouts by year's end (and 127 in 1969). It was Zenkyōtō that made dissensus into their very motto, calling for their own self-negation [*jiko hitei*] as elite students within a hierarchical and compromised educational system that itself required complete disassembly [*daigaku kaitai*, "dismantle the university!"] to end its furtherance of domination.[12]

In short, "1968," in the sense of a global moment, truly begins in this space of restrained policing and daily eventfulness, of diminished state legitimacy and intensified concern to the wrongs such legitimacy previously concealed, both near and far. This politics inaugurates new engagements, with novel perceptions and personal reflections that bring forth new actions and collective identifications. It is at this level that we should consider questions of comparability, of how such politics becomes thinkable, and of the proper approach to address the nature of this politics.

Perceptual Politics and Theorizing Japan's 1968

The present volume's scope happily obviates the need for an explicit survey of the broader field of research and arguments concerning 1968. This piece in particular is intended to be read together with that of my research and archival collaborator, artist and scholar Yoshiko Shimada. The two essays are drawn from our extended empirical investigations and conversations, and they are meant to supplement each other.[13]

12 Beheiren likewise featured a self-critical perspective, calling upon its members to consider their own roles as perpetrators in past and current violence in Asia—the "Vietnam War within ourselves." See Shimada in this volume on the connections of *daigaku kaitai* to Jiritsu Gakkō.

13 The following draws upon two intertwined, ongoing research and writing projects. The first is my forthcoming work on 1968 in Japan, *The Art of Revolution: Politics and Aesthetic Dissent in Japan's 1968*. The second comprises a closely related program of cooperative research, archival preservation efforts, oral history, and joint writings with Shimada. The published works include Yoshiko Shimada, ed., *From Nirvana to Catastrophe: Matsuzawa Yutaka and his "Commune in Imaginary Space,"* Tokyo: Ota Fine Arts Tokyo,

My argument is premised upon recognizing a global 1968, a global moment in which events in Japan operate coevally. In providing the aforementioned account of events within Japan, I fundamentally reject the notion of a distinctive "Japan case" for 1968 in the form of an expansion of a problematic arriving from elsewhere. The particularities of this history need not lead us to provincialization, making a Japanese junior partner to be incorporated within a more familiar and supposedly root-based hierarchy of cases. The particular is, of course, the necessary form of appearance of the universal, so it is an abuse of the two categories to grasp the particular as the universal's opposite.[14] Rather, I argue that events in Japan participated in this global movement in ways that can inform our understanding for an at-once local and global history within this contentious moment. As we saw in the case of both Beheiren and Zenkyōtō, the form of that politics laid claims to universal demands for equality and justice as it grasped the specific details that linked quotidian life and contention to simultaneous far-flung struggles. In this way, 1968 thus takes the form of a global moment of discontinuous solidarity.

In analyzing any scene for signs of a 1968 writ large—that is, a global 1968—we find ourselves facing an epistemological difficulty at the outset—one that has confounded many analyses. First, the form of 1968 politics was that of politics in general, as understood by Jacques Rancière. The unsettling of the boundaries and definitions of the "political," as commonly understood and practiced, is for Rancière the very sign and essence of politics. Politics, in this view, is "an intervention in the visible and sayable," a struggle for visibility and voice out of noise, a shifting of places and designations on the part of claims and groups unnamed, unaccounted for, and disqualified. It is an act of "dissensus" that imagines a speaker, an object, and an addressee predicated on the recognition of the inadequacies of given categories to account for this

2017, exhibition catalog; Mizunuma Hirokazu, Matsuoka Takeshi, and Iwao Yoshinobu, eds., *Akasegawa Genpei no geijutsu genronten: 1960 nendai kara genzai made* ["The Principles of Art" by Genpei Akasegawa: From 1960s to the present], Chiba: Chiba National Museum of Art, Japan, 2014, exhibition catalog; Nakajima Yoshio Syndrome Committee, ed., *Nakajima Yoshio Syndrome: Art Is Always the Next Possibility*, Tokyo: Nakajima Yoshio Syndrome Committee, 2015; and Alice Maude-Roxby, *Anti-Academy*, ed. Joan Giroux, Manchester: John Hansard Gallery, 2013.

14 Such an approach readily obscures structured and structuring forms of social relations. See Moishe Postone, *Time, Labor, and Social Domination: A Reinterpretation of Marx's Critical Theory*, Cambridge: Cambridge University Press, 1993, 366–73.

new vision.[15] One therefore ought to look for it in perceptual and practical transformations, and in deformations of categorical identity—such as "student," for example.[16] Kristin Ross argues that 1968 politics is precisely characterizable as "a flight from social determinations . . . a disjunction, that is, between political subjectivity and the social group." It was a "massive refusal on the part of thousands, even millions, of people to see in the social what we usually see."[17] That is, we find our proper object of analysis not in the pre-given and socially well-recognized forms of belonging, but in the pervasive defections from those categories to as-yet fugitive forms of collectivity. Again and again, politics begins with a recognition of one's own given position as implicated in domination, and in the repetition of injustices near and far, and hence as an inadequate basis for action—and then motion toward something different. And as was the case in the wake of the Enterprise Incident, citizens, students, workers, onlookers, and "nonpolitical" types alike found themselves necessarily drawn to action, and to new subjectivations.[18]

Such politics is by no means exclusive to 1968, even a "long 1968"; it is, again, in Rancière's conception, the very form of politics itself. But 1968 represents a high-tide point for an otherwise rare eventfulness that facilitated such politics in the form of discontinuous, sympathetic exercises in solidarity. Yet, precisely because the most powerfully transformative examples depart from social categories as their very mode of activism, politics itself departs from conventionally identifiable forms and becomes unrecognizable to an analysis keyed to such formalism. In short, as politics, it precisely did not look like what might commonly be recognized as "political."

15 Jacques Rancière, "Ten Theses on Politics," in *Dissensus: On Politics and Aesthetics*, ed. and trans. Steve Corcoran, London: Continuum, 2010, 37; Rancière, *Disagreement: Politics and Philosophy*, Minneapolis: University of Minnesota Press, 1999, 28–30, 58–60.

16 In terms of sheer demographics, by 1967, Japan had over a million students enrolled in some 346 universities—that is, more than in France and Germany combined, without counting the two-year colleges.

17 Kristin Ross, *May '68 and Its Afterlives*, Chicago: University of Chicago Press, 2002, 7, 20–27, 56–61; Rancière, "Ten Theses," 43. See also Davide Panagia, *Ten Theses for an Aesthetics of Politics*, Minneapolis: University of Minnesota Press, 2016.

18 Similarly, while arguing for a strict separation between art/culture activists and political activists, Oguma Eiji concedes that perhaps in absolute numbers, the group that partially engaged with politics, music, and theater alike was the most numerous; see Eiji Oguma, *1968*, Tōkyō: Shin'yōsha, 2009, 93. Such tendencies parallel Hiraoka Masaaki's argument concerning *keisha kekki* and Akasegawa Genpei's reflections on the incomprehensibly blurring line between art and politics (see discussion in Shimada, this volume).

This politics rejected both the administrative politics of an ersatz, single-party democracy and the comfortable conventionality of oppositional groups; it emerged instead in the instabilities of categories that had previously described forms of apoliticality, but which, by 1968, had instead come to indicate an unconventional and hence unbounded critical potential. The *nonpori* or "nonpolitical," *ippan-gakusei* or "typical students," and the *shimin* or "citizens" alike represented sources of profound governmental anxiety, as each had shifted from a normative trajectory of quiescent accomplishment, conventional sociality, and consumption to forms of disidentification and new activism—again, often in the explicitly antihierarchical, nonsectarian organizations such as Beheiren and Zenkyōtō that exploded in membership throughout 1968. Such dynamics were paralleled by a growing new and repurposed vocabulary as the means for solidarity within an expanse of coalescing meanings.[19] And as Yoshiko Shimada details in her companion piece, this was even more the case with those activists targeting perception itself with forms of uncategorizable direct action.

As Ross argues, this has explicit consequences for the retrospective analysis of 1968, as conventional modes of its narration perpetrate "confiscations" by reducing it to biographical and sociological tropes that efface the actuality of its emergent and collective forms. Analyses that cleave to stories of undifferentiated "students" ignore the very modes by which such identities were pervasively rethought in case after case. Again, the University of Tokyo and other students sought to upend their privileged position within a stunningly hierarchical system of university education through *jiko-hitei* [self-negation]; such approaches paralleled similar analyses across the globe even as they helped facilitate making common cause with activists at nearby institutions. The wave of campus seizures exploding in 1968 in Japan was not about self-identity—it was an exploration of possibilities, of new ways of being, one seized from these places of social reproduction, and resonating with similar actions throughout the world.[20] And, if

19 Such contemporaneous usage is documented in Akatsuka Yukio, *Geba an goten* [Gewalt/Underground Dictionary], Tokyo: Jiyū Kokuminsha, 1970, 12–48. In his preface, "*Wakamono bunka wa dokuritsu suru*" [Youth culture becomes autonomous], Akatsuka discusses the differentiation and autonomy of the new culture his dictionary underscores at the level of language.

20 From June of 1968, the weekly *Asahi Journal*, a favorite periodical for activists, featured a nearly thirty-part photo-essay series, "Student Power," documenting scenes of

the immediate triggers for the first instances of such occupations might seem expressly local—in the form of revealed corruption, oppressive administration, labor demands, and the like—the systemic critique that followed rapidly took on an international and global perspective, joining others in developing critiques of the daily practices that reproduce systems of oppression near and far, and then demanding revolutionary solutions.[21]

Such formal resonances within a dissensual politics provide the more obvious manifestations of the global dimensions of 1968. Another is revealed in the related legibility of one scene of such politics to another, whether through the burgeoning media networks (from mainstream to underground) or in the person of traveling activists and dropouts connecting to imagine an antinational subversion of corrupt belonging and its related wars. Even as new political subjectivations proliferated across countless scenes and emergent social roles, their apparent incongruities nonetheless gave rise to mutual solidarity and support. Such obscure resonances were a source of frustration and concern to authorities the world over. The notorious secret CIA report "Restless Youth" noted how a certain shared culture facilitated the transmissibility of radicalism across nations and activist groups. Similarly, according to Yamada Kaiya, a.k.a. "Pon" of the Emerald Breeze Tribe and Buzoku commune, Japanese authorities agonized over the threat posed by American hippie "flower power" communicating its anti-war message to

---

activism around the world. Ranging from Uruguay and South Vietnam to Ghana, India, Senegal, the Philippines, Okinawa, Indonesia, the League of Arab States, Mexico, Denmark, Finland, Sweden, West Germany, France, Turkey, Czechoslovakia, Ecuador, England, and across several pieces on the United States, the series ran as the university occupations spread throughout Japan, presenting a visual confirmation of the discontinuous solidarity of a world joined in revolt. Such sympathetic portrayals contrasted markedly with the national newspaper's newswire-dependent coverage of, for example, the Black Panther Party. See Jason Christopher Jones, "The Black Panther Party and the Japanese Press," *Journal of African American Studies* 21: 1, 2017, 42–70.

21 Vietnam often served as the prototypical measure for complicity—any links between the local and the Vietnam War provided a damning indictment of the former. Late 1960s Japan, with its economic boom benefiting from direct and indirect Vietnam War procurements, a still-occupied Okinawa, extensive American military bases, and supply transits (jet fuel through Shinjuku, for example) provided considerable opportunities for such connections and help make October 21 anti-war day actions highly legible. Yet Vietnam could function equally powerfully in situations with rather less manifest connections—such as in Mexico City—or even in abstraction from such seemingly obvious possibilities—such as in Paris, former metropole for the colony of Indochina.

Japanese youth through the allure of marijuana—and conducted their frequent raids and roundups of hangouts accordingly.[22] Even when it was but a small organization, Beheiren threatened to upend multiyear strategic government plans through its outreach to US service members, garnering police and military intervention radically disproportionate to its size.[23]

Unexpected communications could move in any direction—and even be precipitated by a single individual. A peripatetic artist coming from the early 1960s avant-garde politics in Japan, Nakajima Yoshio brought his practice of radical street performances to Antwerp and Amsterdam. As research is only recently recognizing, Nakajima played an essential role in transforming the conceivable forms of action in a way that catalyzed the actions of the Provo in both cities.[24]

But, again, the thinkability and practical possibility of such solidarities, and new politics, demanded a departure from the identities and categories that would merely reproduce that which activists fought against. And it was here that groups such as those associated with Gendai Shichōsha had their impact—the "thought perverts" who transformed the coordinates of the everyday world and its categories, facilitating new perceptions, both directly and indirectly, through their performative contributions to a sense of eventfulness and radicalized spaces.[25] As artist Akasegawa Genpei argued (see Shimada, in this volume), art and political gazes alike could consider the thrown Molotov cocktail within a rethought field of force and legitimacy, and from that

22 Yamada Kaiya (Pon), *Ai amu hippī: nihon no hippī mūbumento '60–'90*, Tokyo: Morito shuppan, 2013, 63–65. The commune's underground newspaper, *Buzoku*, had printed frequent Japan-visitor Gary Snyder's "Why Tribe" article from the San Francisco *Oracle* in its inaugural issue (December 1967) in English and Japanese translations, together with its own call for defections from nations to a world of communal tribes, written by poet and editor Nagasawa Tetsuo: "We who are within this husk of a national society are forming a society of mutuality utterly different than that of the nation . . . Within a few decades, an alliance of tribes all over the world will be formed, and so we watch over this fated destiny by which nations must pass away."

23 Beheiren's actions also resonated with the pro-desertion "coffee house" underground networks throughout the world.

24 Recent work by Tania Ørum, Peter van der Meijden, and Yoshiko Shimada has begun to document the improbable timely role of this untimely artist. See Nakajima Yoshio Syndrome Committee, ed., *Nakajima Yoshio Syndrome*.

25 Tanikawa Gan's own analyses of "archetypal pattern" [*tenkei*] and its possible creative dissolution in the "nonpolitical politics of the poem"—and the related problems of organization and of troubling repetition—receive thoughtful treatment in Gavin Walker, "Tanigawa Gan and the Poetics of Origin," *Positions* 25: 2, 2017, 351–87.

they could draw intersecting and unstable conclusions.[26] Both radical student and artistic action alike worked to enable new perceptions, and new subjectivations, in ways troubling to authorities precisely for their unclassifiable nature. As politics, they were a departure from the norms Rancière describes as "police," his term for the order of the given and recognized—and its stifling assertion of completeness, to the exclusion of all else.[27]

In a sense, the mass mobilizations, protests, street struggles, campus seizures, and the like can occlude this fundamental dissensual dimension of perception and subjectivation. The achievement of collective action in such scenes of struggle can be mistaken as the verification of politics, which then turns back to a question of mobilization. But if streets full of protesters mark a politics, it cannot but tautologically explain itself. That is, what is the process by which empty streets become full ones? What is the process of subjectivation as an activist? And, just as importantly, what perceptual transformations underlie such engagements? Force and legitimation were key to the activist-police confrontations from October 1967 through January 1968, but it was not a question of numbers, nor of successful opposition. It was a performance of opposition that disclosed the state violence undergirding state policy and an intensified attention leading to new commitments.

The Orthogonal Space of Politics

As Shimada demonstrates with her analysis of publishing house Gendai Shichōsha, an orthogonal perspective on more mainstream and well-recognized forms of "political" thought and action might also serve as the very ground for new thinking and activism. Such politics could also involve spaces of unprogrammed gathering and eventfulness, such as the bustling Shinjuku Ward in Tokyo—1968 saw

26 Shimada (this volume); on Akasegawa, force, and the *objet*, see Marotti, "The Art of the Everyday, as Crisis: *Objets*, Installations, Weapons, and the Origin of Politics," *boundary* 242: 3, 2015, 79–96.

27 Rancière, "Ten Theses," 35–7. His consideration of the police focus on breaking up demonstrations, asserting that "the space for circulating is nothing but the space for circulation," perfectly encompasses state actions against the Shinjuku folk guerrillas in 1969, reregulating the underground "plaza" for their gatherings as a "passageway" [*tsurō*] for circulation alone.

the commencement of construction on the first of the Shinjuku skyscapers (the forty-seven-story Keio Plaza Hotel first tower, completed in 1971) that would come to dominate the space of West Shinjuku, the first planned skyscraper space for Tokyo. The area made available by the closed Yodobashi water purification facility was marketed internationally for its anticipated huge development potential. The newly laid streets, meanwhile, attracted *bosozoku* bikers to their smooth surfaces and strange landscapes. Shinjuku as a whole, by 1968, was seen as an ambiguous site and place of connection for a globalized politics that seemed all around, immanent and yet hard to identify, centered ambiguously in popular and press representations on disreputable figures of youth, activists, hippies, gawkers, idlers, and criminals. But its enormous train station also served as a major commuting hub and rail junction through which millions of gallons of jet fuel passed daily en route to the American air base at Tachikawa, some twenty miles west of the station.

The American military's presence, and the close links between daily commuting and military support, were dramatically exposed in the summer of 1967, when several fuel cars had derailed, crashed, and exploded. On June 26, 1968, the Sōhyō labor federation's railway workers engaged in a labor slowdown and demonstration to draw attention to the prior incident and the continuing shipments.[28] They were joined by representatives from most of the major student movement groups, which, together with members of Beheiren, reached the station platforms and train tracks and disrupted travel for some hours. Newspapers reported that idlers called *fūten* joined the demonstration as well, and after midnight they had allegedly showered the riot police with rocks.[29]

Fūten was the colloquial term for the ambiguous and colorfully dressed young idlers qua hippies who congregated in several locations around and about Shinjuku station. From the summer of 1967 onward, these were figures for alternating castigation and fantasy in the media for their indolence, dirtiness, and drug use (glue, sleeping pills, paint thinner, occasional LSD, and perhaps the recently outlawed marijuana). But, ultimately, the boundaries for this category are ambiguous, since although several hundred thousand people regularly congregated in Shinjuku after midnight, in fact almost no one properly resided there. All were potentially as rootless as the *fūten*.

---

28 *Asahi Shimbun*, June 25, 1968, morning edition, 14.

29 *Asahi Shimbun*, June 27, 1968, evening edition, 10.

Two young idlers popularly referred to as *fūten* in Shinjuku, one huffing glue, thinner, or some such substance. Photo by Hanaga Michitoshi.

The daily practices of a wide variety of people living outside of social norms, drifting through cafe cultures, dropping out, participating in the growing commune movement, engaged at all levels of the informal economy—all casually lumped by media and the state alike into abject and disreputable groupings (*fūten*, criminals, idlers, gawkers, thugs, and so on)—nonetheless demonstrated varieties of dissensual living and brought a sense of eventfulness that contributed to the politicizing potential of the moment. As figures of alternating castigation, fixation, and fantasy in the media, such groups lent their ambiguity to the spaces in which they congregated, drawing in turn attention from all quarters, from the curious and politically interested to plainclothes detectives and riot police.

The proximity of the catch-bars, sex workers, cafe hangouts, and fraught history of a former black-market area imparted an additional sense of norm-breaking, violation, and potential eventfulness to Shinjuku. So too did the sellers of underground newspapers like *Buzoku* [the Tribes], who hung out by the east exit of the station, or in the ground floor corridor of the Kinokuniya bookstore. Lavishly illustrated, *Buzoku*'s inaugural issue of December 1967 had proclaimed the eponymous commune's declaration of transnational belonging through disidentification (written by poet and *Buzoku* editor Nagasawa Tetsuo), encouraging all who read it to drop out and join the tribes of the global commune movement, which would ultimately supplant nations. And, as Shimada notes, a number of the artists and performers who would be featured by Gendai Shichōsha focused their practices on the quotidian eventfulness of key spaces in the Shinjuku Ward: the east and west station exits, the Hanazono Shrine grounds, the underground passageways, Fugetsudō cafe and other hangouts, and Kinokuniya.

Members of group Zero Dimension perform in the ground-floor corridor outside of the Kinokuniya bookstore, Shinjuku Ward, Tokyo, December 9, 1967. Photo by Hanaga Michitoshi.

Such a perspective was perfectly captured by Akasegawa Genpei's succinct description of Shinjuku in Watanabe Hitomi's photo book, *1968 Shinjuku,* as "one station from Yoyogi." This banal geographical fact about train lines had a double meaning: the Japan Communist Party's headquarters was in Yoyogi, and was often colloquially referred to by this location ("Yoyogi's position is . . ."). Akasegawa's comment references both the proximity and distance from Yoyogi. He points simultaneously to Shinjuku's arm's-length difference from the left party politics epitomized by Yoyogi, but, at the same time, its proximity to the longed-for and perpetually forestalled revolution the name metonymically represented. Revolution, just one step—or station—away. Indeed, Akasegawa's formulation suggests that such revolutionary proximity is enabled by this difference.

Rebellion and unstable identities was the theme of *Yui Shōsetsu*, a play by director Kara Jurō and the Situation Theater that enjoyed an extended run into the summer of 1968. This tent theater troupe performed every Saturday within the Hanazono Shrine grounds in their signature red tent to sold-out audiences crammed within its confines. Kara and company's impromptu happenings by the east exit of the station, as advertising for their play, regularly attracted crowds of onlookers. The play is named for a figure of failed rebellion from the early Edo period. In its fantastically abstracted narrative, the question of true and false revolution is doubled in a convoluted story of stolen and unfixed identities, sales of decapitated heads (of the rebels), and violent action. Kara's staging played fantastically with the very notion of anonymous persons stealing and assuming identities of rebellion, creating a meta-play on theater, acting, and political action. The story so attracted Oshima Nagisa, while filming his *Diary of a Shinjuku Thief* (1969), in June of 1968, that he wove interactions with both company and play throughout his film, even having his protagonist come and "steal" the lead role from Kara himself in a scene in which play and film merge. In the wake of the events of June 29, Kara would find his troupe expelled from Hanazono as part of the backlash demanding Shinjuku's "cleanup" [*jōka*, literally "purification"], castigated for attracting *fūten* to the shrine area and encouraging improper behavior.[30]

Shinjuku would remain a key focal point for opposition and authorities alike throughout 1968 and beyond. Events such as that of June 26 both heralded potential coalition building and further expansion among a disparate opposition, providing political possibilities, on the one hand, while enabling a roadmap for the state's recapturing of legitimacy for its force through the ambiguous identities associated with Shinjuku. The presence at the protest of disreputable elements enabled the association of protest acts with the alleged dirty fecklessness of the *fūten*, helping to code them as therefore illegitimate and violent, and

30 See Kara Jūrō, *Karagumi: Jōkyō Gekijō zenkiroku: shashinshū*, Tokyo: PARCO Shuppan, 1982, 78; Maro Akaji, *Kaidanji Maro Akaji ga yuku: ukiyo tawamurete sōrō*, Tokyo: Asahi Shimbun Shuppan, 2011, 80–1. Kara's response would bid a bitter farewell to Hanazono, Shinjuku, and the *fūten* alike.

tying the *fūten* to student violence in turn. During the subsequent protests in and around the station in October, the state indeed managed to regain some of the legitimacy it had lost in January precisely by reassociating protest action with criminality instead of reason.[31] But it is also equally the case that the space for such protest, in the broadest sense, was made invitingly combustible by the overlaid daily practices of provocation, refusal, and imagination, giving the space a paradoxical sense of quotidian eventfulness. And, indeed, the availability of ambiguous identities such as *fūten*, made further ambiguous by such countercultural celebrations of dissemblance, performance, and action, enabled the kinds of disidentification that made much of this politics possible in the first place. And, as a final thought, following Kara's play: perhaps revolutionary subjectivity has to come by way of violation—it must be seized, improperly.

31 See Marotti, "Japan 1968."

5

'68 and the Japanese Women's Liberation Movement

Setsu Shigematsu

This chapter illuminates the revolutionary upheavals and fault lines of Japan's '68 through an exposition of the women's liberation movement. The movement's very name—ūman ribu ["woman lib"]—signaled a break from existing Japanese women's movements and its transnational identification with other liberation movements rising up against imperialism, capitalism, racism, and patriarchy. Along with other radical groups, these activists embraced the task of making and living their revolution, and this chapter describes how *their* revolution was collectively articulated and practiced. Throughout this essay, the term *ribu* is used to refer to this radical feminist movement, its activists, discourse, and praxis.

The chapter has a threefold purpose. First, this discussion contributes to an understanding of the worldwide revolutionary synchronicity of '68 by tracing how ribu's emergence was a response to late 1960s radicalism internationally and domestically. Second, through analyzing ribu's break from and critique of the surrounding movements, we can grasp how its activists exposed the perils and pitfalls of Japan's '68 as it was lived, documented, and remembered. The third part of this chapter discusses ribu's feminist philosophy and praxis as well as its solidarities with other radical movements of its era. In conclusion, I offer some reflections on ribu's own limits and contradictions.

Worldwide Revolution and Ribu's Birth from the Breaches of Japan's '68

This radical feminist movement erupted in the streets of Tokyo in 1970, catalyzed by, and in concert with, existing revolutionary movements, near and far, across the city and the planet. These revolutionary movements manifested as the intercontinental uprisings of 1968—May '68 in Paris arose in the wake of a hundred US cities set ablaze in response to the assassination of Martin Luther King Jr., from the Black Power salute at the Mexico summer Olympics to the victory of the Tet Offensive—rebellions against imperial war, racism, and authoritarianism electrified the collective consciousness with unprecedented images of resistance. As discussed in the other chapters in this volume, Japan's '68 was a complex assemblage of anti-imperialist cross-fertilizations of internationalist Marxist revolutionary and student-led domestic uprisings, at times traversing generations, genders, and classes (bringing together grandmothers, farmers, students, and workers) and crossing ethnic, national, and racialized differences (among Okinawans, Ainu, Zainichi, Buraku and other non-Japanese residents). In its earliest manifestos, ribu's rallying cry attested to its consciousness of the movement's global synchronicity, identifying itself as "one wing" and one part of the other rebellions arising across the world. One of the earliest manifestos, "Declaration of the Liberation of Eros," distributed in June 1970, states: "Throughout the world, people are seeking and struggling for their own liberation . . . for as living beings we are oppressed, confused and endangered by our own structure of consciousness."[1] Other ribu manifestos and writings referred to revolutions taking place, past and present, in other parts of the world, from critiques of the limits of the Bolshevik revolution to detailing the Sanrizuka struggle against the building of the Narita Airport, a movement that was at once domestic and international, imagined as form of resistance against Japan's support for the war in Vietnam.[2]

1 Tanaka Mitsu, "Erosu kaihō sengen" [Declaration of the Liberation of Eros], in *Ribu Shinjuku Sentā shiryō shūsei* [Lib Shinjuku Center Document Collection], eds. Ribu Shinjuku Sentā Shiryō Hozonkai, Tokyo: Inpakuto Shuppankai, 2008, 7–8. Translation published as Appendix i in Setsu Shigematsu, "Tanaka Mitsu and the Women's Liberation Movement in Japan: Towards a Radical Feminist Ontology," PhD diss., Cornell University, 2003. Unless indicated otherwise, all translations are by the author.

2 For the Sanrizuka struggle, see David Apter and Nagayo Sawa, *Against the State: Politics and Social Protest in Japan*, Cambridge: Harvard University Press, 1984; Mizoguchi, Akiyo, Saeki Yōko, and Miki Sōko, eds., *Shiryō Nihon ūman ribu-shi* [Documents of the History of Japanese Women's Lib], Kyoto: Shōkadō Shoten, 1992, 1: 24–8.

Domestically, ribu was born through the contradictions of the radical political formations of the '68 era, including the anti–Vietnam War, New Left, and student movements. Many ribu activists had experienced the radicalism of the student movements and sectarian struggles of the New Left. As defectors from existing leftist movements, ribu activists were conversant and in critical dialogue with the ongoing struggles such as those of the Sanrizuka, Shibokusa, Zainichi, and Buraku liberation activists, the politics of occupied Okinawa, and other movements addressing immigration, labor rights, and pollution. Following other radical movements of Japan's '68, horizontal relationality was privileged in reaction to the rigid hierarchies of the established left and many New Left sects.[3] The movement involved a decentralized network of autonomous ribu groups that organized across the nation, from Hokkaidō to Kyūshū; with no formal leader, its leading activists were Japanese women in their twenties and early thirties.

Ribu's birth was traumatic and exhilarating. Having experienced a spectrum of sexist treatment and sexualized violence while organizing with leftist men, from verbal abuse to sexual assault and rape, ribu activists revolted against the myriad ways that sexism and misogyny were endemic across leftist culture. Women typically supported male leadership through domestic labor, by cleaning, cooking, and other housekeeping duties. There were instances when young women activists were referred to as public toilets [*benjos*] and assaulted and raped by leftist male activists.[4] In some cases, the rape of the women of rival leftist sects became part of the New Left's tactics of *uchi geba* [internal violence or conflict]. In *1968*, Oguma Eiji describes such incidents of sexual violence.[5] Ribu activists spoke, wrote, and testified about their

3 The emphasis on horizontal relationality in the Zenkyōtō student movement can be attributed to Tokoro Mitsuko, a graduate student and activist at the University of Tokyo. See Tokoro's 1966 essay in the October 1966 edition of *Shisō no kagaku* [Science of Thought] titled "Yokan sareru soshiki ni yosete" [The Organization to Come], published under the pseudonym Tomano Mimie. It was republished in Tokoro, *Waga ai to hangyaku* [Our Love and Rebellion], Tokyo: Shinmu Shobō, 1969, 149–59.

4 Ozawa Yōko cites a case in which a male student activist referred to a woman as a "public toilet." See Ozawa, "Ūman ribu no hachijyū nendai" [Women's lib's 1980s], *Gendai no me* 17: 1, 1976, 136–43. This chapter draws from ten years of research conducted for Shigematsu, *Scream from the Shadows: The Women's Liberation Movement in Japan*, Minneapolis: University of Minnesota, 2012, which involved interviews and correspondence with over thirty ribu activists and related intellectuals, activists, and scholars, 1999–2009.

5 Oguma Eiji includes *ūman ribu* as the final chapter of the two-volume series on Japan's 1968, in a section titled "*Ūman ribu to watashi*" [Women's lib and I], 2: 674–774. One well-known case is that of Nagata Hiroko, *Jūroku no bōhyō: hono to shi no seishun* [Sixteen

experiences of sexism, assault, and rape at the hands of leftist male activists.[6] Given such forms of sexual violence that were hidden, too often, in the shadows of Japan's 1968, how did ribu women respond?

Never before in the records of Japanese history had ink sprayed such rage-filled declarations of revolt against Japanese heteropatriarchy and sexist men. The slogans of the movement, like the "liberation of sex" and the "liberation from the toilet" [*benjo kara no kaihō*], unleashed an unprecedented flurry of militant feminist denunciations.[7] With *mini-komi* [alternative media] titles such as Onna no hangyaku [Woman's Mutiny] and art evoking images of vaginas with spikes, ribu activists raised a political banner that had never been so explicit and bold in its declaration of sexual oppression and sexual discrimination.[8]

Ribu activists reacted to the counterculture movement of the 1960s and the sexual revolution. Some of its earliest activists, such as Yonezu Tomoko, criticized the "free love" espoused by male activists even while they emphasized the importance of politicizing sex. Along with her student comrade Mori Setsuko, Yonezu named their cell "Thought Group SEX," and painted "SEX" on their helmets the first time they disrupted a campus event at Tama Arts University in Tokyo.[9] Sex and sexuality emerged as key concepts in ribu's manifestos for human liberation. The politicization of sex was a revolt against the sexism in mainstream society and the Japanese left. Heralding the importance of liberating sex also distinguished ribu from former Japanese women's liberation movements. Tanaka Mitsu, a leading activist and theorist of

Graves: The Spring of Fire and Death], Tokyo: Sairyūsha, 1982, 70. Oguma also recounts the experience of Nagata Hiroko's rape in *1968*, 2: 545. He gives several more examples of how such forms of sexual violence were not uncommon in the New Left. See Chapter 17, 2: 685–6. For the two-volume series, see Oguma Eiji, *1968*, 2 vols., Tokyo: Shin'yōsha, 2009.

6 Other ribu activists I interviewed (like X-san from Hiroshima) also spoke in ribu circles about their rape by male activists prior to their joining the ribu movement.

7 The "Truth Spoken by the Vagina" is a subtitle in the revised version of "Liberation from the Toilet." There are two versions of the pamphlet "Benjo kara no kaihō" [Liberation from the Toilet]: the six-page original (August 1970) and the seven-page revised version, "Benjo kara no kaihō (kaisei ban)" [Liberation from the Toilet (rev.)] (October 1970). The revised version is reprinted in Tanaka Mitsu, *Inochi no onna-tachi e: torimidashi ūman ribu ron* [To Women with Spirit: Toward a Disorderly Theory of Women's Liberation], Tokyo: Pandora, 2001, 333–47, and *Doko ni iyou to riburian: Tanaka Mitsu hyōgenshū* [I Am a Riber Wherever I Am: Collection of Tanaka Mitsu's Expressions], Tokyo: Shakai Hyōron Sha, 1983, 265–80.

8 Mizoguchi, Saeki, and Miki, eds. *Shiryō Nihon ūman ribu-shi*, Kyoto: Shōkadō Shoten, 1994, 2: 45. *Onna no hangyaku* [Woman's Mutiny] was started by Kuno Ayako in Nagoya and lasted for over forty years.

9 Mizoguchi, Saeki, and Miki, *Shiryō Nihon ūman ribu-shi*, 1: 169.

the movement, harshly criticized previous women's movements, saying that the "hysterical unattractiveness" of those "scrawny women" was due to their having to become like men.[10] The brazen and contemptuous tone of their manifestos was a stark departure from past political speech about women's liberation.

This emphasis on sexual liberation evinced ribu's affinity with US radical feminist movements that also exploded in 1970.[11] Ribu activists recognized their shared conditions when they heard news of women's liberation movements emerging in the United States. Information about these movements flowed into Japan via news and alternative media, as documented by Masami Saitō.[12] Japan's largest newspapers, the *Yomiuri* and *Asahi Shimbun*, printed photos of thousands of women protesters in the streets of New York City for the August 26, 1970, Women's Strike.[13] Anti-war posters with defaced US flags decorated the walls of ribu communes and organizing centers.[14] Activists from the United States and Europe visited ribu centers.[15] This cross-border exchange among activists also characterized the internationalist spirit of '68 and a common desire for liberation.

Like so many others around the world, ribu activists were also inspired by the Black Power movement and attempted to follow its lead. This passage from a ribu pamphlet evinces how ribu activists were emboldened by Black Power struggles—as were radical feminists in the

10 Tanaka, "Liberation from the Toilet (rev.)," *Doko*, 267. As I have written elsewhere, although the ribu movement did not have a formally designated leader, Tanaka became its iconic figure and arguably exerted the most significant influence over the direction and politics of the movement. See Chapter 4, "Tanaka Mitsu: The Icon, the Center and its Contradictions," in *Scream from the Shadows*, 103–37.

11 According to Jo Freeman's *The Politics of Women's Liberation: A Case Study of an Emerging Social Movement and its Relation to the Policy Process*, New York: McKay, 1975, 148, radical feminism in the United States took off in the 1970s. See US radical feminist manifestos such as the "Redstockings Manifesto" (1969); Anne Koedt, "The Myth of Vaginal Orgasm" (1970) and "Radical Feminism: Some Male Response" (1969/1970); Robin Morgan, "Good-bye to All That" (1970) in *Voices from Women's Liberation*, Leslie B. Tanner, ed., New York: Mentor, 1970.

12 Masami Saitō, "Feminizumu riron ni yoru hihan-teki disukōsu bunseki (FCDA) no tenkai—ūman ribu undō no media gensetsu o jirei toshite" [Critical Discourse Analysis Based on Feminist Theory; A Case Study of the Media Discourse of the Ribu Movement], PhD diss., Ochanomizu Joshi Daigaku, 2001.

13 *Yomiuri Shimbun*, August 27, 1970; *Asahi Shimbun*, August 27, 1970.

14 Mizoguchi, Saeki, and Miki, *Shiryō Nihon ūman ribu-shi*, 2: 70.

15 Akiyama Yōko, "Yan to ani" [Jan and Annie], in *Ribu shi shi nōto* [Notes from a Personal History of Ribu], Tokyo: Inpakuto Shuppankai, 1993, 15–24.

United States—and drew new lines of departure and separation from the leftist men with whom they had been organizing.[16]

> By calling white cops "pigs," Blacks struggling in America began to constitute their own identity by confirming their distance from white-centered society in their daily lives. This being the beginning of the process to constitute their subjectivity, whom then should women be calling the pigs? . . . First, we have to strike these so-called male revolutionaries whose consciousness is desensitized to their own form of existence. We have to realize that if we don't strike our most familiar and direct oppressors, we can never "overthrow Japanese imperialism" . . . Those men who possess such facile thoughts as, "Since we are fighting side by side, we are of the same-mind," are the pigs among us.[17]

For leftist women to be calling leftist male revolutionaries pigs constituted a kind of declaration of war against sexism in their midst and their newfound enemy—sexist leftist men. When women of the left began to identify this intimate enemy, this moment of disidentification with Japanese leftist men constituted a decisive epistemic break. Their conflict with sexist male comrades forced these women to recognize that they had to redefine their relationship to the revolution from the specificity of their own subject position.

Liberation from the Discriminatory Family-Marriage System

Ribu manifestos heralded a new form of feminist militancy and subjectivity, with declarations such as "the truth spoken by the vagina."[18] Ribu's best-known manifesto, the "Liberation from the Toilet," emblematized the angry renunciation of Japanese heteropatriarchy and its links to capitalist imperialism. According to this manifesto, authored by Tanaka Mitsu, the marriage system "functioned as a system of prostitution,

16 Sara Evans, *Personal Politics: The Roots of Women's Liberation in the Civil Rights Movement and the New Left*, New York: Vintage, 1980. White radical feminists like Sara Evans are criticized by Angela Davis in her classic essay, "Rape, Racism and the Myth of the Black Rapist," in *Women, Race and Class*, New York: Vintage, 1983, 172–201.

17 Tanaka Mitsu, "Shinsayoku to ribu" [The New Left and ribu], in *Inochi no onna tachi e: torimidashi ūman ribu ron*, Tokyo: Pandora, 2001; translation published as Appendix iii to Shigematsu, "Tanaka Mitsu and the Women's Liberation Movement in Japan."

18 Tanaka, "Liberation from the Toilet (rev.)," *Inochi*, 345.

which, parallel to slavery, constituted the background of human history."[19] The marriage system was politicized in a shocking and scandalous manner by calling it a form of prostitution;[20] an emblematic placard from ribu's first public rally asserted: "A Housewife and a Prostitute are Raccoons in the Same Den!"[21] Ribu activists denounced the marriage system, calling it a one-husband-one-wife system, but a form of monogamy that only applied to women. Many refused to enter into marriage based on this political stance and for decades cohabited with partners despite the discrimination their children faced.[22] Ribu activists argued that the *ie* structure—that is, the family-marriage-household system, as the patriarchal and patrilineal family arrangement fundamental to Japanese society from the early seventeenth century to the postwar period—had alienated women from the power of their sexuality and positioned them as subordinate to men.[23] In "Liberation from the Toilet," Tanaka wrote that this system "has been essentially made to limit and confine women's economic independence and women's sexual desire."[24]

While citing Marx and Engels, ribu activists criticized the primacy and theoretical privileging of "economic conditions" over "the problems of everyday living," a mistake that Tanaka argued was a "blatant misunderstanding of the motivating forces of history."[25] In the following passage from the "Declaration of the Liberation of Eros," Tanaka connects the family system to private property, demonstrating the systemic need for women's liberation to be a liberation from the family system and a liberation of sex.

---

19 Ibid., 338.

20 Ibid., 8.

21 Kazuko Tanaka, "The New Feminist Movement in Japan, 1970–1990," in *Japanese Women: Feminist Perspectives on the Past, Present and Future,* ed. Kumiko Fujimura-Fanselow and Atsuko Kameda, New York: Feminist Press at the City University of New York, 1995, 343.

22 The documentary film *Ripples of Change* (New York: Women Make Movies, 2010 [1993]), directed by Nanako Kurihara, includes an example of a ribu family whose children are bullied at school because their parents are not married.

23 Ochiai Emiko notes that the activists of the ūman ribu movement did not seem to make an analytical distinction between what they criticized as the *ie* system and the contemporary male-centered nuclear family system. Ochiai, *The Japanese Family System in Transition: A Sociological Analysis of Family Change in Postwar Japan*, Tokyo: LTCB International Library Foundation, 1997, 101. For further explanation of the *ie* system and its changes through modernity, see Ochiai, *The Japanese Family System in Transition*; Satoshi Sakata, *Ie to Mura Shakai no Seiritsu* [The Formation of Family and Village Society], Tokyo: Kōshi Shoin, 2011.

24 Tanaka, "Liberation from the Toilet (rev.)," *Inochi*, 337.

25 Tanaka, "Erosu kiahō sengen," 7–8.

> It is precisely the patriarchal *ie* (household-family system), based on the principle of authoritarianism, that reproduces the social order through this structure of consciousness and ideology, and comprises the human basis of the system. Given that the basic cause that prevents women's economic independence is the marriage system within patriarchy which is based on the system of private property requiring the preservation and passing on of property leading to the oppression of one sex by the other sex based on the one-husband-one-wife system, women's liberation therefore fundamentally requires the liberation of sex . . . we direct our movement toward the dismantling of the *ie*.[26]

As seen in this quote, marriage was repudiated as the system that (re)produces patriarchy, private property, and authoritarianism. Whether in manifestos like "Declaration of the Liberation of Eros" or in Miki Sōko's rejection of the domestic division of labor (published in pathbreaking ribu publications such as *Onna no shisō*), ribu activists rose up in rebellion, not only against inequality with men, but against the modern family-marriage system itself, where women were supposed to serve men and were largely relegated to the domestic sphere.[27]

Ribu's Critique of Liberal Feminism

In the volume *The Revolution called Ribu,* Kanō Mikiyo opens by making an unequivocal assertion that ribu did not aim for women to be like men or equal to men.[28] Although liberal feminism—which fundamentally advocates for women's equality and equal rights with men—has been the generic understanding of feminism's political aims, this strain of feminist thought was not the heart of ribu's rallying cry. As Ueno Chizuko has pointed out, while the term *liberation* abounds in the literature and manifestos of the movement, in contrast, the word *equality* rarely appears.[29]

---

26 Ibid.

27 Miki Sōko, "Kugitsukerareta nichijo—kaji" [Housework—the daily pounding of the nail], in *Onna no Shisō* [Women's Thought], ed. Saeki Yōko, Tokyo: Sanpō 1972, 198–230.

28 Kanō Mikiyo, ed., *Ribu to iu kakumei: kindai no yami o hiraku* [The Revolution Called Ribu: Uncovering the Darkness of Modernity], Tokyo: Inpakuto Shuppankai, 2003, 1.

29 Ueno Chizuko, "Nihon no ribu: sono shisō to haikei" [Japan's ribu, its thought and background], in *Nihon no feminizumu* [Japanese Feminism], ed. Inoue Teruko et al., Tokyo: Iwanami Shoten, 1994, 1: 3.

To the contrary, if we trace the domestic origins of ribu to what has been described as the "dawn of ribu," the political goal of equality with men had already been rejected as flawed at the outset of the movement.[30] Ribu's critique of sexism was not focused on unequal rights or power between men and women. Rather, ribu's understanding of sexism was informed by a critical feminist response to Marxism in Japan, and activists called for a complete revolution of the sociocultural-political-economic structure. As a radical feminist movement, ribu emphasized a transformation of consciousness and culture, in contrast to Marxist and socialist feminists, for whom capitalism and class conflict remained core tenets.

Like other forms of radical feminism, ribu activists displaced and replaced the primacy of class conflict and economics with sexual discrimination and the importance of creating a woman-centered culture. They asserted that discrimination between the sexes was "the oldest form of class conflict, rooted deeply in the core of human consciousness," and doubted that it would be solved with the "overthrow of Japanese imperialism."[31]

Many ribu activists understood capitalism as a dehumanizing system in which women were required to be "accomplices that made men into slaves of capital."[32] Therefore, it was hardly liberatory for women to follow men in what they denounced as a "slavish mentality" and women were also criticized for their complicity in the capitalist system.[33]

Unlike other leftists and women's movements, ribu critically denounced the modern family system as the foundational reproductive mechanism of a discriminatory society. Discrimination was one of the key words of the movement, and it was theorized in conjunction with ribu's other key concepts: sex, *onna*, and eros.[34] The centrality of the concept of discrimination and, more specifically, *sei sabetsu* [sex/sexual

30 Mizoguchi, Saeki, and Miki, *Shiryō Nihon ūman ribu-shi,* 1:15–95. See discussion of Iijima Aiko in this chapter; also Shigematsu, *Scream from the Shadows,* 89.

31 Tanaka, "Naze 'sei no kaihō' ka: josei kaihō e no mondai teiki" [Why "Sex Liberation"—Raising the Problem of Women's Liberation], appendix ii to Shigematsu, "Tanaka Mitsu and the Women's Liberation Movement in Japan," 298.

32 Tanaka, "Liberation from the Toilet (rev.)," *Inochi*, 343.

33 Ibid.

34 The term *onna* means "woman" and was deliberately used by ribu activists given its sexualized, lower-class, and derogatory connotations compared to more neutral terms for woman such as *josei.*

discrimination] can be attributed to Iijima Aiko, one of the forerunners of the ribu movement.[35]

The important three-volume collection, *Shiryō Nihon ūman ribu-shi* [Documents of Japan's History of Women's Lib], edited by three ribu intellectuals, Miki Sōko, Saeki Yōko, and Mizoguchi Akiyo, begins with the writings of Iijima Aiko's group, the Asian Women's Committee Who Fight Discrimination = Aggression [Shinryaku = Sabetsu Ajia Fujin Kaigi], established in 1969. The group focused on discrimination as aggression toward others and emphasized the importance of a pan-Asian feminist political consciousness that became one thread of ribu's trajectory. Iijima was a longtime socialist activist and former Trotskyist who was married to Ōta Ryū, the founder of Japan's Trotskyist league.[36] She left Ōta after a seventeen-year relationship, saying that she experienced "the oppression of her sex" in her marriage.[37] Iijima questioned postwar conceptions of women's liberation [*josei kaihō*] and rejected how "equality between women and men . . . actually led to an expansion and reproduction of discrimination." In her 1970 essay "What is Discrimination for A Woman," Iijima insisted that women's liberation meant neither "assimilation with men, nor something that would come after class liberation."[38]

Despite the general anticapitalist and anti-imperialist stance of the Japanese left, the majority of men and women failed to reject the nationalized and gendered norms of the family system. Because Tanaka had studied with Iijima, she was able to expand thc women's struggle by articulating a radical feminist critique, gleaning lessons from this lifelong socialist activist.

---

35 Iijima was a predecessor of the ribu movement and influenced Tanaka and other activists; however, she did not personally identify as a ribu activist. Interview with Iijima Aiko, Tokyo, March 11, 2002.

36 Shigematsu, *Scream from the Shadows*, 12. Ōta was considered the founder of Japanese Trotskyism and established the Japanese Trotskyist league [Nihon Torotsukisuto renmei]. See Iijima Aiko, "From Personal Experience to Political Activism in the 1970s: My view of Feminism," in *Gender, Nation and the State in Modern Japan*, eds. Andrea Germer, Vera Mackie, and Ulrike Wöhr, translated, annotated, and with an introduction by Germer, New York: Routledge, 2014, 290–306.

37 Shigematsu, *Scream from the Shadows*, 12. Iijima, *"Shinryaku = sabetsu" no kanata e: aru feminisuto no hansei* [Reflections of a feminist beyond aggression = discrimination], Tokyo: Inpakuto Shuppankai, 2006, 363–65.

38 Iijima, "Onna ni totte sabetsu wa nani ka" [What is discrimination for a woman?], in *Shiryō Nihon ūman ribu shi,* 1: 47–53; Iijima, "From Personal Experience to Political Activism in the 1970s," 295. Iijima rejected the postwar mothers' peace movements, which did not address Japanese women's complicity in the violence to other Asians.

Tanaka expanded Iijima's concept of discrimination to emphasize the importance of sexual oppression in the struggle for women's liberation. Ribu activists deliberately adopted the term *onna* due to its sexualized meaning, lower class, and derogatory connotations. In "Liberation from the Toilet," Tanaka argued that women were divided against each other in the service of men; they were categorized as either good wives who perform the role of "virgin-like" women or they were regarded as "prostitutes" who supposedly lacked the purity to become "good wives and wise mothers" [*ryōsai kenbo*].[39] Tanaka wrote that "aggression and anti-revolutionary forces are sustained by virginlikeness," connecting discrimination to aggression and sexuality.[40] Rejecting this dichotomy of good women versus bad women also entailed a rejection of the existing women's political movements that were premised on the respectable identities of wives and mothers.[41] Ribu, furthermore, distinguished itself from other women's leftist movements by rejecting the given identities of women based on class and marital status, such as *fujin* [lady] or *shufu* [housewife].

Ribu activists criticized the *ie* [family-marriage] system as a microcosm of Japan's male-centered [*dansei-chūshin*] society, which reproduced the blood-based logic of Japanese imperialism.[42] In doing so, they connected marriage and the *ie* system to the ideology of Japanese nationalist imperialism: "The economic system that aims at the preservation and the inheritance of property binds women's sexual desire to men and the *ie,* in order to guarantee the *purity of blood.*"[43] Ribu activists were thus not only criticizing and rejecting what feminists theorize as heteropatriarchy; they also connected marriage to imperialism and their own complicity therein. In "Liberation from the Toilet," Tanaka lambasted the purity of Japanese wives by linking them to the sexual violation of comfort women, stating that "the chastity of the wives of

39 The ideology of good wife/wise mother [*ryōsai kenbo*] was lauded as the national feminine ideal throughout wartime and reformulated in postwar Japan. Kathleen Uno writes, "*Ryōsai kenbo* defined women's contribution to the good of the nation to be their labor as 'good wives' and 'wise mothers' in the private world of the home." See Uno, "Death of 'Good Wife, Wise Mother'?," in *Postwar Japan as History,* ed. Andrew Gordon, Berkeley: University of California Press, 1993, 307–22. This ideology also constituted the core reason ribu rejected the wife/mother identity, given how these identities supported the modern marriage and family [*ie*] system.

40 Tanaka, "Liberation from the Toilet (rev.)," *Inochi*, 344.

41 Ibid.

42 Ibid., 336.

43 Ibid., 5; emphasis added.

the military nation" is part of the same system that created the "dirtied pussies of the comfort women."[44] The sexual explicitness of this manifesto was striking and expressed a new kind of feminist radicalism. This critique of the connected symbolic economy of sexual purity and sexual violence and degradation constituted a fundamental element of ribu's politics and articulated a significant indictment of the imbrication of gender and Japanese imperialism, which would later manifest through its protest actions (against *kisaeng* tourism).

Japanese Women as Complicit Oppressors in Capitalist Imperialism

Ribu's rejection of sexism and heteropatriarchy was not reducible to a protest against the unidirectional sexual oppression of Japanese women. From the outset of the movement, having learned enough leftist theory of self-criticism and self-negation [*jiko hitei*], ribu women recognized their complicities in structural oppression, including a sense of responsibility for past colonial oppression of Korean comfort women. The following quote is from a ribu manifesto distributed at the thirtieth Zengakuren convention in 1972 by Miyaoka Maki. The manifesto expresses how some ribu women articulated their positionality in relation to the violence done to colonized women.

> I am a Japanese woman who made Korean women die from insanity . . . Ninety percent of Japan's military comfort women were Korean women . . . Korean women and Japanese women, however, were placed in this extreme opposition. As part of a race of Japanese oppressors, the women of Japan were opposed to Korean women . . . Am I not on the side of those Japanese women who forced these Korean women to suffer this kind of insane death? I no longer want to add to the misery of my woman's sex by being an accomplice in killing other women.[45]

44 Comfort women is the euphemistic and historical term used to designate women who were required to sexually service soldiers of the Japanese imperial army; most of the women were coerced into this form of militarized sexual slavery. Tanaka, "Liberation from the Toilet (rev.)," 16.

45 Miyaoka Maki, "Zengakuren dai 30 kai teiki zenkoku taikai deno sei no sabetsu = haigaishugi to tatakau ketsuihyōmei" [Raising the issue of sexual discrimination at the thirtieth national Zengakuren conference = declaring our decision to fight against exclusionism], in *Onna no shisō*, ed. Saeki Yōko, Tokyo: Sanpō Books, 1972, 43–4. This manifesto, in a slightly altered form, was republished in *Nihon no feminizumu*, Vol. 1, eds. Inoue et al. The 1994 reprinted edition also does not include the name of any author.

This explicit acknowledgment of Japanese women's positionality as historical oppressors whose identities were formed through gendered colonial violence is an example of ribu's feminist anti-imperialist discourse. Ribu activists also criticized the dual structure of Japanese-US neo-imperialism that forced Okinawan women to serve as prostitutes for US soldiers, connecting the history of the comfort women to the ongoing militarized occupation and sexual violence against Okinawan women.[46]

Ribu's anti-imperialist feminist discourse would later manifest in its solidarity protests against *kisaeng* tourism. This sex tourism involved Japanese businessmen traveling to South Korea to partake in the sexual services of young South Korean women who worked at clubs called *kisaengs*. Ribu's protests against *kisaeng* tourism represented how the liberation of sex combined with ribu's anti-imperialism and enabled new kinds of transnational feminist solidarity based on a concept of women's sexual exploitation and sexual oppression. From ribu's perspective, this form of tourism represented the reformation of Japanese economic imperialism in Asia. They were not against sex work by Japanese women, but opposed to the continued sexual exploitation of Korean women as a resurgence of the gendered violence of imperialism.[47] Ribu activists hence connected imperialism and sexual oppression of colonized women to the continuing sexual exploitation of Korean women in the 1970s. In this way, they were able to expand the leftist critique of imperialism and, at the same time, point to the fault lines and inadequacies of the left.

In her critique of the left, Tanaka points to its failure to have a theory of the sexes.

> Even in movements that are aiming towards human liberation, by not having a theory of struggle that includes the relation between the sexes, the struggle becomes thoroughly masculinist and male-centered [*dansei-chūshin shugi*].[48]

46 Tatakau Onna, "Okinawa to shofu" [Okinawa and Prostitutes], in *Tatakau Onna Metoroparichen kikanshi* [Metropolitan Fighting Women Newsletter] 5, 1971, reprinted in *Shiryō Nihon ūman ribu-shi*, eds. Mizoguchi, Saeki, and Miki, 1: 159–60.

47 Several ribu activists worked in *mizu shobai* (sex entertainment industry) jobs as an experimental part of their feminist praxis, as hostesses, topless dancers, and in Soapland. See Setsu Shigematsu, "The Women's Liberation Movement and Sexuality in Japan," in *Routledge Handbook of Sexuality Studies in East Asia*, eds. Mark McLelland and Vera Mackie, New York: Routledge, 2014, 174–87.

48 "Liberation from the Toilet (rev.)," 277.

According to ribu activists, this male-centered condition infected not only the theory of the revolution and delimited its horizon, but it created a gendered concept of revolution that privileged masculinist hierarchies within the culture of the left. Ribu activists decried the hypocrisy of the left and what it deemed to be the all-too-frequent egotistical posturing of the "radical men" who "eloquently talked about solidarity, the international proletariat and unified will," but did not really consider women part of human liberation.[49] Ribu activists rebelled against Marxist dogma and rejected these gendered hierarchies that valued knowledge of the proper revolutionary theory over lived experience and relationships. Moreover, ribu activists criticized what they experienced as masculinist forms of militancy that privileged participation in street battles with the riot police as the ultimate sign of an authentic revolutionary. While being trained to use weapons, activists like Mori Setsuko questioned whether engaging in such bodily violence was the way to make revolution.[50] Ribu's rejection and criticism of a hierarchy that privileged violent confrontation forewarned of the impending self-destruction within the New Left.

Ribu's Revolutionary Praxis: From Death to Life-Affirming Practices

One of the most radical contributions of ūman ribu involved the movement's response to the United Red Army lynchings. The United Red Army (URA) lynchings became the most notorious case of internal violence within the Japanese New Left. It involved the torture and killing of fourteen members of the sect, most of whom were killed for not proving themselves "proper revolutionaries." What made this case even more spectacular and notorious was the fact that a woman was second-in-command and responsible for many of these killings. That woman was Nagata Hiroko. She arguably became one of the most reviled women in postwar Japanese history and died on death row.[51]

49 Tanaka, "Shinsayoku to ribu," Shigematsu, trans. app. iii, 301.

50 Interview with Mori Setsuko, Tokyo, February 5, 2003. Shigematsu, *Scream from the Shadows*, 5.

51 Shigematsu, *Scream from the Shadows*, 168. See Patricia Steinhoff, "Death by Defeatism and Other Fables: The Psychodynamics of the Rengo Sekigun Purge," in *Japanese Social Organization*, ed. Takie Sugiyama Lebra, Honolulu: University of Hawaii Press, 1992.

News of URA lynchings, released in 1972, devastated the reputation of the New Left in Japan, and many across the left condemned these actions. This case of internalized violence within the left marked its demise. Although ribu activists were likewise horrified by such violence expressed against comrades, many ribu activists responded in a profoundly radical manner that I have theorized elsewhere as *critical solidarity*.[52] Ribu activists had already refused to lionize the tactics of violence; hence, they in no way supported the violent internal actions of the URA. However, rather than simply condemning the URA leaders and comrades as monsters and nonhumans [*hi-ningen*], they sought to comprehend the root of the problem. They recognized that every person possesses a capacity for violence, but that society prohibits women from expressing their violent potential. In response to the state's gendered criminalization of Nagata as an insurgent and violent woman, ribu activists practiced what I describe as feminist critical solidarity specifically for the women of the URA. Ribu activists went in support to the court hearings and wrote about their experience and critical observations of how URA members were being treated. By visiting the URA women at the detention centers, consequently, ribu activists came under police surveillance. Ribu activists enacted solidarity in ways that were not politically pragmatic but instead philosophically motivated. Their response involved a capacity for radical self-recognition in the loathsome actions of the other. Activists wrote extensively about Nagata—for example, Tanaka described Nagata in her book *Inochi no onna-tachi e* [To Women with Spirit] as a kind of "ordinary" woman whom she could have admired, except for the tragedy of the lynching incidents. In 1973, Tanaka wrote a pamphlet titled "Your Short Cut Suits You, Nagata!" in response to the state's gendered criminalization of the URA's female leader; the deliberate publication of such humanizing discourse evinces ribu's efforts to express solidarity with the women who were arguably the most vilified females of their time. Hence, ribu engaged in actions that supported these criminalized others even when the URA's misguided pursuit of revolution resulted in the unnecessary deaths of their own comrades. Through ribu's critical solidarity with the URA, they modeled the imperative of imperfect radical alliances, opening up

52 Shigematsu, "Ribu's Response to the United Red Army Feminist Ethics and the Politics of Violence," in *Scream from the Shadows,* 139–70; Shigematsu, "The Japanese Women's Liberation Movement and the United Red Army: A Radical Feminist Response to Political Violence," *Feminist Media Studies* 12: 2, 2012, 163–79.

a philosophically motivated relationality with abject subjects and a new horizon of counter-hegemonic alliances against the dominant logic of heteropatriarchal capitalist imperialism.

While the harsh criticism of the left was warranted and urgently needed given the deep sedimentation of pervasive forms of sexist practice, it should be noted that, at the outset of the movement, there were various ways in which ribu's intimate relationship with other leftist formations characterized its emergence. At ribu's first public protest, which was part of the October 21 anti-war day, some women carried bamboo poles and wooden staves as they marched in the street, jostling with the police.[53] Ribu did not advocate pacifism; its newspapers regularly printed articles on topics such as "How to Punch a Man."[54] During ribu protests from 1970–2, some ribu activists—as noted, with Yonezu and Mori—still wore helmets that were markers of one's political sect and a common student movement practice.[55]

Moreover, not all Japanese men were equally sexist, and some men sought to practice antisexism, and to be liberated from the binary gender norms that oppressed men as well. There were various ways men could be involved in ribu's activities. For example, during the 1974 Witch Concert, organized by lesbian ribu activist Iwatsuki Sumie (a.k.a. Asatori Sumie), men who were supportive of ribu's politics were trained to be in charge of childcare during the concert.[56] This demonstrated one concrete way that the ribu movement sought to reverse certain gender norms and liberate men from the confines of their prescribed gender roles.[57] Since childcare was deemed feminine labor, typically unpaid and insignificant compared with hardcore revolutionary direct action, the reversal of such a division of labor is a gentler form of revolution that remains an undervalued aspect of a longer gender revolution. As stated in the earliest manifestos, ribu activists clearly grasped the interconnectedness of gendered subject formations: "As we design our own subjective formation, we would like to aid in the (re)formation of men's

53 *Shūkan Asahi*, November 13, 1970, 18.

54 Ribu Shinjuku Sentā shiryō Hozon kai, ed., *Ribu Nyūsu, konomichi hitosuji—Ribu Shinjuku Sentā shiryō shūsei* [Ribu News—Ribu Shinjuku Center Document Collection], Tokyo: Impakuto Shuppankai, 2008, 152, 164.

55 Mizoguchi, Saeki, and Miki, eds., *Shiryō Nihon ūman ribu-shi*, 1: 99, 2: 181.

56 Shigematsu, *Scream from the Shadows*, 96.

57 Ibid., 96–7. The final section of *Shiryō Nihon ūman ribu shi*, vol. 3 is devoted to *man ribu* [men's lib] and contains writings such as "Men's thoughts on sexual liberation," "Let's think together about raising boys," and "The act of crying"; see Mizoguchi, Saeki, and Miki, eds., *Shiryō Nihon ūman ribu-shi*, Kyoto: Shōkadō Shoten, 1995, 3: 395–418.

subjectivity."[58] Hence, although ribu was a women-centered and woman-led social movement, they included men's liberation as part of their publications and trajectory.

Onna's *Philosophy and Collective Praxis*

While's men's liberation was included in ribu's political trajectory, as an *onna*-centered movement, one of its key revolutionary contributions was its conception and ongoing creation of a women-centered philosophy and praxis. As Miki Sōko states in her introduction to the collected documents of the movement, "Ribu is not knowledge, it becomes part of life." This living embodied philosophy was not based on knowledge or male logic, but conceived as an alternative to the male-centered theories of revolution that did not focus on the praxis of daily living as much as producing tangible evidence of one's revolutionary credentials or proof of one's revolutionary resolve.

The following are the lyrics of a song from a ribu musical:

カクメイ　しょう
あなたが　あなたを　カクメイできる
あなたが　変われば　世の中変わる
世の中が変われば　あなたが変わる
Kakumei　shiyo
Anata ga　anata wo　kakumei dekiru
Anata ga　kawareba　yo no naka kawaru
Yo no naka ga kawareba　anata ga kawaru
(Let's make revolution,
You can revolutionize yourself,
If you change the world changes,
If the world changes you change)[59]

The simplicity, repetition, and seemingly circular logic of the song captures the spirit, dynamism, and interconnectedness of ribu's symbiotic understanding of revolution as an embodied daily struggle connecting one's lived revolution to the other and the world. Rather

58 Tanaka, "Erosu kaihō sengen," 7–8.

59 Mizoguchi, Saeki, and Miki, eds., *Shiryō Nihon ūman ribu-shi*, 2: 92. Activists from the Ribu Shinjuku Center created a ribu musical, performing comedic skits and changing the lyrics to popular songs to address issues of women's liberation. The musical started in 1974 and was performed in Tokyo, Osaka, and Hokkaidō.

than focusing on violent battles with riot police or taking up arms against the state, ribu activists sang, danced, and created transformative art and music that expanded their practices of revolution. Dancing with or without clothes, as part of the Witch Concerts or at ribu's women-only summer camps, their expressions of liberation valued participation in the collective making of a feminist revolutionary culture.[60] This involved affirming life over the abstraction of death as a revolutionary ideal and alternative ways of living that recognized the interconnectedness of the self to the other and the world.

Ribu intellectual Saeki Yōko edited an anthology of writings published in 1972, titled *Onna no shisō* [Onna's Thought]. This volume is an example of the birthing of ribu's radical feminist philosophy. Its first chapter begins with Miyaoka Maki's critique of her New Left sect (Chūkaku), including threats made against her life.[61] Given that beatings, rape, and even death was a possible consequence of rebelling against the Marxist authoritarian structure of her sect, Miyaoka's desertion came only after realizing that the sect sought to permanently silence her criticisms of sexism. This is followed by chapters on the need for women to live independently from men. Saeki writes about the politics of choosing to give birth and become an "unwed mother."[62] This politicization of the status of "unwed mothers" (*mikon no haha)* also foresaw the campaigns ribu activists would wage in support of women's choice to raise their children outside of the *ie* system.[63] Another chapter explores the concept of eros, the body, and family. This Japanese *écriture feminine* incorporated the importance of expressing the body of *onna* and liberating the self from the male gaze and men's approval. Writing about menstruation, sexual experiences, and orgasms also characterized ribu's discourse. *Onna*'s thought did not abstract or devalue the body and nature; to the contrary, it elevated the expression of bodily desires, intuition, and valuing natural rhythms. This return to the body and nature was also part of a larger

60 The ribu movement organized women-only summer camps in 1971 and 1972. The first one was held in Shinshū, Nagoya, with 250 participants attending from across Japan. The second camp was organized in Hokkaidō from August 17 to 21, 1972. Dancing featured at both camps, including outdoor nude dancing at the first camp.

61 Shigematsu, *Scream from the Shadows*, 60.

62 Saeki Yōko, "Oto naki ko o umu—mikon no haha" [Giving birth to a child without a man—unwed mothers], in *Onna no shisō*, ed. Saeki, Tokyo: Sanpō Books, 1972, 166–96.

63 Ribu activists were involved in sustained campaigns to support "unwed mothers" (*mikon no haha*). They coined the term *hikon no haha* (nonmarried mothers), which used the Chinese character 非, which means negate. See Mizoguchi, Saeki, and Miki, eds., *Shiryō Nihon ūman ribu-shi*, 2: 195–218.

rejection of a modern industrial capitalist society that valued economic gain above all else and utilized technology to control the body and nature. This return to the body and nature anticipated the ecofeminist thread within ribu's thought and, likewise, how many activists would later become healers.

The potential revolutionary essence of the philosophy and praxis of *onna* inhered in its politicized identification of the sexualized body of *onna* as an abject subject. The reclamation of the abject enabled the movement to forge radical alliances with criminalized subjects such as Nagata Hiroko and *kogoroshi no onna* [child-killing women]. At the outset of the movement, ribu activists also organized in critical solidarity with *kogoroshi no onna,* attempting to understand and articulate the root causes of why women had become so alienated from their sex and sexuality that they would kill their own.[64] The philosophical connections between ribu's critical solidarity with *kogoroshi no onna* and Nagata involved an openness to become identified as abject by virtue of embracing this relationality with those who have been vilified by the rest of society. This kind of feminist solidarity rejected the division of good and bad women and the dominant logic that demanded that women remain properly domesticated to reproduce the hetero-patriarchal state.

Ribu also sought to ally with groups such as Aoi Shiba no Kai, a grassroots group of cerebral palsy activists.[65] This alliance was initiated by ribu activists who were able to connect disability to capitalist productivity. One of ribu's protests in 1974 included the spray painting of the *Mona Lisa* that was on display at the Ueno Museum in Tokyo because officials had barred disabled persons from entering the exhibit. Yonezu, a disabled ribu activist, vandalized the case that contained the *Mona Lisa* with red spray paint in symbolic protest against the dominant capitalist logic of a society that deemed the disabled, elderly, women, and children as nuisances, weak, and unproductive.[66] Such direct action

64 From the early 1970s, ribu activists supported mothers who killed their children—*kogoroshi no onna* [child-killing women], demonstrating their willingness to stand with criminalized women—and thereby rejecting the politics of respectability affiliated with existing housewives' [*shufu*] and mothers' [*haha*] movements, instead choosing to be affiliated with such criminalized women. See Shigematsu, *Scream from the Shadows,* xxi, 4, 25–8; and Mizoguchi, Saeki, and Miki, eds., *Shiryō Nihon ūman ribu-shi,* 1: 164–5, 184, 240–6, 353–4; 2: 24–5, 68–9, 246–7, 363–5, 279–81; 3: 35–6.

65 Mizoguchi, Saeki, and Miki, eds., *Shiryō Nihon ūman ribu-shi* 2: 61, 90, 128, 171, 173–4, 236.

66 Ibid., 87–91.

protests were emblematic of the '68 era and evinced ribu's own radicalism through its willingness to break the law and forge alliances with abject others in protest against the dominant norms of the capitalist state.

The ribu movement also politicized the expression of eros between women. Its long-standing journal, *Onna erosu,* which combined two of ribu's keywords in its title, circulated translated articles about lesbian love.[67] The Ribu Shinjuku Center newspaper also published an interview about woman-to-woman lovemaking, and another group published a proto-lesbian manifesto in 1973.[68] Other ribu activists, such as Wakabayashi Naeko, would become leaders in Japan's lesbian feminist movement. That said, ribu did not espouse lesbian separatism as its end goal or as the only way to be liberated from men. Much of its discourse, as noted above, sought to liberate women and men from the heteronormative coupling tied to the *ie* system. Many activists continued to partner with men, but some refused to marry based on ribu's critique of marriage. Many ribu activists also encouraged, practiced, and wrote about nonmonogamy in their relationships, as feminist women who maintained their own lives and sexual independence.

Conclusion

Ribu sought to first revolutionize the self while on the necessary path to revolutionizing the world, but one of the constitutive tensions in ribu's notion of revolution involved the subject's process of self-determination and self-definition. While it made sense to begin by revolutionizing the self and one's relationship to the other, this transformation was one that existed in the tension of the self's subjective revolution in relation to the collectivity of the movement. In the case of ribu, as in other liberation projects, the movement would lose its vitality and its radicality when the liberation of the self (and the

67 The earliest editions of *Onna erosu,* volumes 2 and 3, published Amano Michimi's translations of the sections about lesbian sexuality from *Our Bodies, Ourselves* and Matsumoto Michiko's photographs of lesbian couples in New York City. *Onna erosu,* Vol. 4, Tokyo: Shakai Hyōronsha, 1974–5. The journal was published from 1973–83.

68 Group Kan's bulletin, published in 1973, is written from the viewpoint of "a woman who loves women," protesting how same-sex love is considered taboo. Mizoguchi, Saeki, and Miki, eds., *Shiryō Nihon ūman ribu-shi* 2: 115.

problem of egoism) took precedence and became disconnected from the collective struggle for liberation.[69]

This focus on the liberation of the self initially prevented ribu from forging alliances with non-Japanese women, whether Zainichi, Okinawan, Ainu, Burakumin, or other non-Japanese women. In this way, the Japanese-centric tendencies of the ribu movement were analogous to how white feminist movements often failed to consciously practice antiracism and create intentional solidarity with women beyond their own ethno-racial group.[70] Although this was part of the limits of the early days of the movement, as noted previously, there was also a consistent anti-imperialist feminist consciousness throughout, which led many of its activists to engage in long-term actions to promote solidarity with other Asian women (as we saw in the protests against *kisaeng* tourism). Many ribu activists maintained such practices over the years, such as Miki Sōko, who continued to organize feminist film festivals with Korean feminist filmmakers, and Ayako Kano, the editor of *Onna no hangyaku* [Woman's Mutiny], who volunteered in a shelter for Filipinas. In these ways, ribu's revolution was one that was sustained through the lifelong practices of its activists, who, half a century later, continue to hold regular gatherings. These activists still identify and live as ribu in a world where the revolution they began remains unfinished. The legacy and longevity of the movement lives on through the writings and sustained praxis of its activists, five decades after its birth from the breaches of Japan's '68.

---

69 Oguma Eiji criticizes Tanaka Mitsu's place in the movement as a bridge to a kind of self-centered consumerist culture. This criticism invited her scathing rebuttal, which was published as a harsh critique of Oguma in "Tanaka Mitsu, *1968* o warau" [Tanaka Mitsu laughs at 1968], *Shūkan kinyōbi* 781, December 25, 2009, 22–30.

70 Ribu activists read Euro-American feminists available in translation and traveled to the United States and Europe. For a critique of the relative "whiteness" of Japanese feminism, see Shigematsu, "Rethinking Japanese Feminism and the Lessons of Ūman Ribu: Toward a Praxis of Critical Transnational Feminism," in *Rethinking Japanese Feminisms*, eds. Julia C. Bullock, Ayako Kano, and James Welker, Honolulu: University of Hawaii Press, 2017, 205–29.

6

1968 and the Postwar Regime of Emperor-System Democracy

Hidemi Suga

Introduction

It goes without saying that "1968" in Japan generally shared its origins and overall direction with the other movements that arose around the same time in the advanced capitalist nations. At its core, 1968 in Japan was centered on a student movement that called into question the structure of the educational system and opposed the Vietnam War. It was a movement that took place against a countercultural background that included new directions in film, theatre, music, and modern poetry; it was likewise a movement that resonated with the thought of Mao Zedong and Che Guevara, and it attempted to ally itself with young workers.

It could be said that this resonance was the result of the increasing unidimensionality of TV and other media at the time, but that is not the whole story. If we embrace all aspects, 1968 could also be said to include a movement against Soviet Marxism and students' adoption of a theory of alienation based on Marx's early writings. Japan was not an exception to this trend. In France, Louis Althusser pointed to an "epistemological break" in the *German Ideology*. In Japan, somewhat before Althusser, the philosopher Hiromatsu Wataru (1933–94) made a similar (and widely accepted) observation in a rather different context. Unlike Althusser, Hiromatsu was not a Communist Party member but was quite clearly a member of a New Left faction.

In so far as 1968 was a simultaneous global uprising—as Immanuel Wallerstein put it, the twentieth century's sole world revolution—it was both inevitable and something that needed to occur. In fact, one powerful Marxist theory that guided the Japanese 1968 was very much akin to Wallerstein's world systems theory (although the Japanese version preceded Wallerstein's). This was Iwata Hiroshi's (1922–2012) theory of world capitalism, which was a critical reconstruction of Uno Kōzō's (1897–1977) Marxist economics. Uno's Marxist economics, in turn, had its roots in the distinctively Japanese reading of Marx's *Capital* that developed out of the debates over the origins and nature of Japanese capitalism around 1930 and which I will touch on later. During the 1960s, Iwata covertly directed the political bureau of a Japanese New Left party but his influence on the Japanese 1968 went far beyond that narrow scope.

Nevertheless, even if it did share much with the other 1968s around the globe, the Japanese '68 clearly had a number of unique characteristics—in particular, the student movement's critique of postwar democracy. The students (of whom I was one) were skeptical and critical of the post-1945 political system and the "democracy" that grew out of it. This analysis borrowed much of its language from Marx and Lenin's critique of bourgeois democracy, but it was clearly of a different character. Unfortunately, Japanese students left very few records of their critique of postwar democracy, and much of their work has by now almost completely disappeared and can therefore only be approximated. Today, the prime minister, Abe Shinzō, wants to "escape the postwar regime" by revising the postwar constitution. Abe's left-liberal parliamentary opponents, who now lean to the right after a process of "Pasokification," defend the constitution and denounce Abe's trampling of democracy. It is therefore fair to say that, among Japan's intellectuals, the 1968 left has almost completely vanished. In concealing or forgetting 1968's critique of postwar democracy, then, the academic liberal left (which is close to what Richard Rorty called the "cultural left") reduces 1968 to a moderate citizens' movement or an existentialist search for the self that is based on a simplistic theory of alienation.

Prehistory and Assumptions

The Japanese 1968 produced a critique of postwar democracy in a large part as a result of the country's historical peculiarity as the "first" Asian state to turn capitalist, and then the first to turn imperialist in the latter half of the nineteenth century, after the Western nations had undergone similar transformations. In contrast to the preceding modernizations in the West, which produced generally secular nationalisms—in a process Max Weber called the "disenchantment of the world"—Japan's modernization, known as the Meiji Restoration (in 1868 and which came with a degree of democratization), installed the emperor as sovereign. The emperor was a "living deity" descended from a supposedly unbroken imperial lineage, and this gave the process strong overtones of religious nationalism. Modern Japanese nationalism is not based on a profound mystery. However, the emperor fundamentally still functions as a "living deity." By and large, Japan's prewar leftist movement was destroyed by the Greater East Asia War (World War II), fought in the name of this emperor as living deity. In order for the authority and power of the emperor to be negated or at least bracketed, Japan's defeat in 1945 and the occupying army required a thorough democratization. Through the constitution promulgated under the direction of SCAP (the Supreme Command of the Allied Powers), the GHQ (the 'general headquarters' of the postwar American occupation), and its commander Douglas MacArthur, Japan's people became sovereign for the first time (and this 1947 constitution is still in force).

Japan's postwar constitution extolled the virtues of peace, renounced war, and declared that Japan would not hold military power; however, since 1947, Japan has often departed from this ideal under the pretext of changes in the world situation (for example, Japan has a military called the Self-Defense Forces). Nevertheless, to this day, the vast majority of Japanese generally support the constitutional ideals of peace and demilitarization. The popular support for these ideals is part and parcel of what is called "postwar democracy." Now that the left has been destroyed, the postwar constitution is the sole reference point for Japanese liberals.

I will not give a detailed account of Japan's postwar history, but after the war, Japan's conservative majority (the Liberal Democratic Party [LDP] and others) as well as the minority reformists (the Socialist and Communist parties) generally defended the system of postwar democracy and accepted its merits. Except for an exceedingly small minority of communist martyrs, Japan's people cooperated with the wartime regime. Nevertheless, in the face of the occupation's policy of democratization, they turned into democrats overnight. For their part, conservatives used the postwar constitution's pacifism as a shield behind which they could advance Japan's economic recovery (made possible by having America pay for military expenditures). Liberals outwardly rejected the Pax Americana while in fact accepting it by pushing a policy of further democratization. Even the Japanese Communist Party, then under the guidance of the Soviet Union, once defined the occupation forces as an army of liberation. The Communist Party, which first became legal after the war, believed in a Stalinist two-stage revolution. Under this theory, the party would pursue communist revolution only after a bourgeois democratic revolution. This implied further pursuit of occupation policy. However, if that policy were taken to its logical conclusions, then the emperor, newly redefined under the occupation as "symbolic," would have to be scrapped.

In the debates that took place around 1930 among Japan's Marxists (who were as sophisticated as any in the world at the time) about the nature of Japanese capitalism and Japan's modernization, Communist Party–affiliated theorists known as the Kōza faction, taking their cues from the Comintern, argued that the emperor system was a (quasi-) feudal remnant signifying an Asian stagnation. Even if the emperor lost his place as sovereign in the postwar constitution, because the emperor was preserved as symbol of the Japanese state and people, Japan's bourgeois revolution could be said to be incomplete. In this sense, the postwar Communist Party preserved its theoretical inheritance: the prewar theory of a two-stage revolution. Even if this historical vision has been watered down to an extreme degree, the Communist Party still maintains this position. (Moreover, the idea that Japan is still behind the West in terms of capitalist development is widely believed, even among conservatives.)

The Japanese New Left, which emerged out of its 1956 critique of Stalin (of course, its historical roots in the re-evaluation of Trotsky and Marx's early work can be traced even further back), despite its radical façade, did not escape the framework of postwar democracy. With its militancy symbolized in its world-renowned, tightly packed "zigzag" demonstrations, the Communist League, popularly known as the Bund, led the Zengakuren's protests in a major mass struggle: the movement against the renewal of the United States–Japan Security Treaty in 1960. The Bund was a Trotskyist student group that broke from the Communist Party after the critique of Stalinism. In contrast to the Communist Party's theory of a two-stage revolution in one country, the Bund's revolutionary program called for a single worldwide revolution. Nevertheless, in several respects, the Bund Zengakuren inevitably bore the birthmarks of its origins in postwar democracy.

"Zengakuren" is an abbreviation of Zen-Nihon gakusei jichikai sōrengō [All-Japan Federation of Students' Self-Governing Associations].

As the name suggests, it was an alliance of undergraduate student governments from each university in Japan. The Zengakuren was a unitary national organization formed in 1948 as a result of a combination of efforts on the part of students—chiefly Communist Party members—who had awoken to postwar democracy, and the occupation's policy of democratization. The Zengakuren was the group that fought most militantly against the rightward turn in occupation policy and for democratization of the university. The Bund, which had wrested control of the Zengakuren from Communist Party hegemony during the 1960 anti-Anpō struggle, inherited its radicalism from the postwar Zengakuren movement, both in terms of personnel and theory. In that sense, it was the leftmost faction of postwar democracy. However, it must be noted that, in the Bund's theoretical departure from the Communist Party, the problem of the emperor, one of the party's most important strategic targets, was almost completely left behind.

As I have already pointed out, the Kōza faction ideology, which both the pre- and postwar Communist Party shared, held that feudal remnants (including the emperor system) with their social base in the agricultural village, had been preserved throughout Japan's modernization—in fact, these feudal remnants had been used to advance modernization. The Bund based itself more or less in the ideology of the Rōnō [Labor-Peasant] faction, which opposed the Kōza faction in the 1930s by arguing that Japan's modernization amounted to an achieved bourgeois revolution. In the postwar years, the Rōnō faction's argument became the position of the left wing of the Socialist Party (now known as the Social Democratic Party), which was to the Communist Party's right. Insofar as it did not advocate the abolition of the emperor system, the Socialist Party could be considered a moderate social democratic party. Broadly speaking, Uno Kōzō's economic theories, mentioned above, could be placed within the Rōnō faction ideology. Starting with the Bund, the question of how to interpret Uno's economics was an important topic for the Japanese New Left. Thanks to its adoption of Uno's economic theories, the Bund was able to understand the renewal of the United States–Japan Security Treaty differently than the Communist Party and other opposition parties—that is, not as something that would retard Japan's democratization and strengthen its fealty to the United States, but rather as a moment in which Japanese capitalism won its independence within an imperialist framework. Also as a result of their adoption of Uno's economics, the Bund and the New Left were able to claim that they stood for a world proletarian revolution. However, at the same time, the Bund and the New Left also picked up a hidden "social democratic" element with the adoption of Uno-school economics: they ceased to question the emperor system. By *social democratic* I mean "more in line with the values of postwar democracy." By the time the Bund was formed, the reconstruction of Japanese capitalism was under way, alongside its conversion into a "mass society" [*taishū shakaika*] by means of military procurements for the Korean War and the development of postwar economic policy. The argument that Japan was a quasi-feudal state was losing its grounding in reality. This was especially true for students who had their social base in the cities. For the Bund, the dilemma was that the emperor system was curiously—one could say fetishistically—wrapped within postwar democratization in such a way as to make it beyond questioning. To varying degrees, this was also a problem in other New Left groups.

Of course, the students organized by the Bund did perceive the hypocrisy of the postwar democratic system. Their doubts were richly expressed in the early works of Nobel Prize–winning novelist Ōe Kenzaburō (b. 1935), who, though he was a little older, was widely read among students at the time. Like the beatniks and "angry young men," Ōe worked into his novels the sentiment of stagnation in mass society created on the flip side of postwar global economic growth; however, at the same time, he was also one of the leading defenders of postwar democracy. Nevertheless, Ōe continually raised the problem of the emperor system in his novels. His best work, *The Silent Cry* [*Man'en gannen no futoboru*], could be said to demonstrate the convergence of Ōe's various and connected *problématiques*.

Zengakuren/Zenkyōtō

According to journalistic opinion, Prime Minister Kishi and the LDP's parliamentary scheming to force through approval of the renewal of the United States–Japan Security Treaty was "dictatorial" and "antidemocratic," and their hard-line stance made the anti-security treaty protests into a national-popular struggle. The Zengakuren, under the Bund's leadership, was the furthest-left radical faction in the anti-security treaty mobilizations. Toward the end of the protests, in fact, public opinion about "defending democracy" changed its focus from disparaging Kishi's despotism to critiquing the Zengakuren's radical militancy. With this turn in public opinion, the anti–security treaty protests came to an end and the Bund split into several factions.

Just as the protests had reached their high point and were entering their final period, the well-known opinion leaders of the time tossed out the question: "democracy or dictatorship?" Needless to say, the intent of this question was to defend "the people" from the Kishi government's "dictatorship." However, in the final stages of the protests, the message of defending democracy was stood on its head and became a journalistic critique of the Zengakuren. Put bluntly, the Bund, which was ostensibly a Marxist party, was, at this juncture, unable to raise the issue of dictatorship—that is, dictatorship of the proletariat. This inability was a theoretical limit imposed on the Bund insofar as it represented the leftmost faction of postwar democracy. (Of course, realistically speaking, raising the issue of the dictatorship of the proletariat during the anti–security treaty protests would have been almost impossible.)

After the movement against the United States–Japan Security Treaty had been defeated, the Bund splintered as it tried to take stock of what had transpired in the protests. Other New Left groups were relatively stagnant during this period. The term "frustration" [*zasetsu*] was ubiquitous at this time. Nevertheless, efforts to break through the stagnation continued and, with issues such as opposition to the war in Vietnam and problems on individual university campuses providing motivation, the student movement gradually began to recover its energy. What merits special attention in a discussion of the historical roots of 1968 is the October 8 1967 "Haneda struggle", against the then prime minister Sato Eisaku's tour of Southeast Asia (including Vietnam), which was organized by several thousand student activists in the area around Tokyo's Haneda Airport. This protest was the first in which the Japanese New Left appeared in the streets wearing helmets and carrying long pieces of squared lumber (called *gebabō*, a portmanteau of *Gewalt* [German for violence] and *bō* [stick]). In a move that was called the "return to violence," the weapons of the 1968 student radicals demonstrated the intensity of the street battles during the October 8 protests.

During the 1960s, Japanese people were mobilized to participate in two main events staged by the Japanese ruling class: the 1964 Tokyo Olympic Games and the 1970 World Exposition in Osaka. In a nutshell, Japanese capitalism used the 1964 Tokyo Olympics as a means to transform its image from "feudalistic" to that of a high-growth economy, by dismantling in one fell swoop its largely rural base. By 1968, Japan's gross national product had become the world's second largest, and the conditions for viewing the emperor system as a vestigial feudal institution were becoming weaker by the day. All the while, the Showa emperor

(1901–89) carried out his role as a "symbol" by presiding over high-profile national events. Nuclear power plants—of the type that exploded in the 2011 Tohoku earthquake—made their public debut by powering the 1970 Osaka World Exposition. Many leftist and avant-garde architects and artists were mobilized to participate in the Osaka event; however, the student activists of the time were relatively unconcerned with the implications and consequences of these political affairs. Providing this context for the years leading up to 1968 is essential to understanding the later events.

Like the 1960 protests, the 1967 Haneda struggle was also fought under the banner of the Zengakuren. The New Left parties were swept into disarray by the end of the 1960 protests. The formerly unified Zengakuren was dissolved and each New Left faction had an alliance consisting of student organizations on the university campuses that were under its control, each of which was called "the Zengakuren." The Haneda struggle was fought by these various "Zengakurens," which had allied for the protest.

The defining characteristic of 1968 in Japan is that it was fought as a comprehensive and provisional alliance (Zenkyōtō) that went beyond the protests of the various New Left Zengakurens. With the factionalization of the New Left parties after the 1960 anti–security treaty protests, each New Left party tended to establish a kind of dictatorial martial law within the undergraduate student governing bodies it controlled. These groups would not countenance even the mere presence of rival parties or activists. It goes without saying that the ideal of student governments formed of representatives freely chosen by students in a secret ballot had become an empty formality. However, for each New Left party to take dictatorial control within a student self-governing body required abandoning "democratic" methods: each faction tended to segregate itself within each faculty of each university, and the frequency of disputes eventually became an impediment to the operation of the university. From the perspective of the New Left factions, though, if they could monopolize student self-governing bodies, they would have a rather tidy sum of student fees at their disposal without much effort on their part—and they could use these funds for their own organizing.

In 1968, non-party-affiliated students referred to these types of student governing bodies as "Potsdam student councils," and called for their destruction. The emergence of these students, who were called "non-sect radicals," gave the Japanese 1968 its defining characteristic.

The Zenkyōtō movement, which began in 1968, started in the large national universities and Japan's largest private university, Nihon, and then spread like wildfire to nearly all Japanese campuses. Though the Zenkyōtō movement included the New Left sects, who clustered around the burgeoning numbers of non-sect activists, the movement made a definitive break with the earlier Zengakuren, which represented for them something imposed from above and a restraint on student activism, after Japan had capitulated to the terms of the Potsdam agreement. For this reason, Zenkyōtō students believed the self-governing bodies should be destroyed, and this idea was an important component of the 1968 critique of postwar democracy.

The term Zenkyōtō was abbreviated from All-Campus [Zen] Joint [Kyō] Struggle [Tō] Councils. Each Zenkyōtō was formed as an alliance or front [*kyōtō soshiki*] of groups with diverse interests, similar to the new "soviets" or *Räte* forms of organization that popped up all over the world in the years around 1968. In this sense, it is possible to say that 1968 and Zenkyōtō was a movement inclined toward a radical and direct democracy, one that opposed forms of representative democracy. However, as I will discuss, Zenkyōtō carried a latent directionality toward dictatorship that created a more radical and important confrontation with postwar democracy.

The Japanese 1968 included a critique of postwar democracy that did not stop at the expression of a desire for a restoration of radical democracy. It was certainly "fraudulent" for Japan to have a military under a postwar constitution that renounced Japan's possession of military force. However, denouncing this hypocrisy implies strict adherence to the postwar constitution. In other words, this sort of critique expresses a desire for completing the project of postwar democracy, which is a criticism found in the Beheiren ("Peace in Vietnam!" Citizens' Committee), formed to oppose the Vietnam War along with the 1968 students. The students who belonged to Beheiren often became Zenkyōtō activists at their universities, but, as a rule, the older liberal intellectual leadership of Beheiren was favorably inclined toward postwar democracy. For the leadership, the democracy within citizens' movements represented the best of postwar democracy. In contrast, for at least the avant-garde of Zenkyōtō, postwar democracy was something to trample mercilessly underfoot. Though merely an acting out of an infantile fantasy, Japan's 1968 students (from the Red Army Faction to the non-sect radicals) even went so far as to form armed-struggle organizations.

Mishima Yukio/Zenkyōtō

One of the most straightforward expressions of the 1968 critique of postwar democracy occurred during the University of Tokyo's Zenkyōtō movement. The event involved the destruction of the University of Tokyo professor Maruyama Masao's (1914–96) office and a physical attack on his person. Maruyama was a liberal political scientist and the most renowned champion of postwar democracy. The majority of Beheiren's intellectual leaders deeply respected Maruyama, and Maruyama himself had an affinity for Beheiren. The attack on Maruyama shows the uniqueness of Zenkyōtō's critique of postwar democracy.

Since there is much that is still unclear about the attack on Maruyama, I will limit my discussion to an overview of the more widely known event, the destruction of his office. On January 18 and 19 of 1969, there was an intense battle between Zenkyōtō students, defending their nearly total control of the University of Tokyo's Hongō campus with a rain of rocks and Molotov cocktails, and the riot police who were trying to clear them out. This battle was called the "defense of Yasuda Tower." Yasuda Tower symbolized the University of Tokyo, and perhaps for this reason, the conflict is understood as the peak of the 1968 protests in Japan. After the battle, it was discovered that "valuable" academic research materials stored in professors' offices had been completely destroyed by the Zenkyōtō students occupying the tower. One of the Zenkyōtō's slogans was "dismantle the university" (although this really meant destroying the university in its capacity as an ideological arm of the state). To borrow Lacan's term, this slogan was interpreted "hysterically" and put into action materially. On seeing the destruction, Maruyama described it as an act of "barbarism that not even the Nazis would have committed." Maruyama's comment was widely reported by journalists, and public opinion largely supported Maruyama.

Comparing the actions of students in 1968 to those of fascists or Nazis is a common tendency of left liberals around the world. However, what makes the situation in Japan unique is that the students had the ardent support of novelist Mishima Yukio (1925–70), who was then emerging as a right-wing activist. Mishima, along with Ōe Kenzaburō, was one of postwar Japan's representative novelists; however, the two authors had completely different political positions and saw each other as rivals. Though Ōe had a deep interest in how 1968 played out, as a postwar democrat, he did not express his support for the movement to the degree that Mishima did.

Even among the small number of intellectuals who supported the Zenkyōtō, not one expressed their support as much as Mishima. At a roundtable immediately after the battle at Yasuda Tower, Mishima praised what Maruyama had called Zenkyōtō's "barbarism" as "thrilling." (For this, he earned the scorn of the conservative ideologues in attendance.) The following May, Mishima attended a debate at the invitation of the University of Tokyo's Zenkyōtō students. This was because what Mishima had described as "thrilling" was Zenkyōtō's complete rejection of the postwar democracy that Maruyama represented. At the debate, Mishima even went so far as to declare that "if you all would just say the word 'emperor' I would gladly join hands with you."[1] Here the Japanese New Left was forced to confront the emperor system that it had left almost unquestioned. Naturally, the students who had invited Mishima could do almost nothing but express bewilderment.

As the entire world knows, Mishima would go on to infiltrate the Self-Defense Forces base in the Ichigaya neighborhood of Tokyo in November 1970 along with several members of his private army, and after giving a speech urging the soldiers to carry out a coup d'état, shouted "Long live the Emperor!" and disemboweled himself. By the time of the debate with Zenkyōtō, Mishima had published a play titled "My Friend Hitler" and made no effort to hide his affinity for fascism. That being the case, Mishima's sympathy for Zenkyōtō, as Maruyama had perceived, was because he saw the latent fascism in 1968. Even if that is true, it is still possible to ask whether what Mishima saw in Zenkyōtō was the form of something hidden by postwar democracy but thrust into daylight by fascism. Would it be wrong to say that although the name of the emperor has since been debated in the same manner that Heidegger's was, it was first questioned in the historical context of postwar Japan in 1968? Moreover, as I will discuss later, Mishima's emperor-centered politics rejected both fascism and Stalinism as "totalitarian."

The roots of Mishima's sympathy for 1968 and the New Left are surprisingly old and deep, as the following two examples show.

First, in 1949, Mishima wrote a short story entitled "Shinsetsuna kikai" [The Nice Machine], which attained unusually large importance among Mishima's many works. The plot was based on a murder case that occurred immediately after the war. The model for the story's

1 Mishima Yukio and Tōdai Zenkyōtō, *Mishima Yukio vs. Tōdai Zenkyōtō*, Tokyo: Shinchosha, 1969.

protagonist was Yamaguchi Kenji (1925–99), who was then a student and would later become an anarchist. Yamaguchi is rumored to have led the strategizing during the battle for Yasuda Tower and was also entrusted by Beheiren to play an important role in its program of sheltering American soldiers who had fled the US military during the Vietnam War era. Yamaguchi is a shadowy figure who traveled the entire world. I will not go into detail, but there are several pieces of evidence pointing to Mishima's awareness of Yamaguchi's activity during the 1960s. (And, of course, Yamaguchi would naturally have known of Mishima.) Mishima was something of a patron of 1960s underground artists and Yamaguchi was also in the same milieu.

In a second example, immediately following the anti–security treaty movement in 1960, Fukuzawa Shichirō (1914–87), a "nativist" [*dochaku*] writer sometimes likened to Kafka and Borges, published the short story "Fūryū mutan" [Dream Tales] in a prominent magazine. The story relates, in a blackly humorous style, some absurd dreams about the serial beheading of the members of the imperial household during a political and social upheaval reminiscent of the 1960 security treaty protests. Right-wing forces objected furiously as soon as the story was published. In fact, the maid of the president of the magazine's publishing company was even murdered in an act of right-wing terror. Fukuzawa had no choice but to flee and live a nomadic, underground life. To this day "Fūryū mutan" has never been published in book form (although it is now easily read on the Internet). In 1968, students used some of their funds to publish "Fūryū mutan" in underground publications. It is now known that it was Mishima Yukio who urged the magazine to carry "Fūryū mutan"—his emperorism was evidently not so strong that he would reject this type of writing. Quite the opposite, in fact: Mishima went so far as to endorse the disorder and anarchy of the work. In addition, in his *Bunka bōeiron* [On the Defense of Culture], which appeared in 1968, Mishima wrote: "The greatest enemy of culture is a political establishment that does not guarantee the freedom of speech."[2] Mishima's statement rejects the totalitarianism of both left and right—that is, Stalinism and fascism—but this should also be understood in the context of his sponsorship of the publication of "Fūryū mutan." When "Fūryū mutan" touched off right-wing terrorism, Mishima himself had to flee to escape the threat. For Mishima, only

2 Mishima, *Bunka bōeiron*, Tokyo: Shinchōsha, 1969. First serialized in *Chūō kōron* in July 1968.

freedom of speech could guarantee the totality of culture. This is because in his view, "culture" and "totalitarianism" were diametrically opposed ideas.

Let us now examine Mishima's scandalous and "rightist" declaration of himself as an "emperorist" in his *Bunka bōeiron* before we investigate how it was a critique of postwar democracy; then we may determine whether he tried to express it in harmony with the 1968 students.

Bunka bōeiron begins with an insult directed at the sclerotic nature—this in spite of Japan's economic maturation—of Japan's cultural and political situation in the late 1960s. Mishima's feelings in this regard are not especially unique. Many, beginning with Ōe Kenzaburō, expressed similar sentiments. What I would like to emphasize is that Mishima rejected not only the postwar emperor system, but also the prewar emperor system as a modern constitutional monarchy. So, what precisely is Mishima's ideal emperor system, a system he called "the emperor as a cultural ideal"?

Immediately after Japan's defeat in 1945, the most pressing concern of the country's ruling class—beginning with the reigning Showa emperor himself—was how to preserve the emperor system. When the American occupation, acting on a political conjecture, converted the emperor from "sovereign" to "symbol" of the state and people, powerful liberalist conservatives rationalized this change by arguing that it was unusual for the emperor to be the political sovereign and that the emperor had generally been a symbol of Japan's cultural unity. In other words, it was the Meiji constitution that was the exception and the postwar constitution that restored normality. This idea is close to Mishima's idea of the "emperor as cultural idea." Though the emperor system may be only latent, it runs through all of Japanese history. One implication of this argument is that, under the postwar constitution—a form of reflection on the prewar experience urging the building of a liberal, cultural state—defending the emperor system can be interpreted to mean "defending democracy." Mishima was wary of this argument, as it was identical to the prewar argument that because the polity, which included the emperor system, was based on a system of private property, the emperor system was synonymous with capitalism. Mishima rejected both the prewar and postwar emperor systems.

Our next issue is the question of what distinguishes the "cultural state"—which Mishima rejected as "culturism"—from Mishima's "emperor as a cultural idea." Mishima believed that the emperor as a cultural idea was not necessarily on the side of state power and established hierarchy, but it also contained an element of anarchy. Japanologists around the world have debated the aestheticization within Mishima's political idea of elegance. If we are to use Walter Benjamin's terminology, Mishima "aestheticized politics" and, in the final analysis, was therefore a fascist.

However, here we must think more concretely. According to Mishima, under the postwar constitution's democratic system, "disorder" (which Mishima called a blood-stained "anarchy")—or, in other words, Carl Schmitt's "state of exception"—could not be understood. Mishima was irritated by what had become by the 1960s an overdeveloped postwar system, and he was therefore attracted to the 1968 students, in whose protests he saw a glimpse of "disorder" or "state of exception." The several-thousand-strong battalion of armed students who appeared in the street battles in Shinjuku on October 8, 1968, pulled in tens of thousands of people and touched off a riot. One could say that the 1968 students who expressed their critique of postwar democracy by upgrading their weaponry from wooden staves and helmets to Molotov cocktails and homemade bombs dreamed a dream that was not so different from Mishima's.

The Emperor System/Democracy

The legitimacy of the postwar constitution that made the emperor into a symbol and ushered in postwar democracy was based on the legal theories of Carl Schmitt's theoretical opponent, Hans Kelsen. This was none other than the birth of an "emperor-system democracy." As is well known, Kelsen was close to Freud and occasionally participated in his seminars. Even if Kelsen included critiques of Freud, a major part of his legal theory rested on Freud's work. Kelsen, who wrote in *God and the State* that he had no doubts about "the inner connection between religious and social phenomena," surely had Freud's *Totem and Taboo* in mind when he wrote that "the theory of popular sovereignty may be sophisticated and refined but it is a mask for totemism."

As I have mentioned, the Japanese people first gained sovereignty under the postwar constitution. One could very well ask, then: to what degree was Freud's Oedipal parricide completed and peace returned? Moreover, one must also consider whether the emperor was totemized out of existence, worshipped as an ancestor out of regret for his murder. It is a fact that the drama described in *Totem and Taboo* was reenacted most faithfully in postwar Japan—as fiction, of course.

Immediately after the war, there was a slogan: "the collective penance of 100 million." Of course, the slogan meant that the 100 million would repent to the emperor.

Soon after the war, Maruyama Masao developed an argument for an "August revolution." According to this argument, Japan's defeat in August 1945 was something akin to the French revolution, in which the monarch was killed. With the annihilation of the emperor following the war, Japan was reborn as a peaceful democratic state with a sovereign people. But this argument has several weak points: most would not consider Japan's defeat a regicidal revolution and would tend to believe that popular sovereignty was something bestowed by the American occupation.

Nevertheless, the very act of dragging the Showa emperor down from the status of a "god" to that of a "person" was regicide. (And, in any case, Japan would not have lost the war if the emperor had really been a god.) But, because he did lose this status, defeat itself was regicidal, and it can be argued that defeat also brought peace. The occupation army, for its part, denied the fact that it had committed regicide, as the Potsdam Declaration had stated that the "Japanese people freely express their desire for the establishment of a responsible government with a proclivity for peace" and because the postwar constitution rested on the basis of the legal fictions of the nation and the state. On top of these fictions was the emperor, who had been totemized as a "symbol," having been converted from being a "deity." The human emperor, who had survived defeat, worshipped this ancestor/totem and became a deity symbolizing peace. In other words, under the emperor system, the emperor is doubled, transformed into two symbols: one a mortal totem, the other a living deity. As this doubling extended into the postwar era, the double image of the emperor meshed with the received wisdom of the ethnologists who considered emperor-centered ancestor worship to be the Japanese people's unique religion. And in fact, ethnologist Yanagita Kunio (1875–1962), who witnessed the promulgation of the postwar constitution as one of the last advisors to the Privy Council, very quickly began to emphasize ancestor worship after the war.

The theory of an August revolution tries to rationalize the fiction of the postwar emperor-system democracy. In other words, it was a logic that deceptively attempted to establish domestic harmony with the form of popular sovereignty dubbed "postwar democracy" coming after the regicide. Naturally, Maruyama Masao was aware of the stark emptiness of the August-revolution argument; for this reason, he declared that, as a democrat, he placed his bets on the fiction of postwar democracy, and the theory would later come under attack from many other directions. Nevertheless, in order to accept postwar democracy, one had no choice but to accept the theory of an August revolution. And once that was done, as Mishima feared, the emperor became a symbol of democracy and shone all the more brightly for it. In fact, this is the reason many of the left liberals who attempt to oppose the LDP conservatives (many of whom are veterans of 1968) have a strong affinity for the emperor.

There is no evidence that Maruyama Masao referenced Kelsen directly as he was developing the theory of an August revolution. On the contrary, Maruyama had absorbed Schmitt's theories early on and it is possible to read Schmitt's influence behind his well-known remark that democracy was a fiction. However, the influential constitutional scholar Miyazawa Toshiyoshi (1899–1976), a central figure during the creation of the postwar Japanese constitution and who subscribed to Maruyama's theory of an August revolution, was himself unmistakably influenced by Kelsen. He may have believed that it was "disrespectful" to define the postwar emperor system as a form of totemism. Miyazawa's connection to Kelsen was indirect, but we can see an important link in his close relationship with famed ethnologist Yanagita Kunio, for whom J. G. Fraser—often cited by Freud in *Totem and Taboo*—was a crucial source. And as an ethnologist, Yanagita traced the problem of regicide in the emperor system back to antiquity.

In any case, it is not a mistake to regard the emperor system as defined in the postwar constitution as a kind of totemism in Kelsen's sense of the word. In modern Japanese constitutional theory, which was derived from German constitutional theory, the prewar liberal theory was based on Jellinek's theory of state corporations [*kokka hōjinsetsu*] or, in other words, the "organ theory" of the emperor [*tennō kikansetsu*], which held that the actual emperor was a mere "organ" of the broader emperor system. This theory lost its power under the postwar constitution's transformation of the emperor into a symbol, and hegemony was shifted to the Kelsen faction. However, as is the case with Freud's theories, this argument was largely limited to one national community [*kyōdōtai*] and is therefore a bit like the arguments for "peace in one country." Nor could this theory elude a critique such as the one given by Schmitt in his *Political Theology*, which held that "the Sovereign is the person who decides matters during a state of exception." It is by now unnecessary to say that Mishima Yukio's critique of the postwar democracy's emperor system was reminiscent of Schmitt's thought. Mishima was a graduate of the University of Tokyo's Faculty of Law, and it has long been pointed out that Mishima's political romanticism resembled that of Schmitt. Mishima's conception of the "emperor as cultural idea" allows for an anarchic state of exception to arise within the nation and sets up the emperor as a potential authority during the state of exception. In contrast to Schmitt, whose "person who decides during the state of exception" was, in extreme cases, a dictator, with Mishima, the emperor was something akin to a zero symbol, permitting any and all anarchy. For Mishima, this quality of being a zero symbol was what he called "elegance." In other words, the emperor was a non-dictatorial dictator. In this sense, Mishima's theory of the emperor as cultural idea is similar to what Roland Barthes developed in *L'Empire des signes*, his travelogue about Japan. However, Mishima's notion of the emperor as zero symbol preceded that of Barthes.

Having developed this theory of the emperor, Mishima should have understood in the way that Bakunin had, that the anarchy of the 1968 students was an example of Schmitt's "anti-dictatorial dictator." Yamaguchi Kenji, mentioned previously, may have understood the Mishima of 1968 as a sort of doubled image of Bakunin. It was certainly not a joke when Mishima told the University of Tokyo Zenkyōtō students that "if they would only utter the name of the emperor he would gladly join hands with them." It is in this sense that it is possible to call Mishima an anarcho-fascist. Mishima did not distinguish between Zenkyōtō and the Zengakuren, but he did grasp the anarcho-fascist element of Zenkyōtō.

Kaseitō Critique/War of Position

No matter how radical their self-presentation, the 1968 students did not question the role of the emperor within the system of postwar emperor-system democracy. For this reason, it is fair to say that they kept the problem of the emperor in suspended animation, and their protests therefore remained within the framework of a provincial nationalism. Only a shock from the outside could break through this nationalistic stasis. This shock came about a year after Mishima's debate with the University of Tokyo Zenkyōtō students and a few months before his suicide.

The Zenkyōtō and the New Left movements attempted to practice what Gramsci called a war of maneuver, but by July 1970, they had objectively reached an impasse. On July 7, a coalition of New Left and non-sect groups held a rally to commemorate the thirty-third anniversary of the Marco Polo Bridge incident, which marked Japan's imperialist invasion of the Asian mainland. Among the sponsoring organizations was the group Overseas Chinese Youth Struggle Committee [Kakyō Seinen Tōsō I'inkai, abbreviated to Kaseitō]. Kaseitō was made up of Chinese and Taiwanese Maoists who aimed to prevent passage of the Immigration Control Bill through the Diet.

However, an incident occurred during the rally's planning stages. A "slightly" discriminatory remark was made by one of the members of the New Left factions, and this precipitated Kaseitō's withdrawal from sponsorship of the event. In response, non-sect radicals severely reprimanded the members of the New Left sect for the remark. The non-sect group was made up of young activists who had emerged from the margins of the Zenkyōtō movement, far from its anarcho-fascist sensibilities. The exclusion of Kaseitō prevented the participation of Chinese people, the very people who had suffered from Japan's imperialist war in Asia. Ironically, the meeting was planned as a forum for a declaration that the participants would not permit another Japanese invasion of Asia. On the day of the event, July 7, a member of Kaseitō appeared at the rostrum and severely criticized the Japanese New Left for claiming to fight for "world revolution" and "internationalism" when they were nothing more than narrow-minded, prejudiced nationalists. This critique became known as the "Kaseitō critique," and on the day, each sect was driven to apologize and submit to self-criticism.

Not only did the Kaseitō critique greatly change the form of the New Left movement that came afterwards, but it also brought major turns in philosophy. It would not be an exaggeration to say that how one interprets these philosophical changes is to pose the question of how to evaluate the Japanese 1968. And this is not just an issue limited to the New Left; it is also relevant to the current issue of racism that is now gaining strength around the world. With the Kaseitō critique, a problem—common to the citizens' movements but, until then, uncommon in the 1968 student movement—came to the foreground. The Kaseitō critique eventually grew into something that even the bourgeoisie had to accept bitterly: so-called political correctness.

The New Left sects, which had run into a dead end in their attempt to create a situation of exception, began to set their course for minority movements with antidiscrimination as their focus. And, in fact, the Kaseitō critique marked the opening of a war of position within civil society over such issues as the immigration status of Chinese and

Korean residents of Japan, feminism, those with disabilities, Burakumin, and ecology. There was likewise a movement centered around the 1970 "return" of Okinawa, which had been under US military occupation, to Japanese sovereignty, but by this time a philosophical re-evaluation that recast Okinawans as a minority was under way.

According to a feminist who gained admittance to journalistic circles in the 1980s and who experienced the 1968 movement firsthand, the New Left and Zenkyōtō movements during the era of their war of maneuver were blatantly androcentric. Within the student-occupied universities, female activists were given only unpaid, housemaid-type roles. As mentioned, while avoiding the problem of the emperor, who was a "feudal remnant," the Japanese New Left, including Zenkyōtō non-sect radicals themselves, had attitudes left over from feudal times.

Another consequence of the Kaseitō critique was, finally, to open up a space for problematizing the emperor within the New Left. The July 7 rally to commemorate the Marco Polo Bridge incident took as its slogan "prevent the re-invasion of Asia by Japanese imperialism," and put into question a war that was fought in the name of the emperor. Whether the Kaseitō critique was of this nature or not, it criticized the Japanese New Left for not permitting the participation of Chinese people and thereby indulging in a nationalistic narcissism. This was pointed out in the following way:

> The Japanese New Left talks about smashing Japanese imperialism and world revolution, but you think of yourselves as the only actors capable of doing anything about it. And you exclude others. That's the same structure of thought that was in the idea of the Greater East Asian Co-Prosperity Sphere.

For example, the most militant of the 1968 groups was the Japanese Red Army, which was known for flying to North Korea and the Arab countries in an attempt to build an international base. In other words, in the final analysis, the Red Army's revolutionary theory was a fantasy that placed Japan at the center. In raising the question of the historical and "racial" responsibility of the metropolitan nation, the Kaseitō questioned the positionality of the Japanese people and proposed the investigation of the emperor's war responsibility. With the Kaseitō critique, the New Left finally had to face the issue of the emperor system.

The problem of re-evaluating modern Japanese history along the axis of the Showa emperor's war responsibility also implied a re-evaluation of the idea of a "postwar" era. This is an inquiry that connects back to the critique of postwar democracy that preceded the Kaseitō critique. In the 1970s, Japan and China had not yet restored diplomatic relations—so, legally speaking, both countries were still at war. In this sense, the idea of a postwar Japan was a fraud.

It was Maoist student activist Tsumura Takashi—the country's most brilliant ideologue produced by 1968—who took up the Kaseitō critique and developed it on the Japanese side. Tsumura was a prolific writer who, against the backdrop of the Cultural Revolution in China, made use of contemporary French thought that had just been translated into Japanese—even if he had not yet completely digested it. Tsumura opened up a critique of the postwar discourse by arguing that it was not yet "post" war, and he began and persistently pursued a citizens' movement to restore Sino-Japanese diplomatic relations.

Tsumura's thought was close to his situationist contemporaries, but one can also see him going further back and carrying on the work of Benjamin and Brecht in 1968, as well as presaging a kind of postcolonialism. In the 1970s, Tsumura was an early organizer behind the antinuclear movement, and he committed himself to a variety of other movements as well. However, following the United States' lead, the LDP realized a restoration of China-Japan diplomatic relations through its hegemony in the Diet. Furthermore, Mao's Cultural Revolution, to which Tsumura had become attracted, suddenly fell from favor, and Tsumura was forced to change direction. Presently, Tsumura is a qigong trainer and subscribes to a New Age philosophy. In the sense that he has been influenced by the early Mao, who was familiar with Taoism, one could say that Tsumura remains consistent with his earlier beliefs. At the same time, his course symbolizes one path that the Japanese 1968 traversed—but this reality is one that could be retrieved from any number of examples around the world.

After the Kaseitō Critique/The Present

Japan's "1968," which was cut off by the Kaseitō critique of July 7, 1970 understandably shifted to a war of position, with citizens' and civil rights movements. That it had become impossible to produce a situation of exception through a war of maneuver was now something that had to be confronted. Many attempts were made, until 1990, but the traditional New Left "zigzag" demonstration became impossible. Even at the university campuses that had been the focus of the student movement, the Zenkyōtō tendency to "smash the Potsdam student self-governing bodies" was paradoxically realized. Today, hardly a single student government exists on Japanese university campuses, and university authorities are able to control their campuses without the mediation of student leadership. At almost all Japanese universities, student political activity is prohibited, and students cannot even distribute leaflets. The Kaseitō critique was a necessary shift in paradigm for 1968, but it also resulted in the retreat of the entire New Left, both in theory and on the streets. (The New Left sects, on the other hand, pursued a war of maneuver even after the Kaseitō critique, but they fell into intra-New Left battles with gruesome "internal violence" [*uchi geba*], which I will not discuss here.)

Finally, I would like to touch briefly on the issue of the emperor system, which became a focus following the Kaseitō critique. The emperor system was not only problematized theoretically, but it has also included assassination attempts by several small radical groups. However, the Showa emperor himself never brought up the issue of his own culpability in the war. When asked about his responsibility for the war, he even went so far as to reply, "I don't know anything about such academic problems." In fact, under the prewar constitution, the emperor lacked all responsibility, something Maruyama Masao defined as "the system of irresponsibility"—but this was because the Meiji constitution was based on von Stein's constitutional theory, under which the sovereign was placed in a position of no responsibility. And then, once again, for the sake of controlling postwar Japan, the occupation failed to question the wartime responsibility of the Showa emperor, who was seen as the symbol of postwar democracy under the postwar constitution.

As if compensating for his father's responsibility, the Heisei emperor Akihito, who acceded to the throne in 1989, just as the Berlin Wall fell (and abdicated in spring 2019), has visited the battlefields of Okinawa and Southeast Asia, offering condolences to all the dead—and not just to the spirits of fallen Japanese soldiers—as well as to the descendants of residents who were caught up in the war. After the great earthquake of 2011, not only did Akihito visit the stricken areas, but he even spoke in a way that could be construed as critical of the government's pro-nuclear policies. This occurred in spite of the current constitution's prohibition of emperors speaking out politically.

It is therefore not surprising that the current emperor has arisen as something like the sole symbol of those Japanese people opposed to the

Abe government's anti-liberal LDP, which subordinates Japan to the United States. (Almost the entire left now argues that the LDP has actively facilitated this subordination.) In 1969, the then prince regent Akihito, rather than having an arranged marriage, was the first member of the imperial family to marry for love. He married a commoner, a daughter of the bourgeoisie, giving rise to something of a national obsession with the couple (it also marked the creation of an incest taboo within the imperial line). Through these moves, the emperor's family came to symbolize postwar peace and democracy. As mentioned, not a few intellectuals of the 1968 generation, in professing their liberalism, have declared themselves loyal to the throne. It is as if, after the Cold War, the ideals of communism were lost and the phantasm of the emperor rose to take its place.

We have reached a kind of end-point of the postwar emperor-system democracy, under which, as Mishima Yukio warned, a defense of the emperor implies the defense of democracy. Insofar as this is expressed within the premises of a theory of popular sovereignty, it amounts to nothing more than the completion of the project of totemism described by Kelsen. As such, it cannot escape a critique of the sort used by Schmitt. The postwar emperor-system democracy has now been accepted, even by the 1968 generation, which should be its harshest critic. This generation's acceptance thus marks the completion of another project. The LDP and Abe slyly allude to a "situation of exception" created by the threats of China and North Korea as they spew out the slogan "escape from the postwar regime," but not even Abe can argue for abandoning the emperor system.

Translated by Guy Yasko

7

The Japanese Communist Party since 1968: Between Revolution and Reform

Yoshiyuki Koizumi

The Library Doesn't Burn (1968)

In an article entitled "Wild Battle Between Students: Zenkyōtō Unable to Barricade Library," about the battle for the University of Tokyo's main library, the *Asahi Shimbun* contained the following passage on November 12, 1968:

> On the night of the 12th, Zenkyōtō (Anti-Communist Party faction) students aiming to blockade the entire campus and students from the Tōdai Tōsō Shōri Kōdō I'inkai [Victory in the University of Tokyo Struggle Action Committee] (Communist Party affiliated) who oppose the blockade fought violently for thirty minutes with wooden staves and other weapons. Around forty students were wounded. Although the blockade was unsuccessful, university leaders hardly showed their faces. In spite of the recent re-organization of the university, the administration has yet to find a clue as to how to bring the situation under control. Now the worst has occurred and student blood has been spilled at the hands of other students.
>
> Also on the 12th, around four in the afternoon, anti-Communist Party students held a meeting at Yasuda Tower where they called a "Rally to Begin the Blockade of the Entire Campus" where they reconfirmed their intent to barricade all of the University of Tokyo. At around 6:30 pm, Building 1 in the Engineering Department was barricaded. In response to the anti-Communist Party students' attempted blockade of the library, about 300 Communist Party–affiliated students,

> with the aid of students from other universities, and, armored in helmets, began a sit-in in front of the library to "Prevent the Blockade with Direct Action."
>
> After 8 pm, anti-Communist Party students began to beat the Communist Party–affiliated students with wooden staves. Communist Party–affiliated students hit back with wooden staves that they had brought and a skirmish broke out. Milk bottles and smoke bombs flew and the sound of yelling and punching could be heard as far away as Hongō Dōri, adjacent to campus.[1]

The Communist Party had previously used violence at Meiji and Hōsei universities, but it had done so under cover of night, not expecting its actions to be reported in the mass media. The battle over the library marked the first time the Communist Party had struck out with force openly against the New Left. The University of Tokyo Zenkyōtō explained its blockade of the university in the following manner:

> On 11 November, Zenkyōtō ended negotiations with university authorities and decided to blockade the entire university. A blockade of the university library was set as the opening move towards a total campus blockade. This is because the library has an important role in the university's research and educational functions, and moreover, it is the den of point-collecting insects who are oblivious to the progress of the campus struggle. Zenkyōtō, which has begun a movement to criticize the university's very foundation, can hardly permit this situation to continue.[2]

According to this document, rather than stopping research and education, the aim of the blockade of the university library was more to blockade the library's reading room, which was the home of the "point-collecting insects" in the Faculty of Law who were preparing for the civil service and bar examinations.[3]

1 *Asahi Shimbun*, November 13, 1968, morning edition.

2 Tōdai Tōsō Zengaku Kyōtō Kaigi, ed., *Toride no ue ni wareware no sekai wo*, Tokyo: Aki Shobō, 1969, 310.

3 Zenkyōtō, especially the assistants' struggle, believed in the possibility of "revolutionary" and "progressive" research and did not completely reject the university's research and educational functions. In this sense, Zenkyōtō did not aim to destroy the library. This parallels the antipsychiatry movement, which rejected existing psychiatry but believed in the possibility of a different form of psychiatry. The antipsychiatry movement even advanced psychiatric care as a form of clinical practice and psychological therapy. On this issue, see

If this is the case, then from Zenkyōtō's perspective, the Communist Party's use of force would appear all the more like a reactionary defense of the "point-collecting insects" who sided with the establishment. In fact, the battle over the library was an action the Communist Party must have prepared for. The conflict began with a sit-in by students in the Faculty of Law. The Communist Party organ *Akahata* [*Red Flag*] reported on the battle in an article entitled "Zengaku heisa no sakudō boshi—Seitō boeiken no kōshi, Torotsukisuto gekitai" ["Prevention of a total blockade of campus—Use of force in self-defense, Trotskyists repulsed"]:

> After a fierce demonstration, undergraduate and graduate students carrying placards saying "Prevent the Blockade of Campus," "Let's Fight and Win Real Democratization of the University of Tokyo," and "Unity and Solidarity" held a sit-in in front of the university library and protested its planned blockade.
>
> In front of the library were more than ten students from the Faculty of Law who had been using the library. These students were enraged by the Trotskyist announcement that the library would be blockaded and began a sit-in to prevent it. They applauded the demonstrations of the Victory in the University of Tokyo Struggle Action Committee and the Tōdai Daigakuinsei Kyōgikai [University of Tokyo Graduate Student Council], who joined their sit-in.
>
> At 7:30 pm and 8:30 pm, the Trotskyist students who were attempting to force through a blockade of campus threatened them twice with wooden staves and fire extinguishers containing toxic substances.
>
> However, the majority of students who supported the Tōitsu Daihyō Junbi Kaigi [United Representative Preparatory Council] stoutly rose against this violence and repelled the Trotskyist attack, delivering a blow against the plot to blockade the entire university and thereby preventing it.[4]

The Communist Party did not see its defense of "point-collecting insects" or its use of violence as a repressive measure benefiting the status quo.[5] In

Koizumi Yoshiyuki, "Seishin eisei no taisei no seishin shi—1969 wo megutte," in *Taisei no rekishi—Jidai no sen wo hikinaosu*, eds. Amada Jōsuke, Yōhei Kadosaki, and Satoshi Sakurai, Kyoto: Rakuhoku Shuppan, 2013, 205–32.

4 *Akahata*, November 11, 1968.

5 The Communist Party had a policy of sending undercover party members into the establishment. It chose these undercover members while they were still undergraduates in the Faculty of Law and had them sit the civil service exam. Considering this

the battle for the library, the party had used force as a means of resistance to indicate that it rejected violence and as a way of realizing the goals of the university struggle. The party translated its general policy of "waiting until the enemy starts something" to the campus setting. In essence, the party held that, if its enemies were to use violence, the party would resist with the violence necessary to defend itself.

Communist Party member students quickly picked up this new policy and began to use it themselves. The party made it official policy in July 1968 in its keynote report from the Nineteenth Meeting of the Communist Party–Affiliated Zengakuren. In the report, the party took the position that "in all their despicable machinations, such as their rigged elections run by various anti-Zengakuren factions, their unfair retention of executive committees/administrations, their violent occupation of student self-governing bodies, their phony parallel student self-governing bodies are not to be taken lightly; if the Trotskyists are to resort to violent means, we will smash them." The party wiped away all compromise: "We will not bend to their use of violence, run away from it, change our stance or fly into a rage because of it. If they continue to come at us with violence, we will marshal our student allies and firmly execute our right to self-defense and smash them with force."[6] And then, as if to confirm, the JCP's Central Committee announced a policy of "justified self-defense" in an article entitled "Shuchō" on September 13, 1968, in *Akahata*.[7] On the battle for the library, *Akahata* stated the following on November 14, 1968, also titled "Shuchō":

> On the night of the 12th [of November, 1968] at the University of Tokyo, students supporting the Unified Representative Group arose to defend themselves and beat back the attacks of violent Trotskyist groups. In the process they bravely prevented the Trotskyists' violent plan to blockade the entire campus. This action has had large repercussions.[8]

---

strategy, the Communist Party had a motivation to defend the lair of its "point-collecting insects."

6 Tokyo Daigaku Zengaku Daigakuinsei Kyōgikai—Tōdai Tōsō Kiroku Kankō I'inkai, ed., *Tōdai henkaku e no tatakai*, Tokyo: Rōdō junpōsha, 1969, 148.

7 "Shuchō: Seitō bōeiken in motodzuku dankotaru kōdō wo—Hōsei Daigaku de no chikaradzuyoi keiken ni narabou," *Akahata*, September 13, 1968.

8 "Shuchō: Gakuen kara no boryoku isso wo—Torotsukisuto no buso kaijō koso senketsu," *Akahata*, November 14, 1968. See also "Shucho: Gakuen no minshuka to boryoku no mondai," *Akahata*, November 22, 1968. At the very least, around January 1969, just

The Communist Party's use of its right to self-defense certainly did bring "large repercussions." On one hand, the government, the Liberal Democratic Party (LDP), and the mass media were now able to treat both the New Left and the Communist Party as violent organizations. On the other hand, the possibility of expressing one's revolutionary stance in action by exercising one's right to self-defense had a liberating effect on Communist Party students. Moreover, the battle for the library was the first large-scale clash between the New Left and the Communist Party, and it was the first in which party-affiliated students were victorious. Not only did this battle in November 1968 become an important turning point for Zenkyōtō's strategy of blockading the entire campus, but it also marked an important turning point in the Communist Party's strategy for the student movement.[9] First, within that movement, before November 1968, the New Left and the Communist Party had sometimes shared the same strategy vis-à-vis student self-governance, but subsequently, this sort of cooperation became almost impossible.[10] Second, as the student movement spread to universities all over Japan, violent confrontations between Communist Party-affiliated students and the New Left arose on many levels and over various small and large issues. The strategies and tactics used in these clashes during this period were sometimes devious and dark, and this provided a deep, emotional background to subsequent clashes between the old and New Left. Third, the conflict over the use of the right to self-defense between student activists and the central party came into relief. The first indication of this was a change in the leadership of the student movement at the University of Tokyo. According to the testimony of Miyazaki Manabu, the central party criticized the University of Tokyo Communist Party cell's competition

---

before and after the battle for the University of Tokyo's Yasuda Tower, the Communist Party's Central Committee had not dropped its policy of justified self-defense. See "Seitō boeiken e no kogeki ha yurusarenai," *Akahata*, January 15, 1969.

9 Tōdai Tōsō Zengaku Kyōtō Kaigi, ed., *Toride no ue ni ware ware no sekai*, Tokyo: Aki Shobō, 1969, 318.

10 In meetings involving entire student bodies, the Communist Party and the New Left sometimes agreed about the direction and form of protests—for example, on the use of tactics such as the indefinite strike and strike committees. Even after November 1968, the New Left and the Communist Party were frequently seen to be cooperating during the early stages of protest at provincial universities and high schools and before conflict arose over the tactic of barricading whole campuses. Among a few student party members, a sense that they were members of the same "left" was preserved and students did not view each other as enemies.

with Trotskyists over who was more revolutionary as "ultraleft adventurism." Immediately after the battle for the library, the Tōdai Tōsō Shōri Renkō I'inkai [University of Tokyo Struggle Victory Alliance Committee] was dissolved and reorganized into the Tōdai Minshuka Kōdō I'inkai [University of Tokyo Democratization Action Committee]. Afterward, the party's central committee took direct control of the University of Tokyo Communist Party cell.[11] Fourth—and this is important—both the Communist Party and the New Left, by moving toward using organized violence in their movements, indicated that they were considering the possibility of an armed struggle, which would have expanded the university struggle toward the labor and political movements. This is critical when considering the transition from the 1968 campus struggles to the 1970 security treaty struggle and the 1971 Okinawa struggle.

Security Treaty Renewal and Okinawa (1970–1)

At least until the anti-security treaty and Okinawa movements of the early 1970s, the left believed in the utility of continuing the tactic of indefinite campus strikes. The histories of 1968 and afterward, though, have completely neglected the politicization and expansion of campus struggles to nearly all universities in Japan. To this day, the majority of those who research the history of the student movement say nothing about the 1970 anti-security treaty movement or the Okinawa struggle.[12] The majority of researchers understand the movements from 1968 to the early 1970s merely as precursors to the citizens' and social movements that came later. They completely ignore the political processes by which the campus protests became the 1970 anti-security treaty and Okinawa protests. Not only that, but the political movements of the times were portrayed as if they had all fallen apart due to *uchi geba* [internal violence]. Consider several incidents from this period: the November 1971 Shibuya riot, the mail bomb sent to a police chief in December 1971, the actions of the East Asia

11 Miyazaki Manabu, *Toppasha—Sengoshi no kage wo kake nuketa 50 nen*, Tokyo: Gentōsha, 1998, 1: 255.

12 The analysis of the movements of the various parties has been neglected. In particular, the LDP's social democratic and welfarist elements have been ignored. Socialism and social democracy as goals within the political process of the 1970s have fallen completely out of the historical field of vision.

Anti-Japanese Armed Front [Higashi Ajia Han-Nichi Busō Sensen], and the bombing of Mitsubishi Heavy Industries headquarters. These were extreme actions, and the people who carried them out were similarly radical. Nevertheless, the majority of intellectuals have ignored the political meanings of these events and have interpreted them as part of a process of increasing militancy and violence in the New Left's internal battles. Moreover, these researchers make no distinction between intra-sect purges and battles between groups. For example, the Red Army incident was treated as an example of growing extremism in the battles between the old and New Left; not only that, but it was portrayed as the only possible outcome of the struggles between these entities. This is the way in which intellectuals reproduced the historical vision of the ruling class, which emphasizes security and defense of the social order. The result of this development was a rather vague historical consciousness that asserted an unmediated connection between the 1968 student movement and the citizens' and social movements of the 1970s. The effect of this historical consciousness has been enormous, as both the New Left and the old left movements cut themselves off from militant protest and became depoliticized, their leftism reduced to a theory of justice. An intellectual who was at the time labeled "a humanist" described the differences between the old and New Left in this manner: "The New Left is 'new' because it is different from the old Left, which supports socialism and communism. They have taken from the old left an interest in social justice."[13]

A mutual interest in social justice was presented as the common interest of the old and New Left, and the main body of this argument was to turn both the old and new into versions of the American egalitarian liberal movements of the time.[14] Alternatively, the old and New Left were each seen as movements that merely "resisted," on the level of micro-situations within civil society.[15]

---

13 Oda Makoto, Kazumi Takahashi, and Nobuhiko Matsugi, eds., *Henkaku no shisō wo tou*, Tokyo: Chikuma Shobō, 1969, 2.

14 The classic representative of this egalitarian liberalism was John Rawls, whose theory of justice was an argument that elided the radicalization and politicization of the civil rights and Black liberation movements; see Rawls, *A Theory of Justice*, Cambridge: Harvard University Press, 1971.

15 Foucault's mid-1970s theories of power, resistance, and subjectivity—which are now the framework of the intellingentsia's worldview—have been applied without modification to 1968 and the movements of the early 1970s. However, Foucault himself did not do so. As one can see in the "Collège de France" lectures of the early 1970s, Foucault understood the relation between the Establishment and the movements of 1968–70 to be

In opposition to this dominant historical interpretation, what we must recall and acknowledge is that both the New Left and old left were aiming to broaden the campus struggle by politicizing it and taking it to a national level. Because the movements were connected with the United States–Japan Security Treaty and Okinawa, they were believed to lead inevitably to a revolutionary situation. To put it bluntly, from 1969 to 1970, both the old and the New Left expected a revolution. These were not simply fantasies, though; this expectation was based on a realistic assessment of the situation.[16] What must be remembered, at the very least, is that both the Okinawa and the 1970 security treaty protests were linked to the military. In other words, they were connected to the state's largest violent apparatus. After 1970, when the left won a majority in elections, they were capable of passing a resolution to exit the security treaty, but doing so would have resulted in a military conflict between the United States and Japan. Even if the left were to gain a majority through peaceful and democratic means, an armed conflict with the United States would inevitably lead to the loss of state power. The Communist Party tried to adopt a policy of popular parliamentarism and structural reform, but there was always an aspect of its program that implied armed conflict with the United States. It was for precisely this reason that the party adopted policies of "waiting for the enemy to attack" and "legitimate self-defense." In 1971, Fuwa Tetsuzō, who worked out the strategy of "popular parliamentarism," remarked:

> In a situation under which the Liberal Democratic Party has a majority in the Diet, it's very difficult for us to form a majority to do anything positive. Even if we are able to keep a lid on the things the LDP majority tries to do against the will of the people through our actions within and without the Diet, it is difficult for us to move things in a different direction . . . In a situation where the LDP is trying to use its parliamentary majority, there is no option but to look for the intervention of the people, who after all are sovereign.

---

characterized by the Establishment's reaction to a revolutionary situation. Cf. Koizumi Yoshiyuki, "The Theory and History of the Subject's Domination of the Self and Others: From Althusser to Foucault," *Zinbun* 47, 2017, 81–9.

16 There is a tremendous amount of documentary evidence to demonstrate this. If one wishes, one might say that the left "subjectively" expected revolution, but one must not forget that the ruling class at the time also "subjectively" expected a revolutionary situation to arrive.

> When it comes to extra-parliamentary action concerning important issues like Okinawa, the people who have a degree of sovereignty outside the Diet, the people who cannot approve of the contents on the agreement on the repatriation of Okinawa, take all sorts of actions to reflect their will in the Diet. Their actions combine with our action in the Diet and make us stronger.[17]

Fuwa appears to be giving a simple outline of party strategy, but we should remember that, at the time, the power behind "extra-parliamentary action" was deemed extremely radical. No matter how far the tilt toward parliamentarism, as long as the party foresaw the arrival of a revolutionary situation, it had to emphasize a strategy that included the exercise of an extra-parliamentary "sovereign power." In connection to this issue, I would like to quote a passage from *Kimi no Okinawa* [Your Okinawa], which is the most famous document from the Communist Party-affiliated youth and student movement:

> Make no mistake, the "US–Japan Security Treaty Prosperity" was squeezed out of the sweat and blood of workers on the mainland.
>
> But that is not all. The US–Japan Security Treaty Prosperity was drawn even more from the blood and tears of Okinawans and the blood of the people of Vietnam . . .
>
> Think about it. If you consider Okinawa to be your problem, you can understand the lively crowds of workers fighting for Okinawa in workplaces all over Japan.
>
> The ruling class must be shaking. It's like when that financier, on seeing the whirlpool of the demonstrations in 1960 said "This is a revolution" and dropped his spoon mid-meal. Or like Shin Nitetsu's president Inayama, who, on seeing the results of the provincial 1971 elections said "I no longer understand where Japan is going." The ruling class looks strong, but they are trembling with fear that the anger over pollution, prices, and "rationalization" will flow into the Okinawa protests.[18]

17 Fuwa, as recorded in the debate "Okinawa higunjika koso to kokkai," in *Sekai*, December 1971, 58.

18 Rōdōsha Kyōiku Kyōkai, ed., *Kimi no Okinawa*, Tokyo: Gakushū no Tomo Sha, 1971, 17, 149.

Both the old and the New Left were united in expecting the arrival of a revolutionary situation. Of course, conflict—some of it armed—continued among the groups who called themselves the "vanguard party" and other groups trying to become the "vanguard party," but one must remember that, at least at the level of the mass movement, there were many points of agreement about the political issues confronting the left. Hirotani Shunji, who directed the University of Tokyo struggle but was later removed from his leadership position, attested to the "unity" of the old and New Left:

> They competed with each other in elections for office, but if the results produced, for example, a Minsei council president, a Kakumaru or a Chūkaku vice-president, they would have no choice but to work together . . . The reason they could not accept "Trotskyists" in a unified student front was not because the Trotskyists had an anti-Communist political direction, but because they were groups who trampled over democracy and ripped apart mass organizations. So if the Trotskyists had respected democracy and stopped all their internal violence [*uchi geba*], we should have joined with them in a unified front, yes.[19]

The Communist Party's approach to the New Left was widely adopted by the party's student activists, including during the anti–security treaty and Okinawa protests.[20] However, the central party clamped down on this loose strategy among student party members. The beginning of the clamp-down was the critique of the "new opportunism."

The Critique of the New Opportunism (1972)

In 1972, the central party began to name a tendency then appearing among party members in the leadership of mass organizations that

19 Hirotani Shunji, *Gakusei undō nyumon*, Tokyo: Nihon Seinen Shuppansha, 1971, 219–21.

20 The party's student activists at the time were well versed in the history of cooperation and conflict between Communists and the non-Communist left (particularly anarchists) in the Spanish popular front. In addition, *Sekai Seiji—Ronpyō to Shiryō*, published by the party's Central Committee, often carried bulletins about similar cooperation and conflict during the rise and fall of Chile's Unidad Popular government. When it came to the question of mass movements, even if party members would not unconditionally cooperate with the New Left, they did not believe they should confront all of the New Left at all times.

were connected to the student and youth movements "new opportunism." Many party members were called before hearings and relieved of their leadership positions in mass organizations, and not a few were driven from the party. In the introduction to its writing reflecting on this process, the party's Central Committee wrote:

> In the early 1970s, under the influence of petit bourgeois confusion and the convulsions that accompanied the sudden advances in the struggles of the time, as well as the violent changes in the domestic and international situation, there arose a new kind of opportunism which included the underestimation of the aggressive nature of American imperialism, the theory that Japanese militarism was the main enemy and the idea that the mass struggle was everything. Within many mass organizations there was a factionalism manifesting itself in unorganized actions. The party promptly and resolutely took action and smashed these actions.[21]

Here, "underestimation of the aggressive nature of American imperialism" also refers to underestimation of the Japanese state's fealty to the United States. The central party had decided that the new opportunism went against its definition of Japan as a subjugated nation in its 1961 program. The "theory that Japanese militarism was the main enemy" was a tenet of the New Left, and "the idea that the mass struggle was everything" was a belief among the part of the New Left that denied the need for a vanguard party. In sum, the central party decided that party members in the leadership of mass organizations had changed their revolutionary strategies and tactics in a New Left manner. In that sense, and only in that sense, it would have been acceptable to call it "left" opportunism or even "ultraleft" opportunism, but the central party instead called it "new" opportunism. The reason for this was that the central party was not only battling the rising tide of left opportunism within the party, but, at the same time, it was trying to shake off a right-wing parliamentary tendency that was gaining currency, particularly among party intellectuals. This tendency, under the banner of Eurocommunism and structural reform, held that a peaceful and continuous transition to socialism was possible by means of a popular-front government that would establish political and economic

21 Nihon Kyōsantō Chuō I'inkai Shuppan-kyoku, *Shin hiyorimi-shugi hihan*, Tokyo: Nihon Kyōsantō Chuō I'inkai Shuppan-kyoku, 1973, 1.

democracy. In other words, the "new" opportunism referred to both left and right opportunism.

In this manner, in the 1970s, the central party resisted, on the one hand, the growing sense that "linked the Okinawa Agreement to the complete rehabilitation of Japanese militarism and the establishment of fascism" and took a simplistic "smash the Okinawa Agreement" stance, for all intents and purposes identical to that of the Trotskyists' "organized petit bourgeois radical impatience," and tried to resist the increasingly popular idea that one should convert the mass organizations and movements to which one belonged into a substitute for the vanguard party. On the other hand, the central party resisted the growing sentiment to give up its battles with social democracy and the New Left, instead intensifying its "war on the intellectual and cultural front" and its "intellectual war against the opportunist tendency growing within self-conscious popular forces" that had "dragged mass movements onto a path of mistaken political neutrality." What should be emphasized here is that, unlike in the battle against factionalism up to the 1960s, the central party did not use as its main weapon infractions against party rules as a pretext for revoking party membership. The "new opportunism" was, in the end, a factionalist current or tendency, and, aside from some movement to form factions, there was no reason to cite violations of the party rules. For this reason, from the 1970s into the 1980s, the party carried out its "theoretical wars" widely, all while tearing apart mass organizations. In the 1970s, the central party, distancing itself from both accelerationist revolutionary currents and parliamentary reformism, tried to develop its own expectations for revolution.

Especially in regard to the student movement, the central party determined that it had to rid itself of "Trotskyist influence" over the "strategy, form and direction of struggle."[22] The party abandoned its resistance and violence based on its theory of justified self-defense and changed its position to state that "it would also use legal methods, which are an effective form of struggle for refusing violence."[23] In addition, the central party tried to shoehorn the student movement into a kind of mass-movement form of student self-government.

22 Nihon Kyōsantō Chuō I'inkai Shuppan-kyoku, *Seinen gakusei undō to Nihon Kyōsantō*, Tokyo: Nihon Kyōsantō Chuō I'inkai Shuppan-kyoku, 1973, 100.

23 Ibid., 108.

> One of the biggest weaknesses of the contemporary student movement is its tendency to become a movement of only the most advanced part of the student population. It is highly desirable to have a student movement which aims to realize the common desires of students, is based on the wishes of a truly wide range of students, and can develop into a movement in which the vast majority of students can participate.[24]

Looking back, the origins of the critique of ultraleft opportunism within the student movement can be traced to November 1968, when Ōkubo Kazushi attested to a major change in party direction:

> "indefinite, confined negotiations" began, but after a few days, without a word, orders were given to retreat through a party member in the Faculty of Literature. The next morning's *Akahata* contained a declaration by Tsuchiya Yoshio, second in command at the party's Central Youth and Student Policy Division, which—again, without any word given to us beforehand—criticized the state of the University of Tokyo struggle and indicated a shift in party policy.[25]

Subsequently, University of Tokyo party members were called to a meeting, where those seen as having ultraleft tendencies were criticized.

> After this action was unilaterally forced through, all University of Tokyo party members were called to a meeting under the name of the Central Committee Secreterial Bureau. The meeting was held at night in a large lecture hall in the Faculty of Agriculture. At the meeting the Secretarial Bureau gave a one-sided critique of the University of Tokyo party cell in which its ultraleft tendencies were labeled "problematic."
>
> . . . According to the notes I took at the time, the central party's critique of the University of Tokyo cell contained the following points. I will quote directly from my notes:
>
> 1. Confusion of a revolutionary line with a mass line. The University of Tokyo cell had fallen out of line with the principle of the mass line, namely that the direction of the mass struggle should

24 Ibid., 88.

25 Kawakami Tōru and Ōkubo Kazushi, *Sobyō: 1960-nendai*, Tokyo: Dōjidaisha, 2007), 202–3. This section was written by Ōkubo.

> be established by the masses themselves, be based on the desires of the masses and be fought from the perspective of realizing those desires. Instead, the University of Tokyo cell had pursued only the revolutionary nature of desires. From there, the content of its desires had developed into something which was impossible to realize in the current struggle. They were in fact impossible to realize under the reigning social order.
>
> 2. The Permanent Revolution tendency and underestimation of the Trotskyists. As an inevitable result of the University of Tokyo cell's desire to escalate towards revolution, and because it did not look at all to the objective situation—instead emphasizing only the structural subjective conditions for fighting the struggle to the end—the cell raised no concrete terms to settle the University of Tokyo struggle. It had abandoned the perspective of resolving its struggle. From this developed a tendency to compete with the Trotskyists to reach the same level of "revolutionism." In this manner, the University of Tokyo cell alienated itself from the masses. On the reverse side of this tendency was an underestimation of the Trotskyists' antirevolutionary qualities, leading to a mistaken belief that the Trotskyists had a base in revolutionary forces.
>
> . . . We could not express any opinion at all at the meeting. We came to hold a fundamental mistrust of the central party which had prohibited us from speaking.[26]

The central party developed a policy that the moment of establishing a popular-front government should be at "a date not too late within the decade of the 1970s." This view was shaped by the Okinawa and anti-security treaty protests and was given reality by the increased number of Diet seats the Communist Party had won in the 1972 general election. Moreover, in the 1970s, when it would have been possible to issue a notice of withdrawal from the United States–Japan Security Treaty at any time, it was self-evident that a popular-front government would be a transition to a revolutionary regime. For this reason, the central party's policy could itself be said to contain a left-opportunist tendency. However, the central party worked to rid the party of this tendency somehow. Why? Probably because the party was adopting an electoral strategy of changing itself into a "moderate" left-wing party, and this meant avoiding both the social democracy represented by the Socialist

26 Ibid., 204, 218.

Party as well as the accelerationist revolutionary line within the party, and holding to the party's own unique revolutionary line.[27]

Splits in the Mass Movement and the Disaffection of Party Intellectuals (1970s)

Throughout the 1970s, not only did the central party try to eradicate the new opportunism from the mass organizations and labor groups under its leadership, but it also tried to split organizations under the influence of the Socialist Party, mainly under the guise of driving out "Trotskyists" and "fake leftist violent groups." Let us look at some examples.

First, in June 1970, the Communist Party formed the Buraku Kaihō Dōmei Seijōka Renrakukaigi [Council to Bring the Buraku Liberation League to Normality]. This group was formed mostly out of party members belonging to the Buraku Liberation League. At that point and through the 1970s, opposition between the Buraku Liberation League and the Communist Party-affiliated Buraku liberation groups was reproduced on university campuses and its negative effects were felt even long afterward.[28] Second, in the disabled rights movement, the party formed the Zenkoku Shōgaisha Mondai Kenkyūkai [National Study Group on the Problem of the Disabled] in 1968. In 1976, the New Left-leaning Zenkoku Shōgaisha Kaihō Undō Renrakukaigi [National Disabled Liberation Movement Liaison Conference] arose to oppose the party-affiliated group. Among other issues, these groups opposed each other on the matter of compulsory special schools for those with disabilities, and their conflict inflicted wounds on both sides. Third, the Communist Party formed the Tōitsu Sensen Sokushin Rōdō Kumiai Kondankai [United Labor Front Promotion Colloquium], abbreviated to Tōitsu Rōsokon, in 1974. The Tōitsu Rōsokon later tried to combat the rightward drift of the Sōhyō [General Council of Trade Unions of Japan], which was under the control of the Socialist Party, by establishing a separate national labor center. It also split several

27 Cf. Hong N. Kim, "Deradicalization of the Japanese Communist Party Under Kenji Miyamoto," *World Politics* 28: 2, 1976, 273–99.

28 The point of contention between the two camps was whether to consider the elimination of anti-Burakumin discrimination to be a problem of bourgeois democracy or whether to consider it a problem of (industrial) capitalism. This conflict could be seen as a rehash of the prewar debate between the Rōnō [Labor-Farmer] and Kōza [Lectures] factions.

single-industry unions by forming separate unions.[29] Then, at the end of the 1970s, after many progressive local governments had lost and the number of Communist Party members had fallen, and at a time when the possibility of establishing a popular-front government had receded, the central party decided to make the Tōitsu Rōsokon into a national organization.[30]

The background to the central party's change of course was its need to strengthen its criticism of the Socialist Party, which was envisioning a coalition with the Kōmeitō [Clean Government Party] and the Minshatō [Democratic Socialist Party] in a popular-front government in which the Socialist and Communist parties would be the main partners. In September 1979, Chairman Miyamoto Kenji called local party committee chairs to party headquarters and criticized the Socialist Party:

> We must now harshly criticize the Socialist Party, which has become an obstacle to the formation of a unified front. Due to the treachery of the Socialist Party, progressive local governments have collapsed with a thud. The recent events in Tokyo are another example. At a time when it would have been possible to deliver a powerful blow to conservative forces through the formation of a progressive unified front, the Socialist Party's vacillation has become an obstacle. In the next general election, the Socialist Party will be feverishly trying to defend its seats with tears. We have a duty to crucify the Socialist Party for its lack of resolution and to impress the true image of the Socialist Party on the people of the nation through the slogan "Reflect on the treachery in Osaka, Kyōto, Yokohama and Tōkyō." By delivering hard blows to the Socialist Party we will make the appeal to the entire Party organization that "true reform comes only with the Communist Party."

Miyamoto's course for the party clearly abandoned the idea of an alliance with the Socialist Party. While it involved a unified front of mass

29 In 1974, in opposition to the Dōrō, which was seen as New Left, the party formed the Japan National Railway Locomotive Union Federation [Kokutetsu Dōryokusha Kumiai Rengōkai, abbreviated Zendōrō] in Sapporo. A similar antagonism arose in the Kansai region, as well. Parallel to this, the health care, education and public employee unions came out with policies to drop the use of the strike as a tactic. See *Akahata* articles "Kyōshi Seishokuron" (April 17, 1974), "Jichitai Rōdōsha—Zentai no hoshisharon" (March 22, 1974), and "Kōmuin—Kōbokuron" (March 22, 1974).

30 See Chairman Miyamoto's statements at the 1979 Ninth Central Committee Plenary meeting.

and labor organizations as the basis of a national electoral campaign, it was also completely unrealizable for the Communist Party to govern on its own. Miyamoto's position was criticized as rehashing the 1930s theory that social democracy was an enemy of the left, but one could also say that it was almost the only possible way for the central party to exclude left and right opportunism both within and outside of the party while simultaneously maintaining a revolutionary stance.

At this point, the central party's 1970s honeymoon with its affiliated intellectuals and cultural figures, who favored structural reform and Eurocommunism, ended, and their estrangement became decisive. As the central Communist Party pushed forward with its drive to purge right-wing opportunism, it steered away, for example, from the trend of Eurocommunism. In 1977, Miyamoto began to criticize the Italian Communist Party for its "lack of principles" over the question of democratic centralism and its theory of organization. Picking up on this, Fuwa Tetsuzō began to criticize by name Taguchi Fukuji, who had introduced Eurocommunism into the JCP. In the end, Taguchi left the party.[31] The central party likewise discouraged the trend of party intellectuals advancing critiques of Stalinism or democratic centralism. In 1977–8, the magazine *Gendai to Shisō*, issued by a party-affiliated publisher, ran the transcript of a symposium entitled "Investigating Stalinism." Before and after its publication, a series of texts were published that gave the appearance of criticizing the central party under the guise of anti-Stalinism and arguments against democratic centralism.[32] Though they took different paths, by the 1980s these party intellectuals had either lost their party membership or had left the party under their own steam.

31 In 1977, in response to Taguchi Fukuji's "Senshinkoku kakumei to zeneitō soshikiron—'Minshuchūsei' no soshiki gensoku wo chūshin ni," in *Gendai to Shisō* 29, Sekihara Riichirō (a pen name for four writers working together, including Sakaki Toshio and Ueda Koichirō) published "Zeneitō no soshiki gensoku no seimei—Taguchi Fukuji-shi no 'Minshushuch ūsei-ron' no ma daiten" in *Akahata hyōron tokushū-ban* (November 1977). In response to Taguchi's *Senshinkoku kakumei to tagenteki shakaishugi* (Tokyo: Ōtsuki Shoten, 1978), Fuwa Tetsuzō's, "Kagaku-teki shakai shugi ka'tagen shugika—'Taguchi riron' no hihanteki kenkyū" appeared in the January 1979 issue of *Zenei*, and a debate between Fuwa and Taguchi continued until 1980.

32 Fujii Kazuyuki, *Shakaishugi to jiyu*, Tokyo: Aoki Shoten, 1976; Nakano Tetsuzō, Takaoka Kenjirō, and Fujii Kazuyuki, eds., *Sutarin mondai kenkyū josetsu*, Tokyo: Ōtsuki Shoten, 1977; Fujii Kazuyuki, *Minshu shūchūsei to tō nai minshu shugi*, Tokyo: Aoki Shoten, 1978, among others.

In this manner, from the middle of the decade, the central party steered a course away from right opportunism and strengthened its campaign against intellectuals within and outside of the party.[33] In the 1980s and even before the collapse of the Soviet Union, the central party had driven many intellectuals out of the organization.[34]

Between Revolution and Reform

The University of Tokyo College of Arts and Sciences student self-governing body used to take a survey of incoming students' political party preference. In 1973, after the Communist Party's advances in the

33 It was in this period when, in the context of its critique of Taguchi, the central party criticized Maruyama Masao, a representative of postwar modernism, by name.

34 To list them: in 1983, the Communist Party-affiliated literary magazine *Minshu Bungaku* carried an article by Oda Makoto, who was a representative of Beheiren. In response, the central party strengthened its interventions into the editorship of *Minshu Bungaku* and *Bunka Hyōron*, and it forced literary party members out of the party. In 1984, Yoshida Yoshikiyo, spokesperson for the board of directors of the Japan Anti-Hydrogen Bomb Conference, was relieved of his position through the intervention of the central party for allowing a united front with a Socialist Party-affliated group. A worker at Nitchū Shuppan who published a book by Yoshida was thrown out of the party ostensibly for violating party rules. See Yoshida Yoshikiyo, *Gensuikyō de nani ga okotta ka*, Tokyo: Nitchū Shuppan, 1984; Yanase Norihisa, ed., *Senretsunaru taiken—Shuppan no jiyū to Nihon Kyōsantō*, Tokyo: Nitchū Shuppan, 1984. In this process, renowned scholar of international politics Eguchi Bokurō and the well-known philosopher Kozai Yoshishige, who had defended Yanase, left the party. Also in 1984, Nakano Tetsuzō was excommunicated from the party. The backdrop to these moves was the central party's wariness of the direction of study groups organized by party intellectuals, such as the Sapporo Materialist Study Group, the Tokyo Materialist Study Group (which was researching Althusser), and the Osaka Materialist Study Group (which had connections to the Democratic Students' League [Minshushugi Gakusei Dōmei, abbreviated as Mingakudō]). This was connected to the drive to unify all local materialist study groups. There are no Japanese-language documents that chronicle these events, though. In 1985, on the occasion of the twelfth party meeting, a faction of the University of Tokyo Graduate School party organization demanded Miyamoto's resignation. The reasons given for this were, first, his political responsibility for "the stagnation of the last ten years"; second, his responsibility as party leader for pulling the party off its advanced-nation revolutionary line after the fourteenth party meeting; third, for the promotion of worship of Chairman Miyamoto as an individual. Furthermore, it was stressed that the central party, with Miyamoto at its core, could not escape its political responsibility for the series of events unfavorable to socialism dating from the 1970s—namely the massacres in Cambodia, pressure from Solidarność in Poland, the Soviet Union's invasion of Afghanistan, and the rightward drift of nongoverning parties. The representative of the group, Iri Ichi, was thrown out of the party. See Ichihiro Itari (Iri Ichi), *Kibun wa komyunisuto—Miyamoto gichō no taijin wo motometa Tōdaiinsei no hanron*, Tokyo: Nitchū Shuppan, 1986.

1972 general election, the Communist Party overtook the LDP as the most popular party among incoming students. In 1973, after the major protests over Okinawa and the United States–Japan Security Treaty renewal had died down, disappointment in the New Left grew. With the Socialist Party beginning to show signs of decline, those affiliated with the left placed their expectations in the Communist Party. Kojima Ryo was not a member, but he had high expectations for the party during this period. Below, he describes his feelings for the party during the 1970s:

> In general, the reason why everyone voted for the Communist Party was not because they supported it as the vanguard party, but because the Communists seemed to be aiming for the creation of a new civil society. Also, they seemed capable of realizing their slogan of "protecting life and lifestyle." Many expected them to protect the weak, whom a Liberal Democratic Party government would completely disregard. It's possible that a majority of us felt that they wanted no part of a revolution staged by a vanguard party. They were all counting on and supporting a new kind of Communist Party. And as if to reply to those expectations, the Communist Party was revising its party principles; I think there was a honeymoon period in the mid to late 1970s during which people looked to the party with great hope.[35]

However, this hope changed to disappointment, which Kojima summarized as follows:

> The dreams and expectations of a "popular front" which we had from the beginning of the 1970s to the middle of the decade, gave way at the end of the 1970s to the dramatic revival of the conservatives. What was decisive in this reversal was the Liberal Democratic Party's overwhelming victory in Japan's first simultaneous election for both houses of the Diet on June 22, 1980.[36]

Why was the LDP able to win in the 1980s? In other words, why did the 1970s, an era in which the left reorganized, end in the victory of anti-revolutionary reaction? What I would like to emphasize here is that

35 Kojima Ryo's statement in *Garan ga akakatta toki—1970 nendai wo kangaeru*, eds. Suwa Kanenori et al., Kasugai: Chūbu Daigaku, 2012, 57–8.

36 Ibid., 108.

Kojima's politics of "defending life and lifestyle," the politics of "defending the weak," or the politics of "a new type of Communist Party" or a "popular front" were realized by LDP governments.[37] Though it has been frequently observed that the LDP government made 1973 "Year 1 of Welfare" by nationalizing the policy of a handful of progressive local governments to give free medical care for the elderly, scholars have not understood the true import of this. The LDP's welfare policy was not simply one that helped the "weak," but one that, by lessening the economic burden on the retired and elderly, also reduced corporate pension expenses. In other words, this was also a policy that guaranteed corporate welfare.[38] To put it another way, in response to attacks from the old and New Left, the LDP incorporated social democratic and egalitarian liberal policies; in doing so, it succeeded in reorganizing Japan into "a new civil society" centered around the corporation. The political history of the LDP in the 1970s emphasized often the Japanese welfare state or a slide towards neoliberalism. In this sense, the regime is frequently considered to be anti-Keynesian, the antithesis of a welfare state. However, one cannot adequately analyze the 1970s as a reaction to 1968 if one takes this view.

One can use the history of welfare for those with disabilities as an example. The LDP and the Ministry of Health and Welfare spearheaded the 1960s handicapped movement, but by the 1970s, though Communist Party and New Left–affiliated groups split organizations for those with disabilities and fought against each other, as a whole, the disability rights movement had become a leftist and radical

---

37 In the early 1970s, the Communist Party was critical of the theory of the welfare state. The Japan Communist Party Central Committee's Publishing Bureau's *Shin hiyorimi-shugi hihan* includes the following passage: "Recently, monopoly capital and the Tanaka government have been scheming to moderate the process of the intensification of the contradiction between the working class and the Japanese and American ruling classes. On one hand, they have strengthened the tyranny of capital in the workplace. On the other, they have been trying to establish a new axis of cooperation between labor and capital by trumpeting a phony 'welfare policy' and pushing forward discussions with union leadership"; see Nihon Kyōsantō Chūō I'inkai Shuppan-kyoku, *Shin hiyorimi shugi hihan*, Tokyo: Nihon Kyōsantō Chūō I'inkai Shuppan-kyoku, 1973, 121. Also, Koizumi Hiroshi, who was on the editorial board of Communist Party-affiliated journal *Keizai*, wrote that "the welfare State is both a euphemism and another name for state monopoly capital"; see Koizumi Hiroshi, *Fukushi to hinkon no keizairon*, Tokyo: Shin Nihon Shubbansha, 1973, i.

38 Prime Minister Tanaka Kakuei wrote in his *Nihon Rettō kaizōron* (Tokyo: Nikkan Kōgyō Shinbunsha, 1972) that "welfare gives birth to growth and growth promises welfare."

struggle.[39] The LDP and the Ministry of Health and Welfare succeeded in subsuming various disability groups in 1981, the International Year of Disabled Persons. In 1984, the government established the Basic Disability Pension system, taking in both Communist Party and New Left groups for those with disabilities. One sees a similar trajectory in the histories of the Burakumin liberation movement, the education movement, the women's movement, the antipollution movement, and the patients' rights movement. What united and circumscribed the movements that had split into Socialist, New Left, and Communist Party-affiliated groups was none other than the Ministry of Health and Welfare. To put it in stronger terms, the practitioners of Eurocommunism and structural reform policy in Japan were in fact the mainstream conservatives of the LDP and progressive bureaucrats in the Ministry of Health and Welfare.

In retrospect, at least on the level of policy, many intellectuals who left the Communist Party in the 1970s refused to change into "good" conservatives and bureaucrats who would defend postwar democracy. On the other side, the Communist Party, in choosing a path of "honorable isolation" by cutting loose those party intellectuals and strengthening its critique of the Socialist Party, forged a path that allowed it to intervene in political power and gain a degree of political control.

With its critique of opportunism, the Communist Party abandoned accelerationist and ultraleft tendencies that looked toward a revolution in the near future. In doing so, the party walked a lonely line between reform and revolution. Paradoxically, precisely because it did so, it was able to ride out the shock of the Eastern European revolutions of 1989 and—unusual for a Communist Party in an advanced country—was able to preserve the name of the Communist Party.

Whatever one makes of it, when looking back at the history of 1968 and what came afterward, one recognizes again how difficult it was to encode the desire for revolution and the maintenance of that desire into parliamentary strategies and tactics. According to Tamara Deutscher, E.H. Carr criticized both the New Left and Eurocommunism on precisely this point:

39 The Association to Protect Children with Heart Disease, the Association to Protect Children with Disablities, and the Federation of Families of the Mentally Handicapped were formed in the 1960s, but these groups were spearheaded politically by the LDP and the Ministry of Health and Welfare.

> Surveying the contemporary political scene shortly before his death, he expressed his exasperation in a brief sentence which is intelligible enough: "The left is foolish and the right is vicious." He was no reformist and did not believe socialism could be attained through the machinery of bourgeois democracy, but he also deplored as an illusion the idea that the working class would in the foreseeable future be either able or willing to fight for socialism. He saw the labour movement in full retreat and was impatient with what he took to be the "new left" and its "theorizing about a revolutionary situation without enquiring whether it exists." The "unity of theory and practice," he remarked, "cuts both ways." In the late 1970s, he was "shattered"—the word is his—by what he saw as the political naivete of much of the European Left.
>
> Eurocommunism was to him a doctrine which "had no leg to stand on," but was making its own contribution to the outbreak of the new cold war. So, to his mind, was any excessive or uncritical preoccupation with the Soviet dissidents.[40]

In 1968, in opposition to the post-1968 new social movements, bourgeois democracy, and Eurocommunism, E.H. Carr held to his spirit of revolution and wrote:

> Lenin, at first, almost alone even among the Bolsheviks, attacked the assumption that the current upheaval in Russia was a bourgeois revolution and nothing more. The situation as it developed after the February revolution confirmed Lenin's view that it could not be confined bourgeois limits. What followed the collapse of the autocracy was not so much a bifurcation of authority (the "dual power") as a total dispersal of authority . . . It was a mass movement inspired by a wave of immense enthusiasm and by Utopian visions of the emancipation of mankind from the shackles of a remote and despotic power.[41]

From 1968 to 1970, "we" also experienced "immense enthusiasm" and were struck and moved by "Utopian visions." The Japanese Communist Party, through its reactionary period in the 1970s, evaded the New Left and Eurocommunist tendencies both within and outside of the party.

---

40 Tamara Deutscher, "E.H. Carr—A Personal Memoir," *New Left Review* I: 137, 1983, 85.

41 E.H. Carr, *The Russian Revolution: From Lenin to Stalin, 1917–1929*, London: Palgrave Macmillan, 1979, 3.

Nevertheless, it maintained an ideal of revolution by defining Japan as a country subjugated to the United States. From the vantage point of the unity of the party's theory and practice, sticking to a program that defined the Japanese as an oppressed people and adhering to an esoteric theory of "letting the enemy attack first" allowed the party to surpass "bourgeois democracy" and "bourgeois" limits in that it looked to the seizure of state power with military power. In this sense, even the party's core, which had participated fully in the conservative slide of the 1970s, was moved by the memory of immense enthusiasm and utopian visions.

Translated by Guy Yasko

8

Human Liberation or "Male Romance"?: The Gendered Everyday of the Student New Left

Chelsea Szendi Schieder

The New Left in the late 1960s in Japan, as elsewhere, embraced an expansive definition of politics. Activists linked the daily reproduction of social institutions in increasingly affluent Japan with global economic inequalities and the peace of postwar Japanese society with wars for national liberation in the Third World. Within this schema, "the everyday" [*nichijō*] or "everyday life" [*nichijō seikatsu*] became a critical concept for student activists, and it shaped their challenges to state and university authority. Within the campus spaces activists occupied and organized their disruptions of the "everyday" of state and capital; female student participants in particular experienced contradictions embedded in the "everyday" of the New Left. Here, I consider the experiences of female activists in the campus-based movement of late 1960s Japan to explore the various meanings of "everyday life" in New Left activism and also to illuminate how young women's participation exposed some of the gaps between radical theory and practice. The New Left had offered a potential space to break down all mainstream power hierarchies, but it ended up reinforcing a gendered hierarchy of domestic, affective, and sexual labor within its revolutionary framework.[1]

This article will examine the "everyday" as a critical site for the student New Left in late 1960s Japan to explore how that ostensibly liberatory movement perpetuated a kind of leftist male romance by

1 The author would like to thank Setsu Shigematsu, who read earlier drafts of this piece and generously shared her ideas and drafts of her chapter in this volume.

marginalizing female voices and applying gendered values to determine the authenticity of activist commitment. As Mori Setsuko, a woman who participated in the campus-based New Left at Tama Arts University, wrote in a pamphlet in 1970, announcing her new focus on women-only activism: "Humans, humans, humans. In our struggle we said this word over and over. What does this neutered noun 'humans' make real? What are we grumbling about with this neutered noun? [The struggle for human liberation] was certainly our struggle, but at the same time it wasn't."[2] The "neutered noun" *human* extended the promise of total revolution and liberation to male and female activists alike, but Mori, like many young women, came to feel that the "human" in the New Left's imagination retained a male subjectivity.

The New Left in Japan as a "Male" Movement?

It is important to place the sexism of the New Left in Japan at the center of any understanding of how that movement functioned. Through exploring the concept of the "everyday" as it operated in the New Left, we can also see how that sexism lived alongside the potential for liberation in the movement. Since a women-only radical movement emerged not only from the Japanese New Left, but from New Left movements globally in the 1970s, there remains a need to understand what within the New Left—its theories and practices—convinced radical women who participated in campus-based activism that they needed to form a separatist movement. Much like the New Left in Japan, feminism in Japan was not simply a reaction to external influences, although news about activities elsewhere intensified activists' feelings that they were part of a global movement.[3] Male chauvinism proved to be a defining characteristic of many women's experiences of New Left activism around the world, which undermines arguments that Japanese sexism is some kind of immutable and ahistorical feudal remnant handed down to the present and unchanged over time. Indeed, young women growing up under democratizing post–World

2 Mori Setsuko, "Shisō shūdan esu.ii.ekkusu soshikiron? Josetsu [An organizational theory for Thought Group S.E.X.? Introduction]," *Shiryō ūman ribu shi I* [A History of Women's Lib Sources I], ed. Mizonoguchi Akiyo, Tokyo: Shōkadō shoten, 1992, 172.

3 See Setsu Shigematsu's chapter in this volume and her book *Scream from the Shadows: The Women's Liberation Movement in Japan*, Minneapolis: University of Minnesota Press, 2012.

War II reforms that included a radical renegotiation of relations between the sexes often felt optimistic that male chauvinism would quickly become obsolete through new coeducational policies and legally protected egalitarian marriages. The postwar student movement operated in a new context in which men and women studied side by side, and coeducational institutions opened up a new space for young people to experiment with gendered expectations and produced a radical student movement that integrated women to a degree not previously plausible.

Although the scope of participation makes it impossible to generalize the experience of female student activists in the late 1960s New Left, many similarities mark the narratives of women who became involved in campus activism and who also became disenchanted with it. This chapter draws upon accounts written by women involved in the New Left who identified themselves as "ordinary" students and who did not participate in formal sects, as well as those who wrote about their New Left experiences after participating in feminist activism. It is particularly tricky to get at the experiences of female student activists who did not join in the subsequent women-only movement. Female students were active across sects and campuses in the late 1960s student New Left, however, joining for reasons similar to those of their male comrades: they felt compelled by the global situation and the paradoxes they saw in their society, and it felt like a natural part of being a student and a member of their campus community. One survey conducted in the early 1990s published the results of 529 questionnaires filled out by people who self-identified as part of the late 1960s student New Left at eighty-one higher education institutions across Japan. That publication included the testimonies of forty-three female respondents from twenty-four universities, each involved in a diverse range of political activities with varying levels of commitment at the time and afterward.[4] Women-only activism opened up spaces for those who had experienced the campus-based New Left to articulate their experiences. This has resulted in a tendency for personal narratives of 1968 to run along gendered lines: male former student activists publish celebratory memoirs of campus occupations, while their female counterparts have tended to publish accounts that consider how campus activism led

4 *Zenkyōtō hakusho* [White paper on the Zenkyōtō], ed. Project Inoshishi, Tokyo: Shinshioshahan, 1994.

them to feminist activism.[5] For many who were young women in 1968, the barricades were exciting, but the sense of betrayal by male activists and the significance of subsequent women-only activism remain the most salient factors for them. This has resulted in an interpretation that casts the student New Left as a "male movement."

The Everyday as a Critical Site for the Left

Many participants in campus-based activism in the late 1960s in Japan employed the term "the everyday" to indicate both the broad set of institutions and practices they challenged, as well as the links between those institutions and war, capitalism, and global inequality. The student movement in late 1960s Japan attacked the "everyday" perpetuation of systems of power in affluent postwar Japanese society and sought to disrupt them with strikes, campus occupations, and street battles. To give a sense of the scope of disruption at universities and the scale of the police response, riot police entered campuses to break up barricades and quell student unrest 969 times in 1968 and 1969, making a total of 16,175 related arrests in that period.[6] Students at the nation's flagship institution, the University of Tokyo, shut down the school's operations, which prevented a new class from entering and sparked debate in the top levels of national politics. One contemporary source estimated that 40 percent of all university students in Japan were unable to attend classes in June 1969 alone because of "campus disorders."[7] The call to interrupt everyday life was answered by a generation of university students, and barricaded campuses were part of their educational experience.

As students disrupted their universities, they also organized behind the barricades of campus occupations; in these autonomous spaces

5 Kano Akihiro and Kano Kenta, *Omae no 1960-nendai o, shinu mae ni shabettoke* [Tell Me Your 1960s Before You Die!], Tokyo: Potto shuppan, 2010; Mihashi Toshiaki, *Rojō no Zenkyōtō 1968* [Zenkyoto 1968 on the Streets], Tokyo: Kawade bukkusu, 2010; Takahashi Hiroshi, *Tuwamono-domo ga yume no saki* [The Rank and File has Surpassed the Dream], Tokyo: Wayts, 2010; *Zenkyōtō kara ribu e* [From Zenkyōtō to Lib], ed. Jūgoshi nōto sengo-hen, Kawazaki: Inpakuto shuppankai, 1996.

6 Takeda Haruhito, *Kōdō seichō* [High Economic Growth], Shiriizu nihon kingendai-shi 8 [Japanese contemporary history series 8], Tokyo: Iwanami shinsho, 2008.

7 "A Statement on the Current Difficulties at the University of California Study Center, Mitaka-Tokyo, Japan," November 10, 1969, Hans H. Baerwald papers, 1945–1991, UCLA Library Special Collections, Box 22, Folder 22.

emerged the potential to create a new kind of everyday, one in which it might be possible to renegotiate their intimate relationships and challenge hegemonic ideals about how those relations should be structured.

There is a longer intellectual history of engagement with theories about everyday life in Japan, but student activists in the late 1960s seemed to base their criticisms upon their experiences of an increasingly disciplined daily life at the universities rather than explicitly invoking the deeper genealogy of the term *everyday*. The writings of thinkers such as Tosaka Jun in Japan or Henri Lefebvre analyzed the links between capitalism and everyday life in the 1930s in Japan and France, respectively, but I have not found significant references to Tosaka or Lefebvre in the writings of student activists in late-1960s Japan. Artistic practices and products in the 1960s also addressed everyday forms of domination and authority, and encounters with such radically critical art undoubtedly influenced the young people gathered in urban centers as well.[8] In a sense, however, the postsecondary students involved in the New Left responded to their own experiences rather than to any preceding texts, which meant that they employed *everyday life* in a variety of ways. They used the term to refer both to the daily functioning of state and capital that they sought to disrupt and also to their lived experiences, with potential for personal revolutionary change.

The New Left's "Male Romance"

While there is a long genealogy of leftist interest in the everyday, there was also a longer history of a male chauvinist Left in Japan as well. Leftist female intellectuals such as Hayashi Fumiko and Hirabayashi Taiko had written about the limits of the radical imagination in prewar Japan as it regarded female participation and women's issues, and many female participants in the early postwar student Left had criticized the sexual politics of the movement before the campus barricades of the late 1960s. Imai Yasuko, a female member of the late 1950s student New Left, complained that the internal dynamics of their activist groups often held female participants to a different standard. Male student activists expected affection and emotional support from their female

8 See William Marotti for a discussion of Japanese artists in the 1960s targeting "everyday life" in their works, particularly *Money, Trains, and Guillotines: Art and Revolution in 1960s Japan*, Durham: Duke University Press, 2013.

comrades, and she noted that the fight for "human liberation" was shaped by their "male romance," which included expectations that women would conform to male expectations about feminine behavior and support. This extended to expectations that women would observe gendered linguistic conventions to soften and feminize their statements. Imai overheard male leader Shima Shigeo's shocked reaction to a female activist's direct and forceful criticism of a male comrade: "This one's just like a child." Imai interpreted Shigeo's comment as reflecting a more general attitude toward women in Japan: that a grown woman ought to speak in a restrained and gracious manner.[9] This kind of everyday gendered expectation went unquestioned by many prominent men in the movement, despite it limiting women's participation in political debates.

In a pattern established in modern Japan by many politically radical men, Shima Shigeo also organized his political and intellectual work around the economic support of his wife, Hiroko. Indeed, Hiroko recalled how Shigeo praised the wives of Meiji-era (1868–1912) politicians, those selfless creatures who offered up instant hospitality for the guests their husbands brought home with them. Knowing that is what he admired in a wife, she aspired to meet the needs of the hundreds of people that passed through her house (Shigeo had moved in with her and her mother when they married) every year, from 1960 until Shigeo's death in 2010. After his death, Hiroko noted her disappointment that Shigeo had not acknowledged her contribution to his political activism, from making rice balls to raising funds to support both his campaigns and his livelihood. However, she also dismissed herself as having no head for such big thoughts, even noting that she preferred that he did not waste his time explaining things to her.[10] In other words, Haruko affirmed the separation of the "real" politics of intellectual exchange from the practical matters of everyday life.

This division between the recognized labor of the New Left—its intellectual production and direct-action confrontation—and the invisible labor of the New Left—generally care work and support—remained gendered. While the care work of the student New Left in Japan was gendered feminine, the hierarchy with which such daily work was

9 Imai Yasuko, "Bunto to feminizum" [Bund and Feminism], *60-nen Anpo to Bunto wo yomu* [Reading 1960 Anpō and the Bund], Tokyo: Jōkyō shuppan, 2002, 74–5.

10 Shima Hiroko, "Onigiri nyōbō" [Rice Ball Wife], *Bunto shinshi* [A Personal History of the Bund], Tokyo: Hihyōsha, 2010, 222–62.

regarded mirrored the low status accorded to it in mainstream society, even as the movement depended upon it. The late 1960s student movement politicized the concept of the everyday, however, which opened up new spaces to question received ideas about gendered social roles.

Zenkyōtō and a Politicized Everyday in the University

An important organizational shift of campus-based New Left activism in the late 1960s opened up the definition of what it meant to be politically involved as a student. In the late 1960s, what became known as the Zenkyōtō [All-Campus Joint Struggle League] became a popular form for mobilizing student activism on university campuses. The Zenkyōtō that formed on campuses in the late 1960s sought to avoid rigid hierarchies and dogmatic politics through sect-less horizontality and "endless debate." The "Zenkyōtō movement" began at the nation's elite University of Tokyo in early July 1968 when "ordinary" students expressed their solidarity for students occupying campus buildings and formed as "Zenkyōtō." But the phenomenon of "nonpolitical" [*nonpori*] students joining in clearly political actions like strikes and barricades under the title "Zenkyōtō" appeared at campuses across the nation and "Zenkyōtō" quickly became a byword for the student New Left in the late 1960s, representing a political ideal of a radically democratic, non-sectarian organizational structure.[11]

A loosely formed group of like-minded activists appealed to so many students because it contrasted with the structure of the traditional leftist organizations in Japan, which tended toward a hierarchical style and demanded of their members that they follow the "party line" and participate in various actions. The dogmatism of the established leftist parties was at the root of young activists' critiques of the Japan Communist Party (JCP) in the late 1950s and prompted the splintering of the JCP-led Zengakuren (All-Japan Federation of Students' Self-Governing Associations) just before the anti-Anpō demonstrations of 1959–60. While the Bund headed the "mainstream" of the Zengakuren during the mass protests organized to counter the revision of the United States–Japan Security Treaty in 1960, the JCP-organized youth group (Minsei)

11 Sawara Yukiko, "The University Struggles," in *Zengakuren: Japan's Revolutionary Students*, ed. Stuart Dowsey, Berkeley: Ishi Press, 1970, 139. Sawara offers a detailed play-by-play of the University of Tokyo Zenkyōtō movement.

also organized students and formed an "anti-mainstream" faction of the Zengakuren.

After the Bund splintered in July 1960, brief alliances and coordinated "struggles" [*tōsō*] or protests would unite sects' actions, but sectarian competition for control of university self-governing [*jichikai*] bodies also channeled a great deal of activists' energies into inter-sectarian fighting. The late 1960s Zenkyōtō marked the climax of decentralized New Left activism in Japan, although the tension between that and centralization—directed actions and diffuse activism—also defined campus activism in the late 1960s. Inter-sectarian fighting would emerge as a particularly violent legacy of the university-based student movement in the 1960s and into the 1970s, further alienating otherwise sympathetic "ordinary" students from leftist mobilizing.

Many young people at universities in Japan in the late 1960s felt compelled to counter authorities precisely because they made a connection between their everyday lives and larger geopolitical issues. Oda Makoto, a prominent anti–Vietnam War peace activist, remarked that it was often a source of bewilderment for outside observers that student activists in Japan so directly linked their campus-based struggles against rising tuitions and other university policies with assisting the people of Vietnam.[12] But students pointed out the ways in which universities and their policies connected with the "everyday" of Japanese capital and the institutions that supported military intervention in Vietnam. In the late 1960s, student strikes and occupations became strategies to disrupt these links.

A prominent student activist and Zenkyōtō chairman at the University of Tokyo, Yamamoto Yoshitaka, outlined a "philosophy of the barricades" during a protracted campus occupation in autumn 1968 in which he defined the blockades as an attempt to disrupt the rationalist logic of capital and authority as manifested in the university. Yamamoto declared that one of the main goals of the barricades was to "confront the malicious and everyday-supporting ideology on campus."[13] This idea of the barricades mobilized an understanding of the "everyday" as the rationalized time in which contestations between labor and management, between oppressed and oppressing elites were smoothed over and hidden away.

12 Thomas Havens, *Fire Across the Sea: The Vietnam War and Japan, 1965–1975*, Princeton: Princeton University Press, 1987, 188.

13 Yamamoto Yoshitaka, "Barikeedo fūsa no shisō" [Thoughts on the barricade blockades], *Chisei no hanran* [Revolt of the Intellect], Tokyo: Zeneisha, 1969, 79–95.

Student activists, linking the activities of their universities with the larger national project of economic growth, built "barricades" of desks and chairs and occupied campus buildings to disrupt this kind of "everyday life" of the state and capital. The blockades of which Yamamoto wrote (and in which he wrote) in November 1968 were those of the highly visible and long-lasting student occupation of the Yasuda Tower at the University of Tokyo, which endured from early July 1968 through January 1969, when the university administration finally called in the riot police to besiege and dislodge the students.

Yamamoto identified the barricades and unlimited strikes of the mid- to late 1968 campus movements as a key tactic in interrupting the process by which university "factories" produced students who served capital. Fliers on the University of Tokyo campus framed ending campus disruptions as failure: "Isn't a 'return to the everyday' actually a defeat?"[14] Unlike demonstrations, living behind the barricades gave some participants the sense that they could avoid the disheartening reimmersion in an "everyday cycle saturated with paradoxes" that frequently ensued after a march broke up.[15] Unlike temporally limited protest actions, the barricades promised continuous disruption, constant possibility.

Toward an Alternative Everyday?

The promise of the campus occupations lay in their creation of an autonomous area within which students could forge an alternative form of "everyday life"—a second connotation of the term, employed by many New Left activists. Student activists of the 1960s in Japan understood "everyday" life in many senses: the term could indicate both the daily reproduction of the conditions for capital and the state, but also the daily lived time in which they could organize challenges to these systems. For example, although the student activists quoted earlier spoke of barricades and strikes as a way to avoid "everyday life," another student activist described participating in an unlimited campus strike as a kind of "everyday activism" that was fundamentally different from

14 Nonpori hansen shūdan, "Nonpori no gakuyū ni uttaeru" [Appeal to Nonpolitical School Friends], July 2, 1968, Tōdai tōsō shiryo shū, National Diet Library, Tokyo.

15 Ōhara Kimiko, *Tokeidai wa takakatta* [The Clock Tower Was Tall], Tokyo: San'ichi Shobo, 1969, 13–16.

the street demonstrations in which she had previously participated.[16] In this case, she pointed out that, for her, launching a protracted strike rather than a one-off demonstration was both a less spectacular action and was also a more sustainable disruption of the other "everyday life" of the powers that be.

One female activist at the University of Tokyo, Katō Mitsuko, described the spatial disruption of the barricades as something that created a temporal rupture and released her from social expectations: "When in the 'exitless' space of Building 8, I was released from my social positions (as a female, as somebody's child, as a Tōdai student, etc.). I lived only in a 'now' that floated away from its position in connecting the past and the future."[17] Katō's description of her experiences in the occupied spaces of the University of Tokyo's Komaba campus echoes the work of Raoul Vaneigem, writing in 1967 in France about the revolutionary potential of lived everyday life: "lived space filches a small portion of the time sweeping it away and makes a present out of it—or at least it seeks to do so, for the present is yet to be constructed. It seeks to create the unitary space-time of love, of poetry, of pleasure, of communication: direct experience without dead time." Vaneigem contrasted this "lived" time-space of the present with "linear" or "objective" time, which aligns with the concept of the "everyday" of authority: "This is the time of *roles*, that time which, within life itself, fosters disembodiment, the repudiation of authentically experienced space and its repression and replacement by appearances, by the spectacular function."[18]

The barricaded space of the university campus was a formative experience for many young women, who then went on to form a radical women's liberation movement in 1970s Japan, because it opened up a space-time in which they could formulate their own critiques of social expectations. Yonezu Tomoko, who would become a well-known women's lib activist, recalled that she was first able to talk about the physical disabilities that had long convinced her that she'd never live the

16 Tokuyama Haruko, "Watashi ga ugokeba yo no naka ga hitori bun ugoku to iu jikkan" [The Feeling That if I Move One More Person in the World Is Moving], in *Zenkyōtō kara ribu e* [From Zenkyōtō to Lib], ed. Onnatachi no ima o tō kai, Jūgoshi nōto sengohen, Kawasaki: Inpakuto shuppankai, 1996, 85.

17 Katō Mitsuko, "Tōdai zenkyōtō no naka de" [In the University of Tokyo Zenkyōtō], in *Joshi zengakuren gonin no shuki* [Notes from Five Female Zengakuren], Ace Books, Tokyo: Jiyū kokuminsha, 1970, 51–4.

18 Raoul Vaneigem, *The Revolution of Everyday Life*, Oakland: PM Press, 2012, 201.

life of a "normal" wife in the "extraordinarily liberated space" of the student barricades.[19] She felt freed in a place apart from the "everyday" logic that defined a woman's "normal" life course.

The occupied spaces of the late-1960s campus-based New Left allowed young people to break out of the roles they felt expected to play in society—and it was that break, as well as a break from dogmatic leftist politics as they had been organized previously, that attracted many left-leaning students to participate in Zenkyōtō actions. Ōhara Kimiko, an undergraduate participant in the University of Tokyo's Zenkyōtō, described how she came to become involved in the strikes and occupations at that university in a memoir published in the spring of 1969. Ōhara felt drawn to campus-based activism once the Zenkyōtō had driven the JCP-affiliated student activists out of the science department's student council, and she found herself at a council meeting in which the discussion among the 250 or so students gathered went beyond sectarian infighting for the first time and took up issues about the radical democratic goals of the movement and the role of the university vis-à-vis the Japanese state and capital.[20] Many personal accounts by female students involved in the late 1960s student New Left relate similar narratives, in which a shift from entrenched sectarian debates to an earnest attempt at communication influenced their decision to participate. Tokuyama Haruko, a young woman who had joined the anti-tuition-hike strikes of the mid-1960s at Waseda University and went on to participate in the women's liberation movement, described attending meetings that escaped the control of the main sects and in which participants freely expressed their opinions.[21] The organizational ideal of Zenkyōtō as a non-hierarchical movement appealed to many young people—especially young women, who felt particularly hemmed in by the expectations of mainstream society.

However, female student activists' descriptions of their experiences in the student-occupied campus barricades demonstrate again and again the contradictions they experienced in a space both liberated from the "everyday time" of Japanese society in general and also defined by gendered expectations. The desire to usurp "everyday life" in the barricades came up against the requirements of daily living in the

19 Yonezu Tomoko, "Barikêdo wo kugutte" [Passing through the Barricades], in *Zenkyōtō kara ribu e*, Jūgoshi nōto sengohen, Kawasaki: Inpakuto shuppankai, 1996, 121.

20 Ōhara, *Tokeidai wa takakatta*, 98–9.

21 Tokuyama, "Watashi ga ugokeba," 85.

barricades. The promises of a greater liberation—from boring lectures, from a rationalized society, from social expectations—attracted many otherwise apolitical students to Zenkyōtō. Young women who were drawn to this expansive call for liberation found new freedoms and also encountered familiar constraints.

Many female students noted the incongruity between the liberated space of the movement's barricades and the quotidian sexism that assigned them tasks because of their gender while increasingly privileging the masculine roles associated with more aggressive strategies of protest. The understanding that women would do the cooking and cleaning was often an unarticulated one. As one male activist remarked to me retrospectively, "no one *asked* the women to cook. No one *told* them they had to clean up." But the many accounts from various student movements at a range of universities describe the expectations that women would manage New Left's "home front." Rice balls, in particular, became a synecdoche for the sexism of Japan's student movement in women's narratives, as women recalled making piles and piles and piles of them.[22]

The responsibilities of feeding the movement often fell to the young women, as did other tasks considered menial but actually critical to the continuation of the struggle: mimeographing the fliers that circulated on the campuses and in the cities, the jail support that coordinated assistance for arrested students, smuggling provisions—such as instant ramen and lemons to soothe tear-gas injuries—into occupied buildings. These tasks made it possible for the movement to continue over time, but the labor involved in them was eclipsed in the narratives about Zenkyōtō that emphasized spectacular street activism, which was gendered masculine. This is part of the New Left's sexism that mirrored the familiar sexism of mainstream society.

The Male Romance of the New Left

As the focus of New Left activism turned toward considering how it was possible to make political claims on the level of everyday life, the observations that young women involved in campus mobilizing made about unequal gender relations became more difficult for them to square with the movement's stated objectives. This was especially the case in the late

22 Tokuyama, "Watashi ga ugokeba," 88; Ōhara, *Tokeidai wa takakatta*, 143–5.

1960s, as the "male romance" of a masculine student activist battling the state's monopoly on violence in the streets grew and in many ways came to define the popular perception and commemoration of New Left activism at that time. In the late 1960s in particular, student activists increasingly emphasized the practice of militant engagement, which they called "gebaruto," a transliteration for the German word "Gewalt," meaning violence or force.

Like the barricades, student activists framed Gewalt—particularly the waging of spectacular street clashes—as a strategy to disrupt the "everyday life" of the nation and capital. Provoking the police was seen as a way to make visible the violence that undergirded ostensibly peaceful postwar Japanese society, a peace that was built upon violence in the Third World. Partly as a practical response to more violent confrontations on streets and campuses and partly as a matter of style, student activists in the late 1960s thus adopted a kind of Gewalt uniform: a helmet painted with one's sectarian affiliation, a towel to protect one's face from tear gas (and police cameras and news cameras), and a "Gewalt stave" [*gebabō*] made of wood or bamboo to wield in battle (against both the police and rival sects).[23]

In the gendered hierarchy that emerged in the New Left, militancy figured as a primarily masculine activity and one that was privileged as the most authentic expression of activist commitment. One female student noted that, although "you're a girl, so you don't have to Gewalt" was never put into words, she felt the sentiment among male activists.[24] Having to hang back and tend the home front cut women out of an essential part of New Left mobilizing, and University of Tokyo student and non-sectarian activist Ōhara Kimiko lamented that her physical weakness meant she could not be a full participant: "I was frustrated that I didn't have a stout frame that could wield a sword like a boy."[25] There remained two clear-cut and gendered roles within the movement: rice balls or "Gewalt staves." The care work overwhelmingly done by women in the barricades, the work that reproduced the "everyday life" of the campus-based New Left, was ultimately obscured by the hypervisibility of spectacular street actions.

23 The "Gewalt staves" were apparently originally employed in sectarian battles and only later came to be used in clashes with the police. William Marotti, "Japan 198: The Performance of Violence and the Theater of Protest," *American Historical Review*, 2009, 97–135, 103 *n*19.

24 Katō, "Tōdai zenkyōtō no naka de," 43.

25 Ōhara, *Tokeidai wa takakatta*, 143–5.

Of course, some women did participate in "Gewalt" even as, within the New Left itself, their participation in these actions did not necessarily trouble the gendered labor division behind the barricades. One female graduate student at the University of Tokyo who became infamous for her activism, Kashiwazaki Chieko, garnered the nickname "Gewalt Rosa," after Marxist theorist and revolutionary Rosa Luxemburg (1871–1919). Kashiwazaki, a student of Polish history, embraced Polish-born Rosa Luxemburg's revolutionary legacy, and "Gewalt Rosa" emblazoned the cover of the memoir she wrote in jail in spring 1969. The title itself—"Sun, Storm, and Liberty"—was from a letter Rosa Luxemburg had written while on holiday, where, she wrote, she had enjoyed "sun, peace, and liberty—the finest things in life—except for sun, storm, and liberty."[26]

In her writing, Kashiwazaki protested the gendered implications attached to being a woman in a radical movement. She described her hostility to a journalist who wanted to interview her "as a woman" in the movement. She responded: "Is it really so peculiar that a woman fights? In this struggle, I haven't been conscious of myself as a woman or as a wife at all." Kashiwazaki rejected the gendered hierarchies associated with kitchen duty, as well: "When I cook for my comrades in the barricades, it's because I really enjoy cooking and am concerned with everyone's health. It's absolutely not because I'm a woman." She declared that wielding a kitchen knife and brandishing a "Gewalt stick" were equally important in the struggle.[27]

But they were *not regarded* as equally important. Some women did write about the pride they took in preparing food for their comrades behind the barricades. They were not unthinking pawns of male activists. But the heroic narratives written by male activists do not consider the significance of rice balls to the struggle. Street fighting remained the clearest and most respected rejection of the values associated with mainstream society and the "everyday life" of state and capital, and participation in or abstention from violence became critical in student movement evaluations of activists' commitment. "Wielding a kitchen knife" against a radish was judged considerably less revolutionary than thrashing a stick against the police or "enemy" students.

Female participants also faced male expectations about their sexual availability, sometimes under the slogan "free sex" and sometimes as a

26 Paul Fröhlich, *Rosa Luxemburg: Ideas in Action*, London: Pluto Press, 1972, 130.

27 Kashiwazaki Chieko, *Taiyō to arashi to jiyū o: Gebaruto Rōza tōsō no shuki* [Sun, Storm and Liberty: Notes from a Gewalt Rosa Struggle], Tokyo: Noberu shobo, 1969, 268–9.

gendered punishment for political disputes. Rape and sexual assault were realities for female activists involved in the New Left. Sexual assault also figured in the *uchi geba* [internal violence] between sects as they vied for control of various campuses. When Kakumaru "lynched" (the transliterated term used for political punishment meted out with a physical assault among the left) a female student member of rival sect Chūkaku at Chiba University, the male assailants concluded their attack by raping her. Their hope was that the shame of enduring a sexual assault would deter her from returning to the campus.[28] While lynchings were generally painful—and, over time, became deadly—affairs, involving not only battering but also torture, the use of sexual assault also incorporated the logic of gendered violence into that of political violence. "Using rape and sexual violence to punish women was an everyday thing," recalled one woman involved in the New Left.[29]

In light of this reality, it also becomes difficult to overlook the significance of cinematic depictions of rape common in cultural works linked to political radicalism in the late 1960s and early 1970s. For example, erotic films that faced censorship for obscenity became linked with other challenges to the state and authority. Oshima Nagisaki was an early champion of the "pink" soft-core pornographic film as a politically oppositional genre.[30] Pink films often faced legal challenges from censors, which the filmmakers and observers interpreted as evidence of their political radicalism. However, as feminist commentators noted in the early 1970s, their works often featured stereotypical gender roles that affirmed the patriarchal status quo. One columnist writing for a feminist publication (*Onna eros* [Women/eros]) about a such a film (Nishimura Shogorō's *The Young Wife: Confessions*) criticized the film's imaginative shortcomings in portraying a "pitiful woman" who succumbs to a rape and her sad fate: "in the end porno film is not able to set foot out of its dark little self-satisfied castle and fly the flag of progressivism."[31] One might add that, while such films attempted a similar disruption of the everyday of the state and authority as did the student-built barricades, without a radically different context within the space-time created, the radicalism can be undermined. In these

28 Cited in Oguma Eiji, *1968*, v. 2, Tokyo: Shinyōsha, 2009, 685.

29 Quoted in ibid., 686.

30 Yuriko Furuhata, *Cinema of Actuality: Japanese Avant-Garde Filmmaking in the Season of Image Politics*, Duham, NC: Duke University Press, 2013, 94.

31 Quoted in Anne McKnight, "At the Source (Code)," *Media Theory in Japan*, Durham, NC: Duke University Press, 273.

cases, it was a masculinist romance that undermined the liberatory promises of the late 1960s New Left.

Toward a Conclusion: Whose Revolution?

Many female student activists who had become sensitive to analyses of labor, everyday life, and alienation found that many New Left interpretations cut them out of the revolution. Young women did not necessarily discover "women's issues" within the New Left—there had been several popular debates about the issues facing women in postwar Japanese society, and even study groups on those themes at various campuses before the rise of New Left activism—but they often left the movement with a new sense of how entrenched the supplementary status of women and women's work were, not only within the structures of society (which was no surprise) but also within the casual practices of comrades who sought to revolutionize everyday life.

As a result of these experiences, women began to question who constituted the active subject of the "revolution." While many young women were drawn to participate in campus-based activism and became caught up in the intensity of building and maintaining barricades and conducting demonstrations and strikes, they also began to name their unease and dissatisfactions with how they felt excluded from the ostensibly universal aims of the movement. As one former activist noted, the University of Tokyo Zenkyōtō was supposed to be a total struggle in the name of humanity, but she felt treated differently within the movement because she was female.[32] This kind of experience led many young women to the conclusion that, even in New Left attempts to forge a radical critique of postwar Japanese bourgeois society, the universal human still meant "man." One young woman concluded that the Zenkyōtō at the University of Tokyo was not necessarily a male movement because of the numbers of male participants as much as it was male in its basic assumptions.[33] These retrospective evaluations would inform a later separation of the history of the 1970s women's movements from the history of the "male" New Left.

32 Ōta Motoko, "Onnatachi no zenkyōtō undō" [Women's Zenkyōtō Movement], *Zenkyōtō kara ribu e* [From Zenkyōtō to Lib], ed. Jūgoshi nōto sengohen, Kawazaki: Inpakuto shuppankai, 1996, 78.

33 Katō, "Tōdai zenkyōtō no naka de," 45.

Ultimately, although the student movement in late 1960s Japan launched a radical critique of systems of power and hierarchy in newly affluent postwar Japan, the persistence of a gendered hierarchy perpetuated the gendering of the "everyday" values of mainstream Japanese society within the radical New Left. The subsequent experience of a gendered division of labor within the movement led many female participants to question the structures that continually privileged masculine modes of activism. Thus, while young women participated in campus-based activism in late 1960s Japan, their contributions often disappeared into the gaps between theory and practice. The idealization, instead, of the masculine street fighter who clashed not only with state authorities but also with other sects reflected the New Left's preoccupation with spectacle and interrupting law and order without a correspondingly urgent concern with forging community through everyday practices. The "everyday" functioned as a critical point at which many female participants felt the contradictions between New Left thought and practice; these deep incongruities convinced them that there was no space for them in the revolution as it was imagined by their male comrades.

9

The Undercurrent of Art and Politics in the 1960s: On Gendai Shichōsha

Yoshiko Shimada

Introduction

In February 1969, a small, private alternative art school, Gendai Shichōsha Bigakkō, opened its doors in Tokyo. Gendai Shichōsha, the radical publishing company, was starting a revolutionary new art school! This was an exciting event for young intellectuals after the tragic end, a month prior, of the occupation of the Yasuda Hall at the University of Tokyo. Bigakkō opened a pilot program with workshops by Nakamura Hiroshi, a painter best known for his "Sunagawa 5-ban" work depicting the struggles of the mid-1950s against the expansion of US military bases, and Nakanishi Natsuyuki, an avant-garde artist and member of the Hi-Red Center, which had staged street events in 1963–4.

In 1970, Bigakkō began its art workshop programming, with three artists teaching in rotation: Akasegawa Genpei, also a member of the Hi-Red Center and famous as the accused in the "1,000-yen banknote trial"; Kikuhata Mokuma, a painter and member of Kyūshū-ha; and Matsuzawa Yutaka, the founding father of Japanese conceptualism. In addition to the workshops, there were morning lectures by scholars and writers whose books were published by Gendai Shichōsha, including Shibusawa Tatsuhiko, a writer and translator of works by the Marquis de Sade; Haniya Yutaka, a writer and political thinker; Kara Jurō, director of the Jōkyō Gekijō [Situation Theater] troupe; Hijikata Tatsumi, the *butoh* guru; Iwaya Kunio, translator and scholar of surrealism; and anarchist poet Akiyama Kiyoshi. Some students came to Bigakkō only to listen to these lectures; and the red silk-screened posters (see the illustration below)

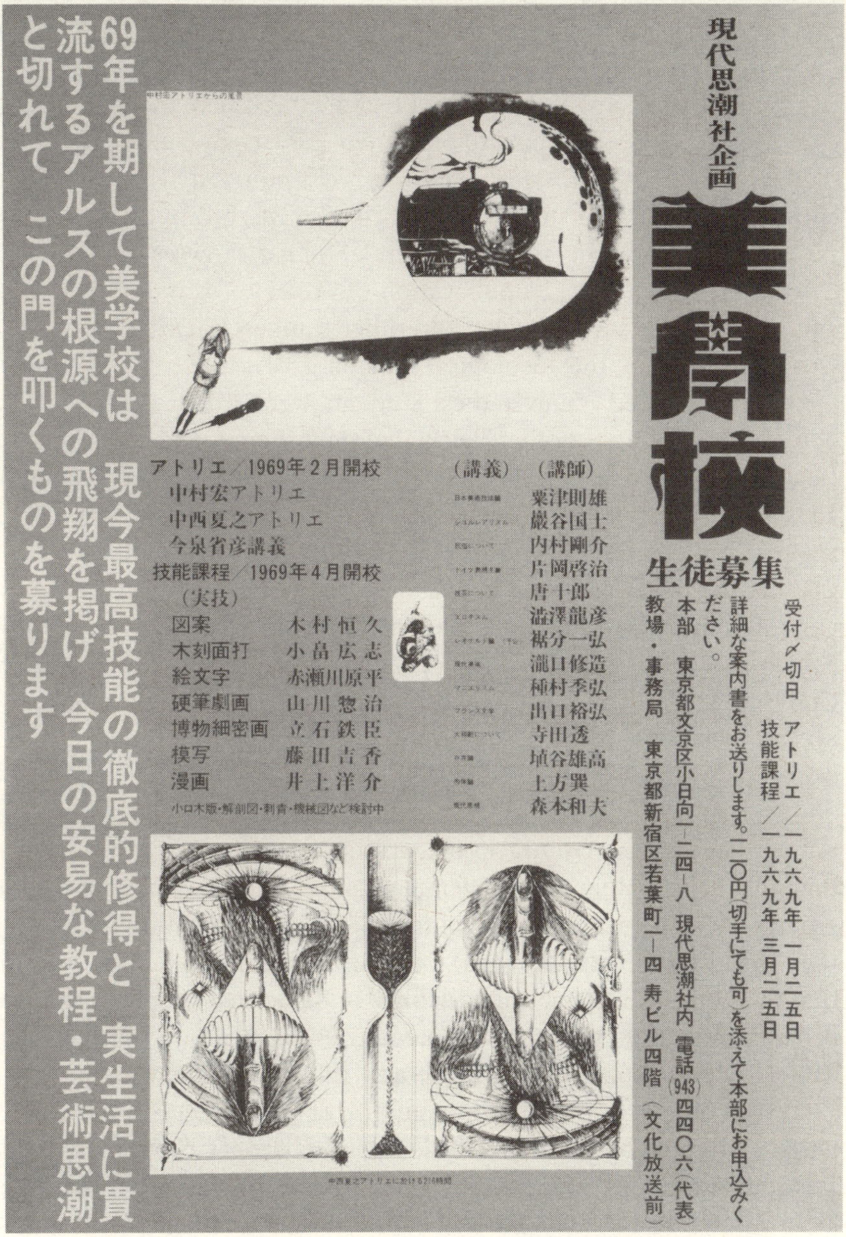

Bigakkō poster 1969 (illustrations by Nakamura Hiroshi and Nakanishi Natsuyuki, logo design by Akasegawa Genpei).

—featuring Akasegawa's faux Taisho period–style logo, *Nakamura*, Nakanishi's design, and Kawani Hiroshi's manifesto—were so popular that they were taken by people as soon as they were put up.

So what made Gendai Shichōsha so attractive to young people in the late 1960s? Ishii Kyōji (1928–2011) had established the publishing company in 1957 but it came to prominence in 1959 when it published the Marquis de Sade's *Histoire de Juliette, ou les prosperités du vice*, translated by Shibusawa Tatsuhiko. The translation was promptly banned as pornographic, and in 1960, Ishii and Shibusawa were prosecuted. During the 1960s, with its publication of Trotsky, Yoshimoto Takaaki, Tanigawa Gan, Haniya Yutaka, and other thinkers, Gendai Shichōsha was often seen as the ideological vanguard of the Zenkyōtō movement—and, indeed, many radical students were ardent readers of its books. However, unlike other "left-wing" publishers, Gendai Shichōsha's catalog did not consist exclusively of political theory; rather, it offered an eclectic mixture of French structuralism, surrealism, eroticism, Russian and Japanese anarchism, and *angura* [under-ground] art that was considered *itan* [unorthodox or even heretical] by mainstream cultural standards of that time. Gendai Shichōsha challenged the established old guard—be it the Japanese government, the Japanese Communist Party (JCP), the good taste of bourgeois intellectuals, or even conventional ideas of "democracy." Ishii Kyōji, the founder, once declared: "We publish BAD books!"

In his voluminous *1968*, Oguma Eiji dismissed the "1968 culture" as a myth because the cultural protagonists of 1968 were not the youth themselves, but rather of an older generation.[1] Indeed, the main actors around Gendai Shichōsha were of the 1960 Anpō generation (that is, in their thirties and forties in 1968). Leaving aside the problematic notion that a cultural movement can be defined or delineated simply by the age of its protagonists, there was an undeniable connection between the leaders of the 1960 Anpō struggle and those prominent in the later Zenkyōtō, as well as in the counterculture of 1968. Hiraoka Masaaki, a writer and a member of Hanzaisha Dōmei [League of Criminals] argued that although there was indeed a generational difference between the 1960 Anpō and the 1968 student movement, the thoughts and questions raised in 1960 continued to be relevant in 1968 and that what really constituted the latter movement originated in the former. Hiraoka hypothesized a tendency for the thoughts and organizational forms of

1 Oguma Eiji, *1968*, Tokyo: Shin'yōsha, 2009, 81.

one era's activists to be taken over not by their direct or "legitimate" heirs but rather by those only loosely or peripherally associated with them. He called this *keisha kekki* [literally, "inclined uprising"] and argued that the direct actions of the Bund movement, Gendai Shichōsha, and Tokyo Kōdō Sensen [Tokyo Action Front, a group and newsletter published by Ishii Kyōji]—among others—were realized by the students, workers and artists of the mid- to late 1960s, albeit sometimes in rather unexpected forms.[2]

With this thesis in mind, I would like to examine the thoughts and actions formed around Gendai Shichōsha and to unravel the intricate connections among the thinkers, activists, artists, and others who confound categorization. I begin by attempting to situate Gendai Shichōsha in the political context of the early to mid-1960s, with a focus on the activism of its founder, Ishii Kyōji. I then look at *Keishō* magazine and the Hanzaisha Dōmei [League of Criminals] as early examples of the meeting of the artistic and the political, followed by a detailed look at the brief but vital existence of Jiritsu Gakkō [School of Autonomy]. I then examine *shisōteki henshitsusha* [ideological perverts] and Akasegawa Genpei's "1,000-yen bill" trial as well as Gendai Shichōsha's own legal troubles linked to the Tokyo Action Front. Finally, I turn to the creation of Gendai Shichōsha Bigakkō as a further attempt to realize artistic and political intervention in the post-1968 era. All of these seemingly disparate actions and activist groups are linked on some level through Gendai Shichōsha , which—as I hope to show—functioned for much of its existence as a kind of clearinghouse for radical ideas and initiatives rather than simply as a publisher of subversive material.

The Myth of Democracy and June Action Committee

The founder of Gendai Shichōsha, Ishii Kyōji, was born in 1928 in central Tokyo and spent his youth among the confusion of postwar Japan as (in his own phrase) a "dealer in the black market." He then joined the JCP and became a prominent member in the early 1950s. However, increasingly frustrated with the party's rigid bureaucracy, he openly criticized the party and in 1953 was stripped of his membership. He decided to fight back by publishing books critical of the very concept

2 Hiraoka Masaaki, "Mittomonai benmei o ippatsu" [One disreputable excuse], in *Jazz yori hoka ni kami wa nashi* [There Is No God but Jazz], Tokyo: San-ichi shobo, 1971, 10.

of a "vanguard" party. In 1960, the anti-Anpō struggle offered the best opportunity for Ishii to present the political ideas that marked a clear departure from the "old left." Rokugatsu Kōdō Iinkai [June Action Committee] (see the illustration below), as the group was known, was a loosely connected gathering of intellectuals and artists in support of direct actions against the Anpō treaty.

Rokugatsu Kōdō Iinkai (From right: Yoshimoto Takaaki and Nakamura Hiroshi). Photographer unknown, courtesy Nakamura Hiroshi.

Ishii said the group started almost spontaneously among those of his friends associated with Gendai Shichōsha. The members were Ishii himself, Yoshimoto, Haniya, Tanigawa, Akiyama Kiyoshi, Matsuda Masao (an editor and later film critic), Oda Tatsurō (an art critic), and Revolutionary Artist Front member Nakamura Hiroshi, as well as some other volunteer members of Zen-ei Bijutsu Kai [The Avant-garde Art Association]. Yoshimoto recalled:

> What we did as Rokugatsu Kōdō Iinkai was to support Bund and their direct actions. Shima Shigeo, the secretary general of Bund at the time of Anpo, told us so-called "intellectuals" not to try to take leadership, not to act as if we were superior to the students. The students were clearly the main players and they took initiative . . . The reasons why I supported Bund were, first, their action style. Their demonstrations were not the traditional lining-up, fist-in-the-air, shouting-slogans

> type. Theirs was more radical and disorderly. It was previously unheard of among the Japanese left. I really liked their new approach. Another reason was they were autonomous—independent of the dogmatic control of the Soviet Union or China. I also thought this was the last chance for Japan to resist the overwhelming power of the postwar capitalist system. The JCP said Anpō enslaved Japan in subordination to the US, but for me, that was not the point. Rather, I thought Anpō would enable Japan to succeed as a capitalist nation equal to the West. Bund tried to stop this uncontrolled expansion of the capitalist system.[3]

Just after the 1960 failure of the anti-Anpō struggle, the main members of the group (Yoshimoto, Haniya, Tanigawa, and others) published through Gendai Shichōsha the anthology *Minshushugi no Shinwa* [The Myth of Democracy], which subjected to critique the conduct of the campaign and became a bestseller among students. In the prevailing atmosphere of defeatism and nihilism, the book had a surprisingly spirited, forward-looking tone. Yoshimoto's *Gisei no Shūen* [The End of a False System] and Tanigawa's *Teikei no chōkoku* [Overcoming Established Form] both clearly saw the failure of the Anpō struggle as the starting point for a new form of the political. In 1966, Ishii published the new edition, with this endnote:

> After five years from the struggle, the existing party leaders are still taking part in the established system, and exploiting the memories of popular movement of Anpō for their credit . . . Recently, their chirpings seem to have finally subsided, and I believe it has become increasingly clear that what was meant and targeted in this book foresaw the whole spectrum of the aftermath of the Anpō . . . We are publishing a new edition to answer the need of the times.[4]

Indeed, the book continued to enjoy a large readership throughout the 1960s and became a "must-read" among the students of 1968.

3 Yoshimoto Takaaki, "Nihon shihonshugi ni sakarau 'dokuritsu-sayoku'" [" 'Independent Left' against Japanese Capitalism"], in *60-nen Anpo/Miike Tōsō*: 1957–1960, ed. Nishii Kazuo, Tokyo: Mainichi Shinbunsha, 2000, 172.

4 Ishii Kyōji, editor's note to *Minshushugi no Shinwa*, new ed., eds. Tanigawa Gan, Yoshimoto Takaaki, Haniya Yutaka et al., Tokyo: Gendai Shichōsha, 1966, 230.

The League of Criminals and *Keishō*

The Bund was disbanded soon after the 1960 renewal of the Anpō treaty. As it had been a loosely connected organization from the beginning, it was hard to control after its focal issue was gone. The majority of students returned to their "normal" campus life to enjoy a few years of relative freedom before going onto the "real world" of work; however, some carried on the quest for change. Waseda University Russian literature students Hiraoka Masaaki and Miyahara Yasuharu had been active Bund members during the Anpō struggle, and after the Bund was dissolved they formed the provocatively named group Hanzaisha Dōmei [League of Criminals] from 1961 to 1963. Their activities were an eclectic mixture of literature, theater and street performance, protest, crime, and pranks. Ishii was intrigued by Hiraoka's declaration that the aim of Hanzaisha Dōmei was to unsettle society in preparation for revolution by staging various "criminal" actions, and in 1962 he published both Miyahara and Hiraoka's essays in *Byakuya Hyōron*, a monthly magazine of criticism published by Gendai Shichōsha. Considering that Hiraoka and Miyahara were still undergraduates in their early twenties, it was quite a feat to be recognized by this cutting-edge publisher, and through Ishii they got to know Tanigawa, Haniya, and other prominent thinkers.

Although Hiraoka and Miyahara's initial focus had been the continuation of the student movement, they became disillusioned by the infighting among the various political factions at Waseda University and sought instead to stage their activities in the streets of Shinjuku—including a "die-in" performance at Shinjuku station during the Upper House election of 1962. Their tactics resonated with the street actions initiated by some avant-garde artists of the time, such as the 1962 "Yamanote line incident," for which Nakanishi Natsuyuki, Takamatsu Jiro, Kawani Hiroshi, and others performed, unannounced, in a crowded commuter train in Tokyo. Such events were attempts at a form of *chokusetsu kōdō* [direct action] that might break through the quiescence that had followed the anti-Anpō defeat and reignite widespread activism.[5] Around this time, Hiraoka became acquainted with Kawani Hiroshi (1933–2003) and Imaizumi Yoshihiko (1931–2010). Imaizumi

5 For an extensive analysis of this politics and experimentalism, see William Marotti, *Money, Trains, and Guillotines: Art and Revolution in 1960s Japan*, Durham: Duke University Press, 2013.

and Kawani were the editors of *Keishō*, a magazine on art and art theory. Kawani declared *Keishō* to be the "synopsis of a plan concocted at the crossing point of political direct action and art action."[6] Indeed, Kawani and Imaizumi were frequent conspirators (sometimes accomplices) in events staged by other avant-garde artists, including the aforementioned "Yamanote line incident." *Keishō* issues seven and eight (both published in 1963; see the illustrations below) focused on "direct action," and in the magazines, Imaizumi urged artists to take their work out of the white cubes of museums and galleries and into the streets in order to "agitate" everyday life. A roundtable published in these issues was the catalyst for both the Hi-Red Center and specifically for Akasegawa's "1,000-yen bill" project; indeed, issue eight included the group's works and a copy of the 1,000-yen print itself peeping through a rectangular cut-out on the cover.[7]

Through Imaizumi and Kawani, Hiraoka got to know Nakanishi, Takamatsu, Kosugi Takehisa (1938–2018), a member of avant-garde music group Group Ongaku [the Music Group], and other avant-garde artists.[8] In November 1962, Hanzaisha Dōmei organized a theater performance titled *Kuroku fuchidorareta bara no nureta kushami* [*Wet Sneeze of a Black-Lined Rose*] at Waseda University's Ōkuma Hall. They asked Nakanishi, Kosugi, Kobatake Hiroshi (a sculptor who later taught woodcarving at Bigakkō), and Takamatsu Jiro to participate. The artists agreed, but they failed to attend the rehearsal and did not appear on stage. Instead, Kobatake pushed his stone sculptures from the balcony seats, while Takamatsu suspended a black rope all over the theater, and Kosugi played his experimental music. Nakanishi, mysteriously absent during the play, was busy painting the urinals red in the men's toilets (see the photograph below). Imaizumi wrote in his diary that he was pleased with the actions taken by the artists: "Artists' participation should not be pre-mediated harmonious collaboration, but should be a spontaneous intervention, even confrontation."[9] The expanding and indefinable practices of groups like Hanzaisha Dōmei continued to blur

6 Kawani Hiroshi, "*Keishō* ni yosete" (About *Keishō*), *Bijutsu techō nenkan* 347, 1971, 72.

7 See Marotti, *Money, Trains, and Guillotines*.

8 On the Music Group, see Marotti, "Challenge to Music: The Music Group's Sonic Politics," in *Tomorrow is the Question: New Directions in Experimental Music Studies*, ed. Benjamin Piekut, Ann Arbor: University of Michigan Press, 2014, 109–38.

9 Imaizumi Yoshihiko, personal diary of November 22, 1962, Imaizumi archive, Tokyo.

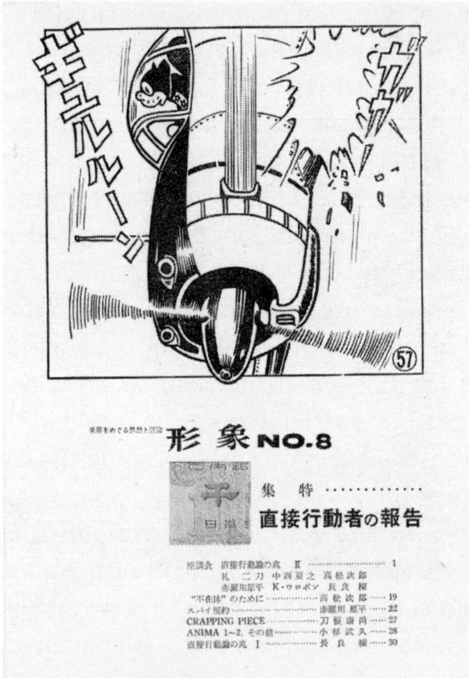

Keishō, issue 8 cover, 1963.

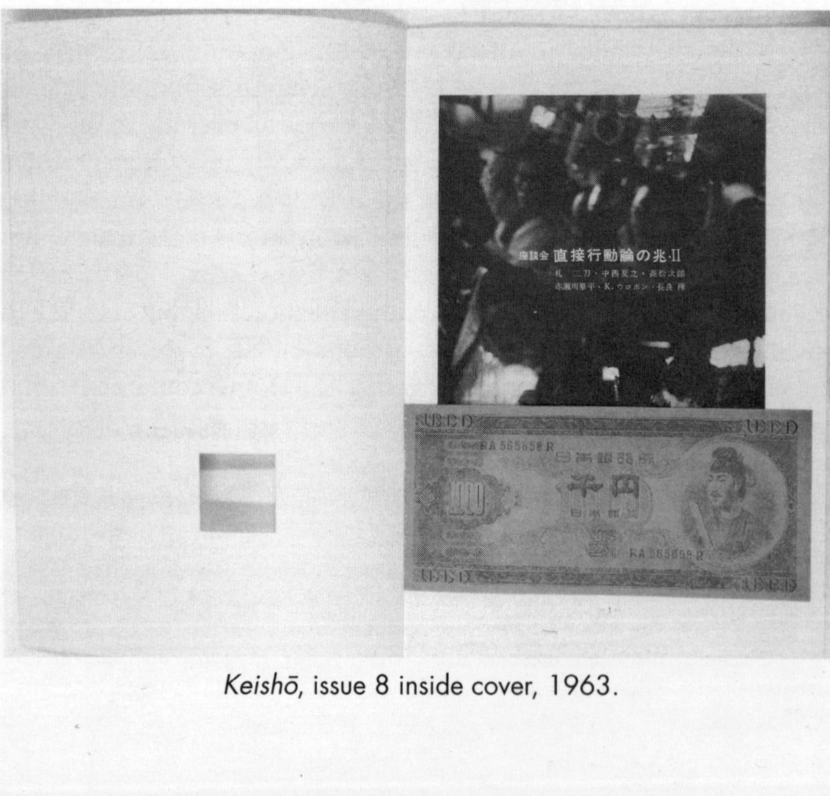

Keishō, issue 8 inside cover, 1963.

Urinals painted red by Nakanishi, Waseda University, November 1962. Photo by Takeda Atsushi.

the conventional borders between the artistic and the political, all while working to give new energies to politics through their peculiar forms of direct action.

Jiritsu Gakkō: The Essence of Contradiction and a Flower of Paradox

Alongside the Anpō struggle, the Miike coalminers' strike was raging in Kyūshū. As commentators and participants repeatedly remarked at the time, the Miike dispute became an all-out battle between labor and capital. But just as in the Anpō campaign, the mobilization of a great number of people meant nothing: capitalists and government bureaucracy succeeded in disempowering yet another group of workers in Japan.

In 1958, Tanigawa Gan set up the "circle village," a workers' cultural group in Chikuhō in Kyūshū, and became heavily involved in the Miike miners' struggle. After the failure of that strike, Tanigawa moved to a much smaller coalmine, Taishō, and organized Taishō Kōdō Tai [Taishō Coalmine Action Brigade] to assist their struggle. Taishō Kōdō Tai was a militant group independent of any political or union organization, and it was unique in including miners already fired by the company. They were striking not to get their jobs back, they said, but to be compensated for the hard work and suffering in the horrific conditions of the Taishō mine. They declared: "No more working in hell! We demand vacations!"[10]

Organizationally, Taishō Kōdō Tai was deliberately anarchistic. Members were not to be registered; if someone claimed to be a member, he was a member. There was no hierarchical system—each individual was both an executive and a member. There was also no majority-decision system. If someone wanted to do something, he and other members who agreed simply carried it out. Participating out of a sense of duty in something you did not want to do was frowned upon. There were no regulations, and the sole principle was "do only what you want to do."

After the failures of Anpō and Miike, Tanigawa's efforts at the Taishō mine gained the attention of radical intellectuals and activists in Tokyo. Ishii felt that Tanigawa was the only one who was doing anything interesting in that post-Anpō period, so he went to see him in Kyūshū. The two hit it off at once and got very drunk together.

Yamaguchi Kenji (1925–99), a legendary anarchist who had been expelled from the JCP in 1959, had likewise become disillusioned with the anti-Anpō movement at an early stage and in 1960 went to Kyūshū to support Taishō Kōdō Tai. Back in Tokyo, Yamaguchi formed Kō-hō no Kai [Rear Supply-Line Group] in 1961 to provide financial and personnel support to Taishō Kōdō Tai. Various organizations, activists, artists, and intellectuals joined Kō-hō no Kai, and the appeal for donations listed Kawani Hiroshi as one of the organizers and Ishii, Yoshimoto, Haniya, and other political and cultural figures as endorsers. Hiraoka and the Hanzaisha Dōmei members also joined the club.

Byakuya Hyōron, published by Gendai Shichōsha from May to December 1962, became an arena for those involved in the group. In its pages, Tanigawa advocated building a "commune" in Tokyo and, in preparation for the commune, proposed to build a Jiritsu Gakkō [School of Autonomy]:

> I don't want to be anything! I want to be something unnamable!
>
> It is impossible to teach or to be taught how to stand on your own

10 Tanigawa Gan, "Eikyū bakansu-shugi" [Permanent vacation-ism], *Katen* 7, 1963, 25: 6, *Kō-hō no Kai.*

> feet. As is well known, a school is a boring place, but the reverse is also true.
>
> Existing schools all try to take your money, acting as if the impossible were possible. Jiritsu Gakkō declares its impossibility. Jiritsu Gakkō is a school that should never exist. You must discard all of your useful knowledge and habits at the gate. Jiritsu Gakkō is the essence of contradiction and a flower of paradox. It is an unattainable school to become an unnamable person. To stand in the middle of this paradox is the only curriculum of this school.
>
> Do you want to fight against those who enforce imperialism in the psychological realm? Do you feel suffocated with labels such as "proletarian" and "intellectual" pasted on your face? If you do, you are accepted to this school.
>
> The tuition of this school is very high—perhaps it will cost your whole life.
>
> It is roadwork for the intelligence, body building of philosophy. If you think these words are false, make your own Jiritsu school.[11]

With this uncompromising cry, Jiritsu Gakkō opened in September 1962 in Tokyo, and it is now widely viewed as the prototype for Bigakkō. As early as 1961, when Kō-hō no Kai started, Yamaguchi was already contemplating some kind of "school" to inform young activists in Tokyo about the new ideas and strategies of Taishō Kōdō Tai. In April 1962, Tanigawa and Yamaguchi sent out an invitation to their friends to discuss starting a school of political thought. The first invitation was sent out from Ko-ho no Kai with Tanigawa's basic plan, which stated that its aim was to create an autonomous organization for political actions and to nurture organizers. The second plan was written by Imaizumi and published in *Keishō* issue six (1962), in which he proposed the following principles:

> 1) We do not exclude any factions, political or religious.
> 2) We do not accept majority rule.
> 3) We expel anyone wanting to teach or to be taught.
> 4) We do not have a class or term system.
> 5) If we were not able to follow the above, we would close.[12]

11 Jiritsu Gakkō Appeal, an appeal letter sent to Imaizumi Yoshihiko, September 1962, Imaizumi archive, Tokyo.

12 Imaizumi Yoshihiko, "Daini no teigen" [The second proposal], reprinted in *Kikan* 11, 1980, 43–4.

Subsequently, Ishii offered temporary office space at Gendai Shichōsha's premises, and Imaizumi, Kawani, and Hiraoka of Hanzaisha Dōmei got involved in the start-up committee of this "school"; Nakamura, Nakanishi, and Kosugi, who all later taught at Bigakkō, each gave a lecture there.

Although it was called a "school," Jiritsu Gakkō did not aim to have intellectuals enlighten the masses. Conversely, the masses were to become teachers. As the aims of Jiritsu Gakkō stated, the provisional lecturers were not only thinkers and artists, but also "a street peddler, the skipper of a riverboat, a bar madam, a comic, a street cleaner, artisans in small factories."[13] Tanigawa also emphasized the "three-way power balance" among those involved: teachers, administrators, and students. The students were not allowed to be passive participants but were to form a group that should have power equal to the teachers and the administrators. Tanigawa insisted that true autonomy could be attained only through severe contention among these three groups. Within a month of Jiritsu Gakkō's launch, however, Imaizumi, Kawani, and Hiraoka had all resigned from the administrative committee. Imaizumi wrote later that the classes, in spite of Tanigawa's initial intention, became more or less "fan clubs" of famous lecturers.

There also seemed to be friction between the political thinkers and the artists, which may also have triggered the resignations. In *Keishō*'s issue eight, Nakanishi recounted the "lecture" he gave at the initial meeting of Jiritsu Gakkō. Nakanishi walked around the audience with a smoke canister in his hand while Kosugi played his music piece by twining a recorded tape around his body. Yamaguchi and Tanigawa were bewildered and, later at the committee meeting, they turned down any further lecture by Nakanishi. Nakanishi explained in a roundtable:

> The reason I went there (Jiritsu Gakkō) was that if it was supposed to be a place for discourses to collide, I could take anything there. I taught them how to make a picture with smoke screen. This is how I express myself so I just took what I do in my work. But later I heard they said it

13 It is not clear if these lectures by the "lower-class laborers" actually happened. A chronicle by Matsuda Masao has no record of this kind of lecture, but Adachi Masao, a filmmaker who was a student, remembers a talk given by a bar madam (interview by Shimada).

> could not be a tool of communication . . . I did not go there to communicate. I thought the meeting was to bring oneself and ask others to bring themselves, which I found interesting.[14]

Imaizumi published the short essay "Can there be a tool for communication?" in the same issue of *Keishō* in which he argued that action, though seemingly incomprehensible, could be a more effective tool for communication:

> if they think Nakanishi's action can't be a tool for communication, then we should doubt if communication itself could be attainable. We should break down this delusion of interpenetration and communication—I had imagined this school might be a place to stir the ideologues in a washing machine with students as detergent . . . For me, nothing conveys one's intention more accurately than a dagger suddenly thrust from behind a door . . . If you can call a sudden action that leaves a strong impact without taking a life a tool for communication, then the bankrupted ideologues can be liberated from using language as a medium.[15]

Thus, the anticipated serious contention and interchange between the ostensibly artistic and political—and among students, teachers, and administrators—could not be fully materialized. However, Jiritsu Gakkō in many ways anticipated the 1968 Zenkyōtō slogan of *Daigaku kaitai* [destruction of universities] and questioned the construct of "learning" itself.

After the departures of Imaizumi, Kawani, and Hiraoka, Matsuda Masao and Yamaguchi Kenji acted as secretaries of Jiritsu Gakkō and they took this opportunity to organize the students into a kind of militia, arming them with helmets. They confronted the riot police at the Ogu Depot railway strike on December 13, 1963, but with this brief clash as the final note, Jiritsu Gakkō was disbanded in 1964.

14 Nakanishi Natsuyuki, "Chokusetukōdō-sha no hōkoku" [Report of direct action], *Keishō* 8, 1963, 8.

15 Imaizumi Yoshihiko, "Karera no sore wa shisō dentatsu no gu ni narieruka?" [Can theirs be a tool for communication?] *Keisho* 8, 1963, 35–6.

Shisōteki Henshitsusha [Ideological Perverts]

A key phrase of the era was *shisōteki henshitsu-sha*, or "ideological perverts," which was first used in a press conference by the national police commissioner. There were groups that defied categorization, such as Hanzaisha Dōmei, the Gendai Shichōsha group, Van film study institute, and the Hi-Red Center. Previously, radical groups had been only "politically" radical; they had no artistic interests. "But things were getting confused [*midareru*] from the authorities' point of view. They felt under pressure because something incomprehensible—groups that made no clear division between politics and art—were lurking around them. We imagined what they were feeling and were inspired by it."[16]

The Hi-Red Center's first exhibition, "The 5th Mixer Plan" of 1963, featured 1,000-yen "banknotes" printed by Akasegawa Genpei, who had made invitation cards and artwork using these printed, single-sided, monochrome "model notes" earlier that year. In January 1964, two police detectives visited Akasegawa's apartment. This was the beginning of the infamous "1,000-yen banknote case."

Prior to this visit, the police had raided the houses of Hanzaisha Dōmei members over an allegedly pornographic photograph in a book titled *Akai Fusen Aruiwa Mesuōkami No Yoru* [Red Balloon, or Night of the She-Wolf] that they had published. There, the police found a printed copy of Akasegawa's 1,000-yen banknote, which was also featured in the book. As a privately printed art book that was circulated only among friends, it should not have been subject to prosecution, but because Hanzaisha Dōmei was one of the groups being monitored by the authorities as "ideologically perverse," Yoshioka, the photographer, Miyahara, and Hiraoka were arrested, and the news was well publicized in major newspapers and weekly magazines (see illustrations below). After making the connection between Hanzaisha Dōmei and Akasegawa, it is likely that the police assumed the latter's 1,000-yen banknote had more than just artistic purposes. The reaction of the press to both cases was similarly scandalized. On January 26, 1964, *Asahi* reported Akasegawa's case as headline news, connecting it to the recent "Chi-37" counterfeit banknote case.[17]

16 Akasegawa Genpei, *Zenmen jikyō!* [Total confession], Tokyo: Shōbunsha, 2001, 128.

17 In December 1961, a very high-quality counterfeit 1,000-yen banknote was found in Akita. From then on, 343 fake notes were found in twenty-two prefectures. Although the Metropolitan Police Department searched in full force, the perpetrator was never found. The statute of limitation ran out in 1973; see Akasegawa, *Zenmen jikyō!*, 160. See also Marotti, *Money, Trains, and Guillotines.*

犯罪者同盟の第一号犯罪

ワイセツ文書頒布罪に…れたある早大生グループの背景

起訴にもあたらぬ"悪書"

"ワイセツ本"をつくって売りさばいていた早大生のグループが、ひょんなキッカケから捕まった。グループの名は"犯罪者同盟"。チャチな名称と笑うなかれ。当のご本人たちは"天下泰平の思想にほとほとイヤ気がさし、混乱こそは我が願い、そのためには自からを犯罪者と規定して……"といたって大マジメ。大学の先生も「初めは驚き心配したが、どうやら主義主張あってのこととわかってホッと安心」したが、いわゆる"エロ事師"たちとは違うとわかったものの、さりとて安心ばかりしていていいものかどうか。"犯罪者同盟"とはそも何事デアルカ。その批判と弁護などを集めてみた――。

Bunshun, January 6, 1963 (recto page and verso page). Recto page (above left): Hiraoka Masaaki (left) and Miyahara Yasuharu (right). Verso page (above right): a Dada Kan page of *Akai Fusen*.

In November 1965, Akasegawa and the banknote's printers were prosecuted for making "models" of the 1,000-yen banknote. Faced with this situation, the "1,000-yen banknote incident committee" was formed to discuss how to deal with the case, with Kawani as chairperson and Takiguchi Shūzo and Nakahara Yūsuke (both well-known art critics) as special defense witnesses. Imaizumi, Nakanishi, Takamatsu, Nakamura, and other artists and art critics were also witnesses for the defense.

Rather than counterfeiting, Akasegawa was accused of violating the obsolete 1895 "Law Controlling the Imitation of Currency and Securities." Although there were numerous commercial products imitating currency, they had escaped prosecution. Akasegawa's charge seems to have been based on the authorities' desire to control the activities of these "ideological perverts." After the court case opened, Akasegawa and his defense team decided to insist that his activities were just "art"—which was ironic, because as a member of the Hi-Red Center, he had been explicitly trying to break out of the confinement of "art," a term the group assiduously avoided.

Meanwhile, Gendai Shichōsha also found itself subject to prosecution due to its association with the Tokyo Action Front. This organization-cum-newsletter was founded in 1965 by Yamaguchi, Kawani, Ishii, Matsuda, and others based at Gendai Shichōsha , and it advocated direct action by organized individuals acting independently of the existing political system. The first issue of June 15, 1965, included the following articles: "From Demonstration to a Group of Personal Battles" by Hiraoka Masaaki; "In the Beginning," a memoir of the immediate postwar years in Tokyo, by Ishii Kyōji; and "Let's Make Life Rich," an agitation to erase everyday life through "happenings" and "actions," by Anaki Teruo (a pseudonym for Kawani Hiroshi, punning on the Japanese pronunciation of "Anarchy Terror"). On November 11, 1965, four members of the Tokyo Action Front, including Matsuda Masao and Sasamoto Masanori, an anarchist employed by Gendai Shichōsha as an editor, were arrested in front of the Gendai Shichōsha building. They were on their way to a demonstration against the anti–Japan-Korea treaty and were in possession of bottles containing ammonia, which authorities suspected would be used against the riot police. Following their arrest, the Gendai Shichōsha building was searched on November 16.

It is worth quoting Akasegawa's (1972) recollection of the "close encounter" between artistic and political direct action at some length:

> As the agents of direct actions of both [artistic and political] sides tried to cultivate their thoughts through actions in everyday life, they separated themselves from their respective authorized fields and went into the street . . . In the street, they gazed at every ordinary object equally, and their gaze eventually changed the nature of those everyday spaces and objects. That was when the "near miss" of the action of artistic expression and the action of subversion occurred; an ammonia Molotov cocktail bottle assumed the guise of an art object; demonstrators burned flags as if staging a "happening"; anti-art 1,000-yen banknotes were produced in the style of a real crime; a pornographic art film premiere took on the appearance of a political riot, and so on . . . These actions had never been "registered" in anyone's minds before and it was hard to classify them as political or artistic incidents, or to determine who was responsible for them. It was as if many similar tails were hanging from many backsides in the street, and a dog [i.e., the police] was frantically sniffing at them to determine which tail belonged to which backside. As the dog could not uncover the nature of the tails, his illusions about them grew out of all proportion. These street actions had no names, and because of that, the dog collected every scrap of evidence carefully to

> determine their identity . . . Some tails seemed to belong to the art world, and others to the political world, and the dog began to imagine that they belonged not to these respective backsides but to the single huge arse of some unknown monster, which he named Shisō-teki henshitsusha [ideological pervert].[18]

"Being unnamable" was an effective way to carry out subversive actions in the streets of Tokyo, but it likewise created suspicion and even fear on the part of the authorities against the agents of these actions. Following Marotti's argument in this volume, this is an instance where Jacques Rancière's "police" are joined by the empirical police against an unnamable politics. Unsurprisingly, both Akasegawa and Gendai Shichōsha faced prosecution.

The Making of Gendai Shichōsha Bigakkō

As Hiraoka predicted, the ideas and actions carried out by Gendai Shichōsha-related groups were partly maintained by the revitalized students' movement, surfacing first at the Nittoku-kin attack by Waseda anarchist students led by ex-Gendai Shichōsha editor Sasamoto in 1966,[19] and then at the Haneda Airport incidents of 1967, and exploding through numerous university barricades set up by Zenkyōtō students in 1968. Sunenaga Tamio, leader of the art/activist group PEAK, stated that he thought the colorful helmets and *gebabō* [wooden poles usable as weapons] were the high fashion of the time, and the graffiti on barricades symbolized an attempt by the students to create a new space, turning the campus into "a new art museum."[20] Ishii had a rather more realistic view of the students' barricades. He went to see the barricade at the University of Tokyo and was disappointed by its flimsiness ("Nihon University ones were better," he said). Unlike their actions in the Anpō struggle of 1960, Ishii and his friends did not form a group in support of Zenkyōtō students.

18 Akasegawa Genpei, *Tsuihōsareta yajiuma*, Tokyo: Gendai Hyōronsha, 1972, 22–4.

19 Nittoku-kin (Nihon Tokushu Kinzoku) was a Japanese weapons manufacturer. On the night of October 19, 1966, thirteen members of Behan-i (Anti-Vietnam War Committee; an anarchist group and no relation to Beheiren) invaded the factory in Tanashi, Tokyo, to protest the manufacturing and export of machine guns to Vietnam. Seven members were arrested. The central figure was Sasamoto, an anarchist activist who worked at Gendai Shichōsha and was a member of Tokyo Kōdō Sensen.

20 Sunenaga Tamio, *Ikinobiru tame no komyūn* [*Commune for Survival*], Tokyo: San'ichi Shobō, 1973, 41–2.

Although he sympathized with them, Ishii had no illusions about the imminent change and revolution some of the students envisioned, and he never intended to pander to them. After Kawani joined as an editor in 1967, Gendai Shichōsha started to give greater publishing consideration to books on art, such as Nakamura's monograph *Bōenkyō kara no Kokuji* [Announcement from a Telescope], Kara Jūrō's first collection of drama and essays *Koshimaki Osen* in 1968 (see illustations below), and Hosoe Eikō's famous 1969 photo book *Kamaitachi* on the *butoh* guru Hijikata Tatsumi. Nakamura's monstrous schoolgirls, Kara's *Tokkenteki nikutai ron* [A Theory of the Absolute Privilege of the Body], as well as Hijikata's writings on the "indigenous" and "premodern" body—all seem to lack immediate political import. None feature the same sort of declared social interventionist ambitions as seen in, say, Hanzaisha Dōmei's street actions of the mid-1960s. However, their primordial negative power was a strong antithesis to the upcoming 1970 Osaka Expo slogan of "Progress and Harmony of Humanity"—a kind of dissensus against a popular conformism of progress and technology.

Ishii was a keen observer of the times, and he foresaw the stagnation and failure of the students' movement of 1968. Ever forward looking, he saw future opportunities in art and education. Almost certainly using Jiritsu Gakkō as a prototype, Ishii tried anew the idea of nurturing autonomous minds—this time not through political theory, but via artistic and physical work. He first tried out this idea on the artist Nakamura Hiroshi in 1968. According to Nakamura, Ishii remarked that what he was trying to do was to "change the world by changing the way the world is perceived" through art.[21] Nakamura also said:

> I think Ishii tried to challenge the post-'68 situation by reintroducing art as a tool for quiet reflection on the internal, and for changes from within. From the beginning, I think Ishii considered Bigakkō not just as an institution for art but also as a movement, where political and artistic activism, thoughts and philosophy were discussed, practiced and realized . . . at a time [when] everything seemed to be sliding down into the bottomless void, we [at Bigakkō] dared to dig our heels in, to stop and think inwardly.[22]

21 Nakamura Hiroshi, interview with Shimada, Tokyo, April 26, 2014.

22 Nakamura Hiroshi, interview with Shimada and Roxby, Tokyo, June 24, 2010.

Bōenkyō kara no Kokuji, cover, Nakamura Hiroshi, 1968.

Koshimaki Osen cover. Designed by Awazu Kiyoshi, 1968.

One of the key concepts of Bigakkō was its emphasis on *tewaza* [hand-skills *te*, hand; *waza*, skill]. What Bigakkō aimed for with the insistence on *tewaza* was consciously to go against the modernist current in search of the "radicals" (in the word's original sense of "root") and the primeval energy from which revolutionary creation could be born. What Ishii saw in *tewaza* was not merely the pursuit of good artisanal skills. Rather, he thought of it as a tool for acquiring "embodiment"—the understanding and realization of ideas through rigorous, disciplined physical experience. Okada Takahiko, an art critic, visited Bigakkō in 1970 and reported:

> The atmosphere of Bigakkō reminds me of the Arts and Crafts movement of William Morris—not in the superficial similarity but in their attitudes. Morris' ideal was not just making good products, but changing the society through development of an Art that was an expression of the pleasure of labour.[23]

Thus, Gendai Shichōsha's quest for free, autonomous minds and society continued even after 1968. Through its publications, support for radical artistic and political groups, and by starting and funding Bigakkō, it created a continuity of radical thought and actions that informed and served as a basis for the radical movement in 1968 and its afterlives beyond.

23 Okada Takahiko, "Bigakkō—waza no shutoku ni gendaibijutsu no ariyō o saguru" [Bigakkō—Search for the existence of contemporary art through mastering skills], *Bijutsu techō nenkan* 343, 1971, 99.

10

1972: The Structure on the Streets

Yutaka Nagahara

> The younger brother screams, facing the death of his elder: "In the end, even *sōkatsu* [self-critique] couldn't save anybody!"
>
> Sakaguchi Hiroshi[1]

> I was forced into despair with myself.
>
> Katō Michinori[2]

> The theme of *Oedipus Rex* . . . lies in the following point: that one divulges to oneself the meaning of *the deeds that one performed unknowingly*.
>
> Nagasaki Hiroshi[3]

Since Then

A half-century has already passed *since then*, but it is still out there, perhaps a totally forgotten or occasionally remembered remnant of an "unmastered history."[4] A few days before writing these words as the

1 Sakaguchi Hiroshi, *Sakaguchi Hiroshi Kakō* [Sakaguchi Hiroshi Poems], Tokyo: Asahi Shinbunsha, 1993, 17.

2 Katō Michinori, *Rengō Sekigun Shōnen A* [The United Red Army: Boy A], Tokyo: Shinchōsha, 2003, 7.

3 Nagasaki Hiroshi, "Higeki no Kōzō" [The Structure of Tragedy], in *Hanranron* [Theory of Rebellion], Tokyo: Gōdō Shuppan, 1968, 214. My emphasis.

4 Edward P. Thompson, *William Morris: Romantic to Revolutionary,* rev. ed., Stanford: Stanford University Press, 1955, 722. Of course it was said regarding the sad and beautiful lines of William Morris (*A Dream of John Ball*, Chapter IV: The Voice of John Ball).

point of departure for this essay, I returned the galley proofs of another essay to my editor. Why mention this? The title of this other piece was "To be a Marxist in Political Economy *after '68*." As might be immediately recognized, I had Louis Althusser in mind while writing it.[5] The subtitle, however, is more specific: "What is the *truth* that so-called Marxian economics could barely manage to demonstrate?" The brief conclusion: what almost all of Marxian economics of the 1960s alleged to *scientifically* prove is the "immaculate conception" of capital,[6] which cyclically or intermittently cries in a delirium, "I'm my own Lord forever and a day throughout heaven and earth." To put it bluntly, there neither can nor must be any *intrinsic* crisis *in and for* capital's self-estimation. *Rational* Marxian economics could demonstrate the structure of our reiterated defeats *scientifically* only because of the way in which it describes capital itself as rationally structured;[7] but for that very reason, it can never imagine and therefore realize the *(ir)rational* reasons people revolt repeatedly in vain. Since then, I essentially stopped expecting anything political from Marxian economics while remaining nevertheless an adamant Marxist, for I came to know that people revolt precisely because of a *politics* of their own,[8] thereby becoming a crisis as such in and for itself against capital, due to the inaugural fact that, in Sylvain Lazarus's terms, "the people think,"[9] as the bearers [*Träger*] of the impossible. Miracle or not,[10] it simply does happen and will be looked back at in one way or another similar to what William Morris dreamt in the name of John Ball. And behind this persuasion, so to speak, there always exists a *politico-theoretical* mapping, perhaps *impossible itself*, with which I side at once: that of Alain Badiou on the one hand and that of Gilles

5 Louis Althusser, *Être marxiste en philosophie*, Paris: PUF, 2015. But see also Jacques Rancière, *Althusser's Lesson*, trans. Emiliano Battista, London: Continuum, 2011.

6 On this point, see Gilles Deleuze (with Félix Guattari), "On Capitalism and Desire," in Deleuze, *Desert Island and Other Texts 1953–1974*, ed. David Lapoujade, trans. Michael Taormina, Los Angeles: Semiotext(e), 2004. Deleuze writes here: "something that has not been discussed in Marx's *Capital* is the extent to which he is fascinated by capitalist mechanisms, precisely because, at one and the same time, it is demented *and* it works" (ibid., 262).

7 "Rational Marxian economist" here does not necessarily mean the protagonists of so-called "analytical Marxism," "rational choice Marxism," and what they called "no-bullshit Marxism"; by saying this, I mean instead that *every* version of Marxism cannot realize the Deleuzian formula of modernity, that "the rational is always the rationality of an irrational" (ibid.).

8 See Alain Badiou, *Peut-on Penser la Politique?*, Paris: Seuil, 1985.

9 See Sylvain Lazarus, *Anthropology of the Name*, trans. Gila Walker, London: Seagull Books, 2015.

10 Daniel Bensaïd, "Alain Badiou and the Miracle of the Event," in *Think Again: Alain Badiou and the Future of Philosophy*, ed. Peter Hallward, London: Continuum, 2004.

Deleuze and Félix Guattari (together with Antonio Negri) on the other. And the third term here—Hegelian or not—is still held by Marx himself, who *politically* fused these tendencies together in a way. I would insist, then: this mapping, and its implications, must hold true for *our* '68 too.

To sum it up as if it were a concluding remark both *at* and *as* the beginning: *since then*, I have been defending the Marxist critique of Marxian political economy, enduring the regressions that followed after the experience of '68 (another "reverse course") by leaning on two connected but antithetical armories as a shield—the work of Uno Kōzō on the one hand, and the work of Nagasaki Hiroshi on the other.[11] *Since then*, the core of the question has been at all times the same: how a politics proper can be possible, even under a stifling and seemingly closed situation. In brief, in terms of political will, *since then* I have been trying to repoliticize the Marx that was depoliticized *then*, and the following chapter revolves around the politics of this *since then* itself.[12]

Taking this *since then* as my point of departure, I gave thought to the dismal role I am supposed to take in this volume while thinking not only of the age and generational composition of these chapters, but also of the political or, rather, partisan histories we all possess, especially the contributors from Japan and their respective political experiences. Having considered that, I set my approach toward a specific target: no matter how deformed in one sense the assembly of this chapter appears, it is above all an attempt to think back over my own *since then*. I should be very quick to add, however, that it is not merely a personal retrospection. It can never be, even if it sometimes appears as such.[13] That is

11 For Uno (and the so-called "Uno School"), see Jacques Bidet, "Kōzō Uno and His School: A Pure Theory of Capitalism," in *Critical Companion to Contemporary Marxism*, eds. Jacques Bidet and Stathis Kouvelakis, HM Books Series, Leiden: Brill, 2007; Gavin Walker, *The Sublime Perversion of Capital: Marxist Theory and the Politics of History in Modern Japan*, Durham: Duke University Press, 2016; and Yutaka Nagahara, "We, the Defective Commodity-Beings," *Journal of International Economic Studies* 26, 2012. I will return in the concluding remarks to Nagasaki Hiroshi's "Hanranron" [On Rebellion] in *Hanranron*.

12 Antonio Negri, "Une Ouverture vers le deleuzisme: Conversation avec Antonio Negri," in *Althusser et nous*, Aloocha Wald Lasowski, ed., Paris: PUF, 2016, 225.

13 I actually tend to be a rather unembraceable "native informant." This standpoint is derived from the sober proclamation of Tanaka Mitsu: "To desire to be understood is a beggar's spirit," in *Inochi no onna tachi e* [To Women of Life], Tokyo: Tabata Shoten,1972, 64–90. She was a precursor of the Japanese women's lib movement. See Mutō Ichiyō, "The Birth of the Women's Liberation Movement in the 1970s," in *The Other Japan: Conflict, Compromise, and Resistance Since 1945*, new ed., ed. Joe Moore for Bulletin of Concerned Asian Scholars, Armonk: M.E. Sharpe, 1997; and Setsu Shigematsu, *Scream from the Shadows: The Women's Liberation Movement in Japan*, Minneapolis: University of Minnesota Press, 2012.

because there exists a sort of depressively imagined intersubjectivity of the '68 generation—some might say an interpassivity—backed up by this historical *since then*. It obliges me to accept being haunted by a thin, quasi-generational group, which did and still does exist, I believe, as a sort of temporally compressed zeitgeist, and to which I happened to belong, fortunately or not. I dub this *quasi*-intersubjectivity—*quasi* because it was violently forced into existence in the wake of the "events" of '68—the thin generation of *hamegoroshi* (a term I will explain shortly), an interpretative mechanism that was retroactively counter-fabricated so as to deal or cope with the "two lost decades"—not theirs (that is, the capitalists) but *ours* (the radicals).

1972, or *Hamegoroshi*

What does this Japanese term *hamegoroshi* mean? It means something "permanently set," whose typical image is a fixed window, but it literally means in Japanese "being tightly *fitted into* a fixed *frame* [*hame*] and thereby *killed* [*goroshi*]." This frame, in a sense, is one that paradoxically gives our intersubjective *I* a hypothetical frame within which to bring out some specific aspects—not the uniqueness or particularity—of '68 in Japan. That is to say, this thin generation of *hamegoroshi,* under whose small flag I would venture to "speak truth"—in the Foucauldian sense—about '68 in Japan, gets caught between two contrastive, if not necessarily contradictory, yet complicit generations: the direct '68ers and the post-'68ers.

To be sure, insofar as most everyone thinks in terms of this generational gap and has a legitimate right to think that way, what I would call the generation of *hamegoroshi* always thinks of itself as being simultaneously too late and too early, and therefore feels located nowhere, like *The Youth Who Came Late,*[14] to borrow the name of Ōe Kenzaburō's novel, thus feeling always-already doomed to miss the right moment, despite the fact that no one can ever figure out what that is supposed to be. In this sense, some, if not all, of the *hamegoroshi* generation were structurally situated behind the '68ers, themselves influenced to some extent by the 1960 Anpō generation through the

14 His *Okuretekita Seinen* [The Youth Who Came Late] was written in 1962 under the situation of the defeat of the '60 Anpō; his *last* best work, *The Silent Cry* (trans. John Bester, reissue, New York: Grove Press, 2016) was published under the '68 atmosphere in 1967.

New Left groups reconstructed around 1965 after the defeat of the '60 Anpō,[15] best exemplified by the formation of the so-called "Three-Faction Zengakuren" [Sanpa Zengakuren] in 1966.[16] This thin generation at the edge of '68 somehow got through the violent—yet, in another sense, apathetically frivolous and apolitical—season of the post-'68 period, in turn leading to the bubble economy of the late 1980s. The process toward the asset-price bubble (from the late '80s to the early '90s) was driven in some senses by certain '68ers being literally sick of the 1970s, alongside certain post-'68ers who somehow felt always awkward in 1968 and mocked the '68ers at heart.[17] The *hamegoroshi* generation was firmly tied to this disastrous crossroad (or fixed nodal point) and caught between two fires. And it was 1972 that was the dividing moment. This is exactly what the politics of the *since then* specifically signifies here. As to this pivotal year, critic Tsubouchi Yūzō gives us a sober periodization, freed from any resentments:

> Although there was a tendency to only emphasize the aspect of the era of high growth that was new and in flux, in another sense, older things and former sensibilities strongly remained . . . Its entanglements were formative for the intensity and violence of the change of the *Zeitgeist*.

15 For the '60 Anpō protest, English materials are too many to count. For now, see George R. Packard III, *Protest in Tokyo: The Security Treaty Crisis of 1960*, Westport: Greenwood Press, 1966; Ellis S. Krauss, *Japanese Radicals Revisited: Student Protest in PostWar Japan*, Berkeley: University of California Press, 1974; and Patricia G. Steinhoff, "Japan: Student Activism in an Emerging Democracy," in *Student Activism in Asia: Between Protest and Powerlessness*, eds. Meredith L. Weiss and Edward Aspinall, Minneapolis: University of Minnesota Press, 2012.

16 See William Andrews, *Dissenting Japan: A History of Japanese Radicalism and Counterculture from 1945 to Fukushima*, London: Hurst & Company, 2016, 79–83; Patricia G. Steinhoff, "Memories of New Left Protest," *Contemporary Japan* 25: 2, 2013; and the meticulously documented essay of William Marotti, "Japan 1968: The Performance of Violence and the Theater of Protest," *American Historical Review* 114: 1, 2009. I appreciate both Andrews and Steinhoff—without their efforts to document and analyze the postwar processes of Japanese radicalisms, I would not try to write about it in Japanese, let alone English.

17 It is reported that "the new generation of activists were understandably estranged from their senior peers. In the words of Fusako Shigenobu [the JRA leader], despite an age difference of only a few years, the students of 1968 regarded the Anpō veterans as 'old geezers.'" Andrews, *Dissenting Japan*, 69. I do not regard "them" as "old geezers" as Shigenobu did, since I knew many "Anpō veterans" and I respect them, but at the same time I totally agree that "an age difference of only a few years" made an enormous difference in terms of "*mentalité*."

> The peak of this intensity was 1968, but what in fact finalized these transformations was the year 1972. In other words, the dramatic cultural fluctuations of the era of high growth began in 1964, peaked in 1968, and reached their completion or zenith in 1972. To put it another way, 1972 was precisely the "end of the beginning" of an era, and also the "beginning of the end."[18]

In this regard, the *hamegoroshi* generation, split between the "the end of the beginning" and "the beginning of the end," occupied a sad vantage point, and it is only in this sense that they are authorized, both by the '68ers who cynically disavowed their past, and the post-68ers who respectfully kept their distance from the '68ers, simply to gaze at the truth of the Japanese '68[19]—after all, every truth is always "post-evental" (especially for the '68ers) and possibly, if not feasibly, "*pre*-evental" (the hope of the post-'68ers).[20] If Badiou is right in insisting that "the reason why interpretations of that event [May '68] differ so much is that *they usually recall one aspect of it and not the complex totality that gives it its true grandeur*,"[21] I can say that the *hamegoroshi* generation that I have adopted as a singular window—albeit fixed and unopenable—through which to view '68 in Japan is just "*one* aspect of it"—without which, however, "the complex totality" could not be grasped, even partially.

If so, then neither masculine grand theories nor heroic tales are permitted here. In fact, their testimony is often lined with traumatic truths, which, for that very reason, in turn could "punch a hole" in the knowledge of the Japanese '68. Their testimony might also be heterogeneous, by nature, according to the places (or sites)—such as factories,

---

18 Tsubouchi Yūzō, *1972—"Hajimari no Owari" to "Owari no Hajimari"* [1972: "The End of the Beginning" and "The Beginning of the End"], Tokyo: Bunshun bunko, 2006, 13–14. Tsubouchi was born in 1958 and belongs to the post-'68 generation.

19 Alberto Toscano speaks his mind stingingly: "Tell me how you survived the 1980s and I'll tell you who you are. This might be an apt adage for the handful of contemporary radical theorists from the 1960s levy (1950s, in Negri's case) who have garnered such attention in the last decade from the younger generation learning to cope with and contest neoliberalism," which must be heard by anyone who boasted of "being there." Alberto Toscano, "The Sensuous Religion of the Multitude: Art and Abstraction in Negri," *Third Text* 23: 4, 2009, 370.

20 Alain Badiou, *Manifesto for Philosophy*, trans., ed. Norman Madarasz, Albany: SUNY Press, 1999, 107, translation modified. See also Nagahara Yutaka, "Shisō wa dekigoto ni okureru" [Thought Is Outstripped by the Event], in *1968*, ed. Suga Hidemi, Tokyo: Sakuhinsha, 2005.

21 Alain Badiou, *The Communist Hypothesis*, trans. David Macey and Steve Corcoran, New York: Verso, 2010, 45–6, my emphasis.

university campuses, prep schools, high schools,[22] junior high schools, the streets, and even the political factions [*seiji-tōha*] themselves—where those who would speak truth *necessarily took the risk* to be or choose without any defined reasons,[23] "but it is also *the sole known source* of new knowledges,"[24] which is precisely what repeatedly trapped and "framed" the *hamegoroshi* generation.

But here, not simply for convenience's sake but rather truly seriously, out of the two brutal aspects of the aftermath (or maybe "after*mess*") of '68 in Japan—the Rengō Sekigun [United Red Army: URA] purge,[25] and murderous inter-sectarian struggles [*uchi geba*, or "internal violence," specifically infighting between the New Left groups][26]—I will take up the former and scratch just the surface of it not merely as a witness myself but also as something that is not an exception in the first half of our "lost two decades." Before entering into it, however, I would like to reinforce my viewpoint here by again referring to Badiou, who understandably thinks it more important to "speak of a 'decade of '68' rather than of 'May '68'" per se,[27] which *literally* has had "no *place*" in

22 On high school organizations, see *Zengakuren: Japan's Revolutionary Students*, ed. Stuart Dowsey, Berkeley: Ishi Press, 1970, 191. As far as I know, there were more Zenkyōtō-affiliated high school organizations or groups across the nation than is reported. They were simply "erased" by school teachers, the prefectural board of education, and the Ministry of Education. Our high school comrades across the nation, if they failed to substantialize their own organizations, rose up individually everywhere and simultaneously struck back against the powers that be together with their unknown brothers and sisters. For the high school situation, see Kobayashi Tetsuo, *Kōkō Funsō 1969–1970* [High School Strife 1969–1970], City: Chūkōshinsho, 2012. There were lots of prep-school Zenkyōtōs, as well, and they were *closer* to the streets than college students. They had no guarantee in terms of social status and were likely to be on the verge of becoming lumpen proletarians or precariats (now called *freeters* in this country). See, David H. Slater, "The Making of Japan's New Working Class: 'Freeters' and the Progression from Middle School to the Labor Market," *Asia-Pacific Journal* 8: 1, 2010.

23 I have in mind here Badiou's concept of "site," *place-lieu*, or *esplace* and *horlieu* as the theory of street and revolt. See Alain Badiou, *Theory of the Subject*, trans. and intro. Bruno Bosteels, New York: Continuum, 2009. See also Alain Badiou, "The Factory as Event Site: Why Should the Worker Be a Reference in Our Vision of Politics?" *Prelom* 8, 2006.

24 Alain Badiou, *Ethics: An Essay on the Understanding of Evil*, trans. and intro. Peter Hallward, London: Verso, 2001, 70. My emphasis.

25 For the URA, see Patricia G. Steinhoff "Three Women Who Loved the Left: Radical Woman Leaders in the Japanese Red Army Movement," in *Re-Imaging Japanese Women*, ed. Anne E. Imamura, Berkeley: University of California Press, 1996; Andrews, *Dissenting Japan*, xxi, 139ff.; and Christopher Perkins, *The United Red Army On Screen: Cinema, Aesthetics and The Politics of Memory*, Basingstoke: Palgrave Macmillan, 2015.

26 For *uchi-geba*, see Andrews, *Dissenting Japan*, xxi, 147–61.

27 Badiou, *The Communist Hypothesis*, 52.

the previous history.[28] It is only through this notion of the "decade of '68" that we can adequately describe not only the post-'68ers, by locating this *hamegoroshi* generation as their predecessors, but also the '68ers themselves, whose own predecessors were the 1960 Anpō generation.[29] Only in this sense can there exist a "temporal indistinction," or "certain indistinct," to borrow the neologism of Sylvain Lazarus,[30] which nevertheless firmly straddles and fixes the *hamegoroshi* generation (as the *disenchanted* Marxist "mediators—'*intercesseurs*' in the Deleuzian sense—" that "the Left needs").[31] Badiou writes:

> There is a sort of *temporal indistinction* [indistinction provisoire] *between what is beginning and what is coming to an end*, and it is this that gives May '68 its mysterious intensity.[32]

This echoes, of course, with Tsubouchi's prior sober evaluation. Our "indistinction" started in 1972 and then triggered the "lost two decades" *for us*. These lost decades are composed of two contrastive yet sequential phases sitting back to back: the "violent and clandestine decade" of the 1970s,[33] which, intriguingly, happened to follow the developmental curve of hyper-economic growth since 1955 on the one hand;[34] and, on

---

28 Gilles Deleuze (with Félix Guattari), "May '68 Did Not Take Place" in, *Two Regimes of Madness: Texts and Interviews 1975–1995*, ed. David Lapoujade, trans. Ames Hodges and Mike Taormina, New York: Semiotext(e), 2006.

29 For the pre-evental, see Nick Srnicek, "What is to be done? Alain Badiou and the pre-evental," *Symposium: Canadian Journal of Continental Philosophy* 12: 2, 2008. In other words, we are now required to theorize the form(ation)s of our struggles under the phase of reterritorialization of deterritorialization. See Alain Badiou, *The Rebirth of History*, trans. Gregory Elliott, New York: Verso, 2012; together with Nagasaki Hiroshi, *Hanranron* [On Revolt]; *Seiji no Genshōgaku aruiwa Ajitētā no Henrekishi* [Phenomenology of Politics, or Pilgrimage of the Agitator], Tokyo: Tabata Shoten, 1977. As to the theory of Nagasaki, see Yoshihiko Ichida, "The Ethics of the Agitator," in this volume.

30 Lazarus, *Anthropology of the Name*, x–xii; and Alain Badiou, "Politics as Thought: The Work of Sylvain Lazarus," in *Metapolitics*, trans. Jason Barker, London: Verso, 2005, 42–5.

31 Gilles Deleuze, *Negotiations: 1972–1990*, trans. Martin Joughin, New York: Columbia University Press, 1995, 126.

32 Badiou, *The Communist Hypothesis*, 55, my emphasis.

33 For the clandestine aspect of the decade seen from a comparative viewpoint, see Gilda Zwerman, Donatella della Porta, and Patricia Steinhoff, "Disappearing Social Movements: Clandestinity in the Cycle of New Left Protest in the United States, Japan, Germany, and Italy," *Mobilization: An International Journal* 5: 1, 2000; Andrews, *Dissenting Japan*, 123ff.

34 It is usually called "stable growth." See Takafusa Nakamura, *The Postwar Japanese Economy: Its Development and Structure, 1937–1994*, 2nd ed., Tokyo: University of Tokyo Press, 1995, Part III.

the other hand, the first moves toward the asset-price bubble in the late 1980s,[35] which in turn prepared *their*—the capitalists'—two lost decades, in which we also necessarily became entangled.[36] It also began the gradual process toward the formation of the neoliberal and rentier-financial capitalist system now globally in full bloom, while the generation of the Zenkyōtō—demographically speaking, baby boomers (or what is called the *dankai no sedai* [generation of mass society])—seems, quite ironically for the younger generations especially, now to be *the last beneficiaries* of the regime that the '68ers tried to dismantle, from the viewpoint of the bio-economic state apparatuses such as the pension system and so on. In the course of all this, we also encountered the two major ends: that is, the self-defeating and seemingly sudden collapse of the Cold War regime and the orthodox Marxism (that is, the many versions of Stalinism) associated with it, on the one hand; and the *natural* end of the *Showa* era, "The Japan of Hirohito," on the other.[37]

An Unavoidable Trauma

1972: no matter how traumatic it is, it can only be an overture. I will simply quote a free-style *tanka* [poem] first:

> The younger brother [*otōto*] screams, facing the death of his elder [*ani*]:
> "In the end, even *sōkatsu* [self-critique] couldn't save anybody!"

35 In fact, it is very important to describe and define the early 1980s in relation to the defeat of the '68, but here is not the place to do so. Simply put, however, the early '80s connects the two phases not simply chronologically but in the sense that it was the era of government austerity measures (administrative reform)—anticipating the recent neoliberal policies—promoted by Prime Minister Nakasone Yasuhiro under the global trend toward neoliberalism (e.g., Thatcherism and Reaganomics) by way of financial deregulation and globalization, and, as the result of that, the Japanese National Railways, Nippon Telegraph and Telephone Public Corporation, and Japan Tobacco and Salt Public Corporation were privatized. For the labor unions in turn, the early 1980s was therefore the last crucial phase where they could *remain and deserve* to be labor unions in the strict sense of the word. See Nakamura, *The Postwar Japanese Economy*, Chapter 7.

36 Originally the capitalist stagnation was simply called the "lost decade," starting from late 1991 after the collapse of asset-price bubble of the late 1980s and "ending" in 2000, but recently another consecutive decade (from 2001 to 2010) was added to it and they came to be called the "lost two decades."

37 See "Showa: The Japan of Hirohito," *Daedalus: Journal of the American Academy of Arts and Sciences*, 119: 3, 1990.

The writer is Sakaguchi Hiroshi, one of the top-ranking leaders of the United Red Army and a death-row convict charged with sixteen counts of murder and one of manslaughter. The "big brother [*ani*]" here is the eldest of the three Katō brothers [*Katō san-kyōdai*], three famed siblings who all joined the URA. Katō Yoshitaka is his name. He was executed/lynched under the name of *sō*katsu, or [self-criticism] at the URA's mountain base.[38] And the "younger brother" [*otōto*] is the youngest of three, only fifteen years old at that moment. His name is Katō Motohisa. He joined the URA together with Yoshitaka and the second brother, Katō Michinori. Motohisa and Michinori attempted to escape from the mountain base together after Yoshitaka's death but failed. As a result, Motohisa and Michinori were forced to hold a Mt. Asama lodge employee hostage in the URA's final stand against the police, and they were finally arrested after having "accomplished" [*kantetsu*] their ten-day "revolutionary war," together with three other surviving comrades. The *tanka* I quote above, freely deconstructing the traditional rules of *tanka*, succeeds in materializing the desperate and grievous scream that exploded from Motohisa during the shootout at the Mt. Asama lodge.[39] Nothing more can be added to it.

The second epigraph, wherein Michinori writes, "I was forced into despair with myself," comes from the book he published after having served out his sentence.[40] He continued to write:

> So many horrifying, gruesome lynchings in the name of *sōkatsu*. And at long last, my brother ended his short life of just twenty or so years right before my eyes. It was an occurrence I couldn't believe, but a hard fact I had to accept. And yet *I don't want to be defeated by this absurd ordeal which forced my brother to accept his own death*.[41]

38 *Sōkatsu* is the "process of ideological evaluation, discussion and conflict leading towards consensus; it took on a new destructive form within *Rengō Sekigun*." Andrews, *Dissenting Japan*, xxi, 139ff. See also Christopher Perkins, *The United Red Army On Screen*, Chapter 3.

39 For the URA, in addition to Andrews' *Dissenting Japan*, see Yoshikuni Igarashi, "Dead Bodies and Living Guns: The United Red Army and Its Deadly Pursuit of Revolution, 1971–1972," *Japanese Studies* 27: 2, 2007; and Perkins, *The United Red Army On Screen*, 34ff.

40 He was sentenced to thirteen years' imprisonment in 1983 and released on parole in 1987. He was underage when arrested.

41 Katō Michinori, *Rengō Sekigun Shōnen A* [The United Red Army: Boy A], 8, my emphasis. From his narratives, I cannot see why he so smoothly made this giant leap toward armed struggle. It looks as if he even made no decision. But what is more important here is that it was an even more merciless experience than the Moscow trials for the revolutionaries, since it was defined by the "executers/leaders" as "death by defeatism." See Patricia G. Steinhoff, "Death by Defeatism and Other Fables: The Social Dynamics of the Rengō

I had no TV set in my flat at that moment, so I watched in the dining room of my friend's boarding house. I was just excited by the *armed* character of this so-called revolutionary struggle against power that was developing in real time at Mt. Asama Lodge without being able to imagine the next scene to come, where heaps of corpses were meticulously, *literally dug up* in the snowy mountainside. It was broadcast in a scandalously dramatized manner.

It is possible that "they" had the complete information about "it" in advance. "They" might have been on the watch for an apt timing through which to *expose* "it" visually to the public through the media. It might have been strategically devised to express the Hamletic ruse that the type of brutal tragedy the public are most fond of had already taken place from the beginning. It was always already finished when it surfaced. It was actually a bloody dramatization with a deliberately manufactured scenario to shatter and dispirit us all.[42] To borrow the title of Gil Scott-Heron's masterpiece—released in 1970—and change its tense, "The Revolution Has Not Been Televised"! Its connotation is exactly the same as his original title: "The Revolution Will Not Be Televised."

In the cold winter of 1972, we were obliged to stand, riveted to this overt revelation of the end of the '68 as "the structure of a defeat," which took place *not* on the streets—actually, that was almost over already—but through live television.[43] I felt as if it were the last notice delivered from the side of power to the public through TV, and this bloody "structure of defeat" in turn gave rise to stark reactions—deeply apolitical reactions—that lasted throughout the 1970s *on both sides*: taking various forms or types of violent struggles such as *uchi geba* [the internal killings between sectarian groups], the armed struggle of the Higashi Ajia Han'nichi Busō Sensen [East Asia Anti-Japanese Armed Front], and other non-sectarian radicals (so-called black-helmet groups),[44] on

Sekigun Purge," *Japanese Social Organization*, ed. Takie Sugiyama Lebra, Honolulu: University of Hawaii Press, 1992; and Perkins, *The United Red Army on Screen*.

42 The entire left, except the JCP and Kakumaru-ha [Japan Revolutionary Communist League Revolutionary Marxist Faction] kept silent, as far as I can remember. Of course, the JCP and Kakumaru-ha heaped all sorts of abuse on the URA.

43 It is said that "the ratings for NHK [Japan Broadcasting Corp]'s non-stop coverage averaged 50.8 per cent and peaked at 89.7 per cent at 6:26 p.m. Vehicle traffic was noticeably lighter throughout the day in Tokyo," see wikipedia.org/wiki/Asama-Sanșō_incident, (accessed September 1, 2017).

44 The so-called black-helmet groups are not necessarily anarchists in Japan; almost all of them are "non-sect radicals." See Fukashiro Junrō, "The New Left," *Japan Quarterly* 17: 1, 1970, 29.

the one hand; and, as I will mention carefully in the concluding remarks, another instance of the incessant self-revolutionization of capital, which incorporated into its function the fruits gathered "unknowingly" by the '68ers or "radical dissidents" of the period.

Actually "it" just happened, or rather *surfaced*, just two months after my discharge from a short stay with the police. I was just a non-sectarian lumpen kid who was pumped up by struggling on the streets—*tan-geba*, or "simple violence" (*Gewalt*)—together with nomadic non-sectarian urban activists gathering from every corner in Tokyo[45] and spreading out.[46] At the time, I was still wondering if I should matriculate to university and leave the *joyous* streets, but I was also well aware that the streets I experienced and experimented with myself were almost gone except for the "scheduled struggles" [*sukejūru tōsō*] set up by the above-ground sections of certain New Left groups.[47] Around 1971–2 was the year of the final disappearance of those streets and that of the clandestine move of the New Left groups that seriously tried to accomplish "world revolution,"[48] but with the mute and hard lesson of the URA case in mind.[49]

In fact, a few months before, a documentary film called *Red Army/PFLP: Declaration of World War*, by Wakamatsu Kōji and Adachi Masao[50] was widely screened and propagandized by the so-called Red

45 As Andrews quotes in the epigraph for his book, "Revolutionary events generally take place in the street"; it is the urban street where everything takes place. Henri Lefebvre, *The Urban Revolution*, Foreword Neil Smith, trans. Robert Bononno, Minneapolis: University of Minnesota Press, 2003, 19.

46 To be sure, we enjoyed even in Japan something akin to what Badiou calls the "libertarian May" together with the "red flag" on the streets, accepting, of course, "violence" that "may well have been defensive and anti-repressive." Badiou, *The Communist Hypothesis*, 46–7, 49, 54–5. See also Nakano Masao, *Gebaruto jidai since 1967–1973* [The Days of Gewalt Since 1967–1973], City: Chikuma Bunko, 2011. Nakano's is the most *badass* recollection (as a literary work) that vividly documents those pleasant and joyful yet sad and tough days.

47 No one can deny that the '70 Anpō protest did not get into swing (see Ōmori Shigeo, "June 1970," *Japan Quarterly* 17: 4, 1970). For the struggles against the so-called Okinawa *Reversion* Agreement, there is a lot of literature; see, for example, Patricia G. Steinhoff, "Student Conflict," *Conflict in Japan*, in E.S. Krauss, T.P. Rohlen, and P.G. Steihoff, eds. Honolulu: University of Hawaii Press, 1984; Miyume Tanji, *Myth, Protest and Struggle in Okinawa*, London: Routledge, 2006; and Andrews, *Dissenting Japan*, Chapter 5.

48 For the "world revolution" and the Bund (New Left groups in Japan), see Kenji Hasegawa, "In Search of a New Radical Left: The Rise and Fall of the Anpō Bund, 1955–1960," *Stanford Journal of East Asian Affairs* 3: 1, 2003.

49 The URA is an "unprincipled coalition" between the Sekigun-ha [Red Army Faction], which was descended from the Bund and the Kakumei Saha [Revolutionary Left]. As was pointed out, Sekigun-ha has been aiming at the "world revolution," but the Kakumei Saha upheld the line of anti-Americanism and patriotism [*hanbei aikokushugi*].

50 *Red Army/PFLP: Declaration of World War*, by Kōji Wakamatsu and Masao Adachi, 1971, available at YouTube.

Bus [Aka-basu] activists. Those who were exhausted and frustrated by the "official" end or wasting away of '68—especially non-sectarian radical street activists—became ideal targets for recruitment, not only by the Japanese Red Army (JRA), but also by other radical groups upholding the line of armed struggle;[51] since the street culture of protest was gone and New Left groups went underground, this recruitment was often carried out through personal relations, or what we called then "pole-and-line fishing" [*ippon-zuri*].

The very smell of the air had changed, and everything seemed to be bound up by closedness and suffocation. New forms of repression and *sanitization*, such as *apāto rōrā-sakusen*, the hunting of activists through door-to-door campaigns conducted by the police and neighborhood associations [Chōnaikai]—which informed on "unusual" or simply eccentric neighbors as potential "extremists"—were rapidly underway.[52] In other words, blatant interpellations overwhelmed the streets. For example, we could no longer stop by diners on the way back from the street with helmets and red flags. It was clear, even for us: around 1972, not only campuses but everywhere that was a place of the left, or even simply a countercultural neighborhood space, had already become either a battleground of armed conflict between the sectarian organizations or a police-led calm and clean "non-event" space.[53] New Left groups were hunted down, went underground, and became clandestine, largely abandoning or being forced out of the sites that they knew. Activists of those days often described their retreat as a "recall" [*shōkan*] from the front.[54] Therefore, I cannot

51 For the JRA, see Patricia G. Steinhoff, "Hijackers, Bombers and Bank Robbers: Managerial Style in the Japanese Red Army," *Journal of Asian Studies* 48: 4, 1989.

52 For the (political) functions of Chōnaikai, see, for example, Theodore C. Bestor, "Tradition and Japanese Social Organization: Institutional Development in a Tokyo Neighborhood," *Ethnology* 24: 2, 1985.

53 As Koizumi Yoshiyuki eloquently documents in this volume, even in the JCP, there was a split—the so-called "New Opportunism" faction problem—and the purge associated with it around 1972. See Kawakami Tōru, *Samon* [*Inquisition*], Chikuma shobō, 2001.

54 It is sometimes misunderstood as the recantation [*tenkō*] (see Andrews, *Dissenting Japan*, 93ff.), but, to be fair, and since I think the concept of *tenkō* does not work anymore here, I have to touch on the other directions that emerged after the post-'68: that is, a kind of the Japanese version of "rustication," such as the antipollution movements, becoming local government servants for the people, antidiscrimination front, "*yoseba* activism," and so on. For the "*yoseba* activism," see Andrews, *Dissenting Japan*, 195, 264–5; and Brett de Bary, "Sanya: Japan's Internal Colony" in *The Other Japan*. For the prewar *tenkō*, Patricia G. Steinhoff, *Tenkō: Ideology and Societal Integration in Prewar Japan*, New York: Garland Publishing, 1991; and Richard H. Mitchell, *Thought Control in Prewar Japan*, Ithaca: Cornell University Press, 1976.

contradict the following statement of both White and Steinhoff below:

> In effect, the people gave the police carte blanche to repress what came to be seen as *homicidal radicals*, not students with reasonable demands . . . The result was a nonevent: the treaty "struggle" was effectively over by the time of the treaty's renewal in the summer of 1970, and the radical students have not since the early 1970s been able to mount a significant attack on the system much less generate popular support.[55]
>
> The retrospective negative collective memory of the whole period of student conflict has served to reinforce the outcome in favor of social order and helped to weaken the potential for social conflict over the still unresolved issues for several decades.[56]

It has also been reported, based on a famous survey conducted in 1997, that "the number one reason" why people "had left student activism was *uchi-geba*, or internal killings [24.8 percent]. The reason with the second highest number of responses was the Rengō Sekigun [URA] purge [16.9 percent]."[57] An ex-activist states:

> I felt that the New Left that I knew and supported was over . . . I tried to put on a brave face for a while but it didn't work . . . It was as if my voluntary muscles were working, but my involuntary muscles didn't . . . I pulled out of all the activities of the movement.[58]

And another activist also recollects her reaction in the face of the exposed URA Purge:

> I shuddered with its horror. Such a thing—mutual critique and self-criticism—was frequent and common among every group in those days, even if it didn't lead to murder. That made it all the more horrific.[59]

---

55 James W. White, "The Dynamics of Political Opposition," *Postwar Japan as History*, ed. Andrew Gordon, Berkeley: University of California Press, 1993, 437, my emphasis.

56 Patricia G. Steinhoff, "Memories of New Left protest," *Contemporary Japan* 25: 2, 2013, 163.

57 Andrews, *Dissenting Japan*, 98, 161. The original source is Zenkyōtō Hakusho Henshū I'inkai ed., *Zenkyōtō Hakusho* [Zenkyōtō Whitepaper], Shinchōsha, 1994, 413.

58 Shibata Hiromi and Akane Saburō, *Zenkyōtō*, Kawadeshobōshinsha, 2003, 127.

59 *Zenkyōtō Hakusho*, 49.

The dysfunction of what are here called "involuntary muscles" could result from a deep somatic trepidation, but I would also insist that it arose from another trepidation: the fear of the possibility that one could, in fact, have been "them" and could have done what "they" did. It is precisely this that "made it all the more horrific." After some time, a rumor spread in the neighborhoods of the left, which had it that Michinori, the second brother of the Katō trio, was born in 1952. He is the exact same age as me. I also came to know eventually that Michinori was a high school classmate of my close friend at the university I entered after my own "recall" [*shōkan*] from the front. In this sense, Michinori was my contemporary and *my unknown neighbor*. The reason I make a personal detour here is exactly the following hard fact: not only in relation to the URA purge but concerning later *uchi geba* or internal killings as well, it was "right out there" for anyone who was more or less involved with the left movements at that time.[60] In other words, we cannot regard it as an exception; it belongs to the structure of '68. Everyone could have been Katō. We could have been members of the URA, the JRA, the radical clandestine groups that rapidly bloomed after 1972, or the New Left groups obsessed with internal violence throughout the '70s.[61] Especially for the *hamegoroshi* generation, it was an experience of actuality because they witnessed its deep cleavages, its openings with still-blurred demarcations, right before their eyes; in other words, they happened to arrive both too late and too early.

In this way, the defeat of the '68 revolt need not be declared aloud because of, or in spite of, the URA tragedy; it was enough just to be whispered. The problem therefore was, far from thinking simply about how to start over from this impaired beginning, to find a way out to remake a new beginning,[62] not by repeating a disavowal of the defeat

60 Ueno Chizuko talked about her trauma like this: "Not just for me, Rengō Sekigun was a real trauma for my generation. We avoided it. We didn't want to see it, hear about it or discuss it." (cited in Andrews, *Dissenting Japan*, 146. The original source is Ueno Chizuko and Kanō Mikiyo, "Dialogue—Feminist and Violence: Between Tanaka Mitsu and Nagata Hiroko," *"Revolution" as Lib*, Tokyo: Inpakuto Shuppan, 2003, 6.

61 Many told me their own experiences of visitors at night knocking on their flat doors. The visitors—almost all of them were not student activists but the members of the Residential Area Antiwar Youth Committee [Chiku Hansen Seinen I'inkai] who were already ready to go underground—showed their weapons like iron pipes and tried to persuade others to go underground for the "war" to come [*uchi geba*]. As to the development of the Antiwar Youth Committee, see Fukashiro Junrō, "The New Left," 31–2.

62 Slavoj Žižek, "How to Begin From the Beginning," in *The Idea of Communism*, eds. Costas Douzinas and Slavoj Žižek, London: Verso, 2010. As to the remaking of the beginning, I clearly remember a reasonable, compelling and encouraging comment from Tanaka

like the postwar Japanese who, along with their government, nonchalantly replaced the *defeat* of the war with the *end* of the war,[63] but by enduring *this unembraceable defeat that is not one.*[64]

To be sure, there might be what Badiou calls the "double obsessive fear" of "May '68": the strict "conceptualization" such as "a tendency towards *political formalism*" coming directly from scientific structuralism (for example, Althusser), on the one hand, and the "poetic surge" of society (for example, the stylish graffiti slogans, "*Sous les pavés la plage*," "*demandez l'impossible*," and so forth) on the other. Badiou concludes, in a bit of a contrived fashion, that "May '68 has Frege on the one hand and Rimbaud on the other. Its singularity, that is the mixture of the two."[65] But we have neither Frege nor Rimbaud, and therefore no mélange of both as its marker of "singularity."[66] All

---

Mitsu. She said, immediately after the URA disaster, in the postscript for her seminal work, that "armed struggle principally seeks power, but where are all those morons yelling 'armed struggle, armed struggle!' when power itself wants to render the entire movement clandestine? At least in the forms of armed struggle that roused certain sectors of the New Left, it was literally nothing but a waste of life." See Tanaka, *Inochi no onna tachi e*, 338. According to the copyright page, it was written after the exposure of Rengō Sekigun purge and before April 25, 1972.

63 See Yutaka Nagahara, "The Corporeal Principle of the National Polity: The Rhetoric of the National Polity, or, the Nation as Memory Machine," trans. Gavin Walker, *Perversion in Modern Japan: Experiments in Psychoanalysis and Literature*, eds. Nina Cornyetz and Keith Vincent, New York: Routledge, 2009.

64 When I say "the unembraceable defeat which is not one," I first of all have in mind the second defeat that immediately ensued from the defeat in World War II and the so-called "reverse course": that is, the defeat of the postwar revolution, whose mainstay was the labor movement, led by the JCP, and its kernel was the struggle for "production control." On production control, see Joe Moore, *Japanese Workers and the Struggle for Power 1945–1947*, Madison: University of Wisconsin Press, 1983, and "Production Control: Workers' Control in Early Postwar Japan," in *The Other Japan*; and John Price, "Production Control: Workers' Control in Early Postwar Japan," in ibid. For the "reverse course," see Evelyn S. Colbert, *The Left Wing in Japanese Politics*, New York: Institute of Pacific Relations, 1952; Henry Oinas-Kukkonen, *Tolerance, Suspicion, and Hostility: Changing US Attitudes toward the Japanese Communist Movement, 1944–1947*, Westport: Greenwood Press, 2003; and Lonny E. Carlile, *Divisions of Labor: Globality, Ideology, and War in the Shaping of the Japanese Labor Movement*, Honolulu: University of Hawaii Press, 2005.

65 Aliocha Wald Lasowski and Alain Badiou, "De la singularité de l'événement à Mai '68: les sens de l'universel," *Labyrinthe* 32, 2009, 151.

66 We also have such a poetic aspect in the form of "graffiti" that the Zenkyōtō left on the walls of Yasuda Hall in the University of Tokyo at Hongō campus, such as "Seek solidarity and don't fear isolation." This phrase is borrowed from an essay by the famous poet Tanigawa Gan, "Kōsakusha no shitai ni moeru mono [That Which Germinates on the Corpse of Operative] in *Tanigawa Gan no shigoto* [Works of Tanigawa Gan], Book I, Tokyo: Kawade Shobō Shinsha, 1996 (1958), 114. As to Tanigawa, see Gavin Walker, "Tanigawa Gan and the Poetics of the Origin," *positions: asia critique* 25: 2, 2017; Wesley

that was overwhelming at that moment was the frightened or even fanatical seriousness [*maji*] with its pressing silence, and the criticisms of the extremisms of New Left groups used as negative examples of '68 in an attempt to deliver the Zenkyōtō movements from disaster; it is exactly this seriousness, joined to a frenzied muteness that, to tell the truth, actually irritated not merely the post-'68ers but even the *hamegoroshi* generation as well,[67] and therefore the problem is how to decipher the fact that this strictness and seriousness caused such mutual damage.[68]

Sasaki-Uemura, "Tanigawa Gan's Politics of the Margin in Kyushu and Nagano," *positions: east asia cultures critique* 7: 1, 1999, and *Organizing the Spontaneous: Citizen Protest in Postwar Japan*, Honolulu: University of Hawaii Press, 2001, 93–4.

67 Truthfully, I was sick and tired of "their" seriousness [*maji*] when I discovered an old slogan on the wall of the main agitating point of Building No. 7 (the so-called Nanahon) in Komaba campus (University of Tokyo) that was squatted together by the non-sectarian groups (black helmets) and the remnants of Tōdai Zenkyōtō. It said, "*Bunshōka seyo!*" [Document and Compose!] I hated this kind of pushy and enlightened seriousness. In that sense, also, I disliked the so-called *jiko hitei* [the denial of the self], *shutaisei* [subjectivity] *tachibasei* [positionality] etc. often stressed by Zenkyōtō people, too, because they seemed so conceited and self-important. All of them were very *uzai* [heavy/gloomy]. For the *jiko hitei*, see Guy Thomas Yasko, *The Japanese Student Movement, 1968–1970: The Zenkyōtō Uprising*, Ann Arbor: UMP, 1998, Chapter 2. As to the two types (of ethos?) of Zenkyōtō, see Takemasa Ando, *Japan's New Left Movements: Legacies for Civil Society*, London: Routledge, 2014, 68–76. He grasps the characteristics of Nichidai [Nihon University] Zenkyōtō as "self-liberation" and that of the University of Tokyo as "self-reflection," which I find superficial and clichéd. I would recommend Ando to read Nagasaki Hiroshi's "Gimanteki de jiyūna gerira" [The deceptive and free guerrilla] in *Kessha to Gijutsu* [Association and Techne], Tokyo: Jōkyō Shuppan, 1971.

68 For example, for us left-oriented high school or prep-school boys and girls, books such as Oku Kōhei, *Seishun no bohyō* [The Grave Marker of Adolescence] (Tokyo: Bungeishunjūsha, 1965) were canonical "tools," along with Boris Savinkov (*Memoirs of a Terrorist* and *The Pale Horse*), and George Orwell (*Homage to Catalonia* and *Animal Farm*). They were frequently exploited to organize [*oruguru*] young, naïve kids. To be honest, I was moved by Oku's work, but at the same time flinched at his "seriousness." For Oku, see, Fukashiro, "Student Thought and Feeling," 152–3. About this situation, Andrews describes it as follows: "As true for Anpō 1960 as it was even more so for the later student and New Left activists, these young people had *an innate seriousness and asceticism* . . . Though not immune to *tenkō* [recantation], their commitment was by and large pure and devout" (Andrews, *Dissenting Japan*, 70, my emphasis). Innate or not, they tended toward a cheap mobilization of the theory of alienation, which can easily touch the heartstrings and raise righteous indignation against social injustice; then they took to the streets, to encounter the riot police *in order to be able to reify themselves as militants*. After all, the streets are the school of revolution. One report tells us apropos of the '70 Anpō that a student activist at a local university dissuaded "an uncommitted student from leaving the strife-torn campus for a picnic," saying that "to go now implies your submission to power which, in turn, means your abandonment of living. The question is whether or not you will live as a human being" (Fukashiro, "Student Thought and Feeling," 151). A familiar scene at that time!

I strategically started *our* narrative of '68 in Japan with the worst, and its "dismal dead end" in 1972 from an unfamiliar viewpoint—that of the *hamegoroshi* generation. We can never let go of starting all over from *here*. We have no choice but to reset the entire problem of asking how the structure descended onto the streets in the form of defeat and that of coping with the ways in which the capitalist incorporation of this structural defeat was realized as the successful "inversion" of what the '68ers *unknowingly* tried to gain,[69] as Luc Boltanski and Eve Chiapello somewhat misleadingly insinuated.[70] For that, however, the next step is to go back a few years and read how the structure was observed through the eyes of economics.

"It" Simply Took *Place*

"It" seemed to take *place* explosively, all on its own. For the observer, it appeared to be an unexpected upsurge and rapid expansion, but I have to be very quick to add that it was due to the "pressure of circumstances" [*Druck der Verhältnisse*], as well.[71] In other words, it was not simply a sort of miracle but the result of patient and cumulative interventions into micro-situations—factories, classrooms, and the streets[72]—from the non-sectarian independent agitators, the *jichikai* [autonomous student

69 The word "invert" is a usual translation of the German *umstülpen* in the Marx industry because it is connected to the Marx who declared the "inversion" of the "dead dog" [toten Hund]. But I have to quote the German version of *Das Kapital* here in order to undeceive the misleading English translation of the German *umstülpen*. Marx actually writes: "Sie steht bei ihm auf dem Kopf. Man muß sie *umstülpen*, um den rationellen Kert in der mystischen Hülle zu entdecken" (Karl Marx, *Das Kapital*, Erster Band, Buch I, Berlin: Dietz Verlag 1993, S.27). The *umstülpen* should be translated literally as "turn inside out" or "roll up" in order to see what is inside because, as Jacques Bidet correctly pointed out, of the Hegelian heritage still haunting Marx. See Jacques Bidet, *Exploring Marx's* Capital: *Philosophical, Economic and Political Dimensions*, trans. David Fernbach, foreword by Alex Callinicos, Leiden: Brill, 2007. I am saying this to go back to the relation between the Deleuzian '68 and the Badiouian '68.

70 Luc Botanski and Eve Chiapello, *The New Spirit of Capitalism*, trans. Gregory Elliott, London: Verso, 2005 (1999), to which I will return in the concluding remarks.

71 Karl Marx, *Capital*, Vol. 1, Harmondsworth: Penguin, 1976, 414.

72 Badiou said about the working class that "given its scale and its general features, the [general] strike took place, in historical terms, *in a very different context from the youth rebellion*" (*The Communist Hypothesis*, 47). For the relations between the New Left in Japan and the labor unions, see Tozuka Hideo et al., *Nihon niokeru 'Shin-Sayoku' no Rōdō Undō* ["New Left" Labour Movements in Japan], 2 vols., Tokyo: Tokyo Daigaku Shuppankai, 1976.

council] activists, or the professional organizers who were sent from the reconstructed New Left after the defeat of the 1960 Anpō struggles.[73]

It was reported, for instance, that "the number of universities involved in major disputes was 6 in 1961, 10 in 1962, 9 in 1963, 13 in 1964, and the figure swelled to *50 in 1965*,"[74] and this rapid upsurge of heightened political tension prepared the ground for the actual arrival of the '70 Anpō, which, paradoxically, paved the way for '68. I have to say, in order to avoid an unnecessary misunderstanding, that '68 was not a simple preliminary skirmish in advance of the '70 Anpō protests or the struggle against the so-called reversion of Okinawa; it simply took place independently, yet in a connected manner.[75] According to the *Asahi Shimbun* Public Opinion Survey, conducted on October 29 and 30, 1968, the "disputes arose in some 110 schools, *more than 10 per cent* of the nation's 845 colleges and universities ... In 65 of these schools, the disputes were still unresolved on 1 January 1969."[76] It was

73 Yamamoto Yoshitaka (a chairperson of Tōdai Zenkyōtō) is absolutely right in saying that the Tōdai Zenkyōtō was "beautified or deified as an 'organization of independent [*jiritsu-shita*] individuals,' but it is a bit of a rose-colored portrait. It was actually a complicated relation that was composed of activists of several political parties and non-sectarian activists" (Yamamoto Yoshitaka, *Watashi no 1960 nendai* [My 1960s], Tokyo: Kin'yōbi, 2015, 149). As to Nichidai Zenkyōtō, Mihashi Toshiaki claims that "I became a member of Nichidai Zenkyōtō by the action I myself have chosen, and I did nothing more than claim to be a member [without any permission from Nichidai Zenkyōtō]"; Mihashi Toshiaki, *Rojō no Zenkyōtō* [Zenkyōtō on the Street], Tokyo: Kawadeshobōshinsha, 2010, 12.

74 Fukashiro Junrō, "Student Thought and Feeling," *Japan Quarterly* 16: 2, 1969, 148, my emphasis. 1965 was the year of the so-called Nikkan Tōsō (the struggle against the Treaty on Basic Relations between Japan and the Republic of Korea).

75 However, at the same time, I have to question Suga Hidemi who wants to privilege '68. Suga insists that it's misleading or even wrong to confound '68 with the '70 Anpō protests. According to him, this confusion is derived from the delusion of some people who project the illusion of the '60 Anpō onto '68. He justifies his insistence in saying that the '70 Anpō was scheduled for automatic renewal. I would agree with Suga in that he emphasizes the difference between '68 and the '70 Anpō protests, but if that is the case, then Suga should persuade Andrews, who correctly describes that "after all, the 1960 treaty was merely a revision of the earlier pact that had been signed in 1951" (Andrews, *Dissenting Japan*, 26), and in this sense, the '60 Anpō is not different from the '70 Anpō. See also Ōmori, "June 1970," 389ff.

76 "The *Asahi Shimbun* Public Opinion Surveys: Strife in the Universities," *Japan Quarterly* 16: 2, 1969, 157, emphasis mine. Please note that the date was just before the apex (qua demise) of the Zenkyōtō movements. Zenkoku Zenkyōtō [National Zenkyōtō] was established on September 5, 1969 in the Hibiya Open-Air Concert Hall (the so-called Hibiya Yaon) and Yamamoto Yoshitaka was elected as the chairperson hiding underground and in his absence. There are various evaluations of the National Zenkyōtō regarding the interventions and the internal struggles of New Left groups: the National Zenkyōtō became the hegemonic space for the New Left groups, and as a result, the non-sectarian radicals

also reported that, "behind the disputes," various problems existed, yet almost all of these seemed to be still *apolitical or moderate*. But, at the same time, it appropriately highlights the fact that:

> The disputes have usually flared up over some minor point which in the course of argument has been blown up into a major issue, the situation being further aggravated by lack of foresight and reluctance to act on the part of university officials.[77]

As far as the Tōdai Zenkyōtō is concerned, as Nagasaki—who frequently put forward his theory of the agitator's *techne* and organization of revolt from the ongoing evental site as a "veteran" of the '60 Anpō protest—adeptly sorts out in this volume, it "flared up," was "blown up," "further aggravated," and in turn became the hard object of politics embodied in concrete slogans, which finally ignited the events that were rapidly to come.[78]

> The unaligned students take no part in the factional struggle [especially between the JCP and New Left groups] but, by and large, their sympathies are with the striking students. As this survey shows, many avoid participation in the violence; but their growing dissatisfaction with the universities has given rise to disputes, and contributes, though indirectly, to the prolongation of the strife.[79]

But what is more interesting here is the students' reaction toward the so-called Shinjuku Incident of October 21, 1968 [the Shinjuku Sōran,

---

literally *recalled themselves from the movements*. Thus, some said that the date of establishing the National Zenkyōtō is that of the end of the Zenkyōtō movement. See Yasko, *The Japanese Student Movement*, Chapter 6.

77 The issues taken up were: 1) the problem of tuition fees; 2) democratization of the universities; 3) the problem of the dormitories; 4) the demands for new and improved facilities; 5) the problem of centralization and relocation of university buildings; 6) the dissatisfaction with university presidents and members of academic governing boards; 7) the internship system for medical students; 8) demands for revocation of disciplinary measures taken against students; 9) student participation; and 10) discrimination in exams. For the selection of teaching personnel, see "The *Asahi Shimbun* Public Opinion Surveys: Strife in the Universities," 157.

78 For the Tōdai Zenkyōtō, see Donald Frederick Wheeler, "The Japanese Student Movement: Value Politics, Student Politics and the Tokyo University Struggle," PhD diss., Columbia University, 1974; Yasko, *The Japanese Student Movement*; and Andrews, *Dissenting Japan*, Chapter 4.

79 "The *Asahi Shimbun* Public Opinion Surveys,"157.

literally Shinjuku Riot].[80] The survey reports that "more than half of those surveyed at all four universities were opposed to the demonstration of 21 of October," mainly because of its "violence," but the point is rather:

> Though as many as 20 per cent of those at Tokyo University supported the demonstration, only 10 per cent of those at the other universities shared the view. Reasons given for support included *"we have the right to hold meetings and demonstrations," "there is no other way to protest against modern society" and "the government and the riot police are bad."*[81]

Apart from evaluating whether the number 20 percent is high, and whether "*only*" 10 per cent is actually low—and I believe it is nonsense to talk solely about some numerical calculation of the question—what is at stake here is that they politically came to think or *sense*, starting from and gradually overcoming their familiar and everyday complaints, and then moving to some sort of leap, that "there is no other way to protest against modern society," which signifies that the problem *overflowed* from the previous sites.

As I will touch on shortly regarding the theories of the political subject in the class struggle hammered out in the specificity of the postwar Japanese situation, the minority often works on and agitates the majority situation, and this political intervention has been painstakingly carried out at least since the defeat of the '60 Anpō protests. A commentator takes up, from the viewpoint of the postwar political processes, the fact of "the nonexistence of genuinely revolutionary left-wing forces in Japan" as the major cause of the *independent* upsurge of the student movements.[82] Concerning this point, John Dower indicates the critical issue at stake: "Despite polemic of the most vitriolic sort, postwar Japan never was split into completely unbridgeable ideological camps" under the postwar regime formed since 1955 by the San Francisco System and the 1955 System, which acted as "code words for the peculiar capitalist context, overseas and at home,"[83] and both of

80 For Shinjuku Sōran, see Andrews, *Dissenting Japan*, Chapter 5.

81 "The *Asahi Shimbun* Public Opinion Surveys," 167. My emphasis.

82 Fukashiro Junrō, "Student Thought and Feeling," *Japan Quarterly* 16: 2, 150, emphasis mine.

83 John W. Dower, "Peace and Democracy in Two Systems: External Policy and Internal Conflict," in *Ways of Forgetting, Ways of Remembering*, New York: New Press, 2012, 189–90. Dower defines the "1955 System" as one that "signifies a domestic political structure characterized by an internally competitive but nonetheless hegemonic conservative establishment and a marginalized but sometimes influential liberal and Marxist opposition."

which have in fact been ultimately backed by the perversely continuing war regime called the 1940 System.[84] As I will touch on shortly, under this situation, those who were expelled and/or defected from the JCP radically took over, together with the students, a crucial and critical part of the class struggle in Japan, especially due to what they understood to be the "betrayal" of the JCP.[85]

Thus, in 1996, approximately three decades after '68 and five years after the burst of the asset-price bubble, in order to review not only the postwar economic processes in particular but the *modernizing* process even since the Meiji Restoration (1868) in general, economist Hamada Kōichi recalled one scene in 1968 to begin a speech.[86] This talk, financially sponsored by Nomura Securities International—which, in turn, let us say, amply demonstrates the "political position" he adhered to by 1996—sounds, nevertheless, as if he yearns for '68. Although I am not interested in whether the young Hamada joined the protest against the Kishi administration in 1960, he actually belongs to the '60 Anpō generation purely in terms of age, and because he was an assistant professor of the University of Tokyo in 1968. Thinking about his current

84 For the "1940 System," which is not so popular as a concept compared to the "San Francisco System" and the "1955 System," see Yukio Noguchi, "The 1940 System: Japan under the Wartime Economy," *American Economic Review* 88: 2, Paper and Proceedings of the Hundred and Tenth Annual Meeting of the American Economic Association, May, 1998, and "Leaving the '1940' System and Moving into a New System," in *The Transformation of the Japanese Economy*, ed. Kazuo Sato, New York: M.E. Sharpe, 1999. As Dower points out, "Both Japan's incorporation into US cold-war policy and the triumph of the conservative elites were evident *from the 1940s* . . . The genesis of both systems is thus *much earlier* than a literal reading of the popular labels would suggest." Dower, "Peace and Democracy in Two Systems," 190. It is an interesting view not only concerning the so-called "reverse course" and the current Abe administration but also the so-called "Client State" (Gavan McCormack, *Client State: Japan in the American Embrace*, annotated version, 2007) because this problem has much to do with the debate on Japanese capitalism in the 1920s and the strategic diverging point between the JCP and New Left.

85 See a compact yet well-framed interpretation of the building of the Bund in relation to the betrayal of the JCP after such extremism as the Sanson Kōsakutai [Mountain Village Operation Corps] movement and the drastic strategy change (deradicalization) of the Sixth Congress of the JCP (1955), including long-standing problems such as the strategy of anti-Americanism and/or anti-Japanism in the postwar revolution (which reemerged as the Higashi Ajia Han'nichi Busō Sensen under a new guise); see Hasegawa, "In Search of a New Radical Left," and "Anti-American Nationalism and Leftist Factionalism in 1950 and 1960 Japan," *Journal of the International Student Center, Yokohama National University*, 18, 2011.

86 Hamada Kōichi was born in 1936, is Tuntex Emeritus Professor of Economics at Yale University and an economic advisor of the Abe administration (the so-called Abenomics).

political status, it is a bit surprising that he starts his arguments with a prosaic statement: "I still remember an Indian-summer day in 1968 when I sat on the steps of the economics building at the University of Tokyo."[87]

This sort of pastoral scene in the Tokyo autumn, which Hamada reminisces over, rapidly culminated in the battle of Yasuda Tower at the University of Tokyo's Hongō campus.[88] But the "prologue" of his paper read at Yale seems full of nostalgic or even bittersweet recollections of the Tōdai Hongō campus at that time and, curiously, there is no direct disparagement against the Tōdai Zenkyōtō; in fact, he even seems somewhat sympathetic to them in an interesting manner:

> *Postwar liberalism in Japan came with the spurt of student movements that peaked around 1968* . . . The student revolt in the late 1960s was *the last spurt of liberalism, and after that liberalism in Japan was about to fade* . . . Japan was cruising on the most rapid growth trajectory in history, but it was *anticipating future changes*. In the socioeconomic sense, 1968 was *a reflection point* of Japan's high growth period.[89]

Although it would be quite easy to do, I am not going to make any ironic remarks that take up Hamada's current involvement with the Abe administration, or pose any cutting questions about what might happen after "liberalism in Japan," and what he meant by saying it "was about to fade."

What is at stake here instead is that Hamada chooses to characterize the Zenkyōtō movement not simply as a catalyst of "postwar liberalism"—which is itself, of course, a very interesting point and one that deserves to be scrutinized as the proper subject of democratization, different from what is often called "postwar democracy" [*sengo minshushugi*]—but as the embodiment of "a reflection point" of "Japan's high-growth period" as well. Of course, it can be interpreted

87 Kōichi Hamada, "Japan 1968: A Reflection Point during the Era of the Economic Miracle," Economic Growth Center, Yale University, Discussion Paper No. 764, August 1996, 1. Gavan McCormack, who stayed in the University of Tokyo from May 1969—immediately after the collapse of Yasuda Tower and the ensuing cancellation of the entrance exam—to August 1970, reported the situation at Tōdai at that moment. See Gavan McCormack, "The Student Left in Japan," *New Left Review* 1/65, 1971.

88 See Shima Taizō, *Yasuda Kōdō 1968–1969* [Yasuda Hall 1968–1969], Chūkōshinsho, 2005 and Steinhoff, "Memories of New Left Protest."

89 Hamada, 2–3, 7, my emphasis.

as the capitalist declaration of a "stable" *victory* announced through the mouthpiece of a political academic, but what must not be overlooked here is the interesting or even *neutral* manner by which he describes the relation between them. That is, he simply writes that "postwar liberalism in Japan came with the spurt of student movements that peaked around 1968" under the section title "Anticipation of Changes"; he merely juxtaposes the two "'68s"—"'68" and 1968, so to speak—in parallel or almost indifferently. That is to say that he, an authoritative mainstream economist, seems careful to not attempt to bring forward any sort of causal chain between the student revolt and "the *last* spurt of liberalism" despite the fact that he closely juxtaposes them and then sees the '68 revolt, at least at Tōdai (Tokyo *Imperial* University), as an event.

In relation to his position, however—which is, of course, likely to be understood from the viewpoint of Japan's high growth—we have to be very cautious not to conflate his juxtaposition of the two with liberals like Oguma Eiji, who manufactured a "phone book"-sized two-volume set on '68 in Japan.[90] In his short English essay, he concludes that "theoretically speaking, the student uprising in Japan in 1968 was a kind of 'reactive revolution' based on an old-fashioned common moral sense" against the rapid economic growth.[91] To make matters worse, his "ideas" and cheaply reductionist conclusion require a peculiar background justification that he attempts to derive, surprisingly, from E.P. Thompson.[92] But it is nothing but an *inverted adaptation* from certain similar simple classifications that Ellis Krauss made regarding the '60 Anpō in 1988. Krauss sees, in a similarly reductionist manner, the '60 Anpō protest as "the crucial transition period to a generation of postindustrial radical youth," and then characterizes "the JCP-dominated

90 Andrews, *Dissenting Japan*, 66, 314. Oguma's book must be criticized or even dismissed not simply for his "being based solely on textual research" but, moreover, for his sloppy and in some sense politically biased textual critiques, which is clearly exposed in his description about the Beheiren (Citizens' Federation for Peace in Vietnam). For the Beheiren, see Thomas R.H. Havens, *Fire Across the Sea: The Vietnam War and Japan 1965–1975*, Princeton: Princeton University Press, 1987.

91 Oguma Eiji, "Japan's 1968: A Collective Reaction to Rapid Economic Growth in an Age of Turmoil," *Asia-Pacific Journal* 13: 12: 1, 2015, 25.

92 E.P. Thompson, "The Moral Economy of the English Crowd in the eighteenth Century," *Past and Present* 50, 1971. If the "reactive revolution" is his own coinage, he should instead refer to the "reactive radicals" discussed in Craig Calhoun, *The Question of Class Struggle: Social Foundations of Popular Radicalism During the Industrial Revolution*, Chicago: University of Chicago Press, 1982, xii–xiii.

student movement (Minsei)" as modernizing,[93] and "the anti-Yoyogi" (that is, anti-JCP) movement as "the emergence of postindustrial youth."[94]

In contrast to Krauss's simplistic model and Oguma's causal repression of an event that radically "evades" history,[95] Hamada, as a conservative economist, *sincerely* concludes his paper with the plain statement that, objectively, "many things that were crucial to explain the basic changes in the Japanese economy in the years shortly to follow were *preparing themselves in 1968*."[96] In a sense, I have already praised Hamada's text too much, but that is because he recognizes on some level that "history grasps in an event *the way it is actualized in particular circumstances*" [*son effectuation dans des états de choses*],[97] which must be strictly defined as *Druck der Verhältnisse* or the "pressure of circumstances." It also resonates, albeit in a conservative manner, with Wallerstein, who accentuates *not* simply what is mistakenly called "the world revolution of 1968," but who carefully stresses that "1968 was a revolution *in and of the world-system*" and its historical "structuredness" was accumulated over a series of events.[98] In relating to this "structuredness," we also have to consider those political interventions that could conceivably turn some accumulated mundane things into a "miracle" event, which, as I previously intimated, has much to do with the practico-theoretical status of the student in the class struggle, newly bestowed by the New Left after the deradicalization of the JCP.

Whether or not Hamada had knowledge of it,[99] it is well known that the JCP traditionally and dogmatically insisted that "students were

93 Nihon Minshu Seinen Dōmei [Democratic Youth League], usually called Minsei Dōmei, is the JCP youth organization.

94 Ellis S. Krauss, "The 1960s' Japanese Student Movement in Retrospect," *Japan and the World: Essays on Japanese History and Politics*, eds. Gail Lee Bernstein, Haruhiro Fukui, Basingstoke: Macmillan, 1988, 112–3.

95 Deleuze, *Negotiations*, 170. Translation modified.

96 Hamada, 21, my emphasis.

97 Deleuze, *Negotiations*, 170. Translation modified.

98 Immanuel Wallerstein, *The Essential Wallerstein*, New York: New Press, 2000, 33, 355. My emphasis.

99 Aoki Masahiko (a.k.a. Himeoka Reiji), two years younger than Hamada and an alumnus of University of Tokyo Economics. He has long titles affiliated with Stanford University, but, what is more important is that he was a leading theoretician of the Bund, and his first book, written at the age of twenty-two—*Nihon kokka dokusen shihonshugi no seiritsu* [The Formation of Japanese State Monopoly Capitalism], Tokyo: Gendaishichōsha, 1960—was canonical for his organization. In this regard, Hamada might have some knowledge of "it" as a form of common sense from those days.

simply a marginal arm of labor" and made them "subordinate to the general party organization of the labor movement." With reference to this "irreconcilable dispute with [the center of] the JCP" over the theory of the main body of militants in the class struggle,[100] Takei Teruo, founder of the Zengakuren, responded to the JCP on the importance of students in the class struggle by proposing a theory he referred to as "students-as-stratum" [sō *toshite no gakusei*], whose practical kernel was that students deserved to be the main *political subject* of the class struggle as a substantial stratum independent of the leadership of the working class and the party.[101] Politically, it amounted to a denial of the idea of the vanguard party, which was obviously unacceptable for the JCP. "Takei's theory" was inherited and more radically modified to cope with the actual situation, such as its utilization during the revolt against the Kishi administration around 1960 by Bund leader Shima Shigeo as the theory of "students as precursor" [*senkusei riron*],[102] which "is actualised in particular circumstances" to make a "miracle-qua-event" happen. It is by the same logic that Deleuze regarded '68 as "an irruption, of a becoming in its pure state," pointing out that "the possible does not pre-exist, it is created by the event."[103]

As I have already pointed out, the process of becoming—whereby minor problems rapidly "flare up," "blow up," and are "further aggravated" toward the apex of struggle—is the emergence-process of the event-qua-miracle, particularly actualized according to its evental sites. As Deleuze insists, "there is always one part of the *event* that is irreducible to any social determinism, or to causal chains," which can create something that mocks the "historians" who "are not very fond of this aspect."[104] Badiou, who sits back to back antithetically with Deleuze, nevertheless says almost the same thing from the reverse side: "political history abhors the void."[105] When we consider the politics of how to deal and cope with a defeat that is inevitably to come, it consists in safeguarding this "void" that becomes the

100 Steinhoff, "Japan: Student Activism in an Emerging Democracy," 63.

101 Takei Teruo, *Sō toshite no gakusei undō* [The Movement of the Student as Stratum], Tokyo: Supēsu Kaya, 2005.

102 For Shima and his strategy, see Hasegawa, "In Search of a New Radical Left: The Rise and Fall of the Anpō Bund, 1955–1960."

103 Deleuze (in conversation with Antonio Negri), "Control and Becoming," 171, 234.

104 Deleuze (with Félix Guattari), "May '68 Didn't Happen," in *Two Regimes of Madness*, 233.

105 Alain Badiou, "The Fascism of the Potato," in *The Adventure of French Philosophy*, trans. Bruno Bosteels, London: Verso, 2012, 193.

post-evental hegemonic field, exactly what we ought to create: a politics of the *since then*.

’68 in Japan was far from a “reactive revolution,” neither simply “the result of a crisis” nor “a reaction to a crisis.” In other words, it was neither the “result of” nor the “reaction to” something previously existent; it was, rather, “the current crisis, the impasses of the current crisis,” just as was said of the Parisian May. If this is the case, then what is at stake here must be the following: what if, along with Badiou, Žižek, Boltanski and Chiapello, and unlike Deleuze, our current crisis *did not necessarily* “stem directly from the *in*ability of” Japanese “society to assimilate” ’68, but, rather, the ability *par excellence* of capitalism to revolutionize itself by *assimilating* what ’68 desired to realize and incorporate into itself as its “inversion”?[106] I will make a few remarks on this point to conclude.

The “Structure” *Did* Descend onto the Streets in the Form of Defeat

As is well known, Lacan attended Foucault’s talk, “What is an Author?,” in February 1969 and intervened as the last commentator, stating, “If the events of May demonstrated anything . . . it was precisely a *descent of structures onto the street*.”[107] This is, of course, not simply a pithy remark about the poetic slogans of the radical left in Paris but more about the expected answer to the question “what is an author?” Žižek refers to this episode and concludes with a Marxian twist by arguing that “the explosive events were ultimately the result of a structural shift in the basic social and symbolic texture of modern Europe.”[108] Badiou, approximately forty years after that, soberly points out: “We are commemorating May ’68 because the real outcome and the real hero of ’68 is unfettered neo-liberal capitalism”;[109] and ends his harsh observation with the statement, reminiscent of

106 Deleuze (with Félix Guattari), “May ’68 Didn’t Happen,” 234.

107 Jacques Lacan in Michel Foucault, “Qu’est-ce qu’un auteur?,” *Dits et écrits* I: 1954–1988, eds. Daniel Defert et François Ewald, Paris: Gallimard, 1994, 820. English translation from Michael Clark, *Jacques Lacan: An Annotated Bibliography*, Vol. I, London: Garland Publishing, 1988, 240–1, my emphasis.

108 Slavoj Žižek, “Acceptance: The Cause Regained,” in *Living in the End Times*, New York: Verso, 2010, 353.

109 Badiou, *The Communist Hypothesis*, 44.

the *Communist Manifesto*, that "this May '68 basically contributed to the dissolution of everything in the icy waters of capitalism."[110] In sum, they insist that the *author* of '68 was the structure itself, which descended onto the streets in the guise of the people there. If this is the case, then is this structure itself an inevitable alias of the defeat?

For me, not only as part of the aforementioned *hamegoroshi* generation but also as an economist by profession and a critic with an odd and passionate commitment to Marxism, I cannot disagree with them. In Japan, as well, ironically speaking, what '68 demanded was almost realized precisely by the system it tried to dismantle,[111] in the sense that "the class of '68" is "in power" almost everywhere.[112] Žižek unerringly describes this bizarre situation within which "capitalism usurped the left's rhetoric of worker self-management," by "turning it from an anti-capitalist slogan to a capitalist one."[113] In other words, ironically speaking, the '68ers *unknowingly* succeeded in their revolution, which in turn has much to do with this defeat which is not one. Thinking of what Žižek said, bearing in mind the slogans of the labor movement in Japan right after the defeat of World War II (that is, the focus on "production control" and control of the factory as their evental site), I cannot help but recall certain lines of William Morris to which I referred at the outset. He states, in the name of John Ball:

> But while I pondered . . . how men fight and lose the battle, and the thing that they fought for comes about in spite of their defeat, and when it comes turns out not to be what they meant, and other men have to fight for what they meant under another name.[114]

This is not a confession of resignation; rather, far from it, it is an introduction of a repeated beginning, and this is closely related to the axiomatic point that informed Lacan's comments on Foucault: "The fact that this slogan is written in the streets proves nothing except that, as is often the case, *within every act is a fundamental misunderstanding of*

110 Alain Badiou, "May '68: Alain Badiou in conversation with Aude Lancelin," *Lana Turner: A Journal of Poetry and Opinion* 9, 2016.

111 The difficulty is, of course, that it is not "totally" but "almost" realized.

112 Boltanski and Chiapello, *The New Spirit of Capitalism*, 168–9, 195ff.

113 Slavoj Žižek, "The Ambiguous Legacy of '68: Forty years ago, what was revolutionized—the world or capitalism?," *In These Times*, June 20, 2008.

114 Cited in Thompson, *William Morris*, 722.

itself."[115] Sophocles dramatized this notion of the inevitable "misunderstanding of itself" as tragedy. The reason we ought not to regard the tragedy of the URA and the murderous history of internal killings within the New Left as exceptions is also here: what is called the structure always descends into the streets in the guise of an exception or miracle, and therefore we have to *deliver politics to this defeat* that is structured post-eventally.

Nagasaki Hiroshi, making use of Marxian economics or Unoist theory (the concept of "pure capitalism") as a pretext, proposed on September 20, 1968—just before the zenith of the Zenkyōtō movement—the autonomy of politics by insisting that "the paradoxical influence of Uno's theoretical work is to liberate *politics* from the theoretical field [of causal relations or scientific formalism]." He goes on to say that:

> We departed from the point where Uno consciously [i.e., logically] stopped. In other words, the radical theoreticism of Uno which absolutely lacks actual relations with practice in turn influenced our [political] practices [their autonomy].[116]

It is exactly the distinct, autonomous field of politics that must be questioned for its possibility, as Badiou did.[117] This paradoxically resonates with Boltanski and Chiapello, who argue that "the history of the years after 1968 offers further evidence that the relations between the economic and the social . . . are not reducible to the domination of the second by the first."[118] It is this "inversion," so to speak, that '68 made happen on the structured streets.[119]

In this sense, I cannot easily agree with Andrews, who stated recently, in rather a reductionist manner, that the lost two capitalist

115 Jacques Lacan in Michel Foucault, "Qu'est-ce qu'un auteur?," 820–1. Clark, *Jacques Lacan*, 241, my emphasis.

116 Nagasaki, "Hanranron" [On Revolt], 83–4.

117 See Badiou, *Peut-on Penser la Politique?*

118 Boltanski and Chiapello, *The New Spirit of Capitalism*, 168–9.

119 The immediate materials of my essay I referred to at the outset of this chapter are Alain Badiou, "Capitalism Today," in *The Rebirth of History*, and *Qu'est-ce Que J'entends par marxisme? Une conférence donnée le 18 avril 2016 au séminaire Lectures de Marx à l'École normale supérieure de la rue d'Ulm*, Paris: les éditions sociales, 2016; Antonio Negri, "La construction du commun: Un nouveau communisme"; Alain Badiou and Slavoj Žižek, *L'Idée du communisme, II: Conference de Berlin, 2010*, Paris: Nouvelles Éditions Lignes, 2011.

decades (the 1990s–2000s) "did not bring a return of political anger and radicalism. Instead, [they] engendered pessimism, timidity, pusillanimity."[120] It would also be too easy to quote Heinrich Mann here—"The vanquished are the first to learn what history holds in store"—which Wolfgang Schivelbusch utilizes as an epigraph for his famous book in order to prove that people almost unquestionably embrace defeat *as if* they constituted *the subject meant to embrace defeat.*[121] On the contrary, we have to listen carefully to the meaning of Badiou's stern warning that "if the people do not have their own politics, they will enact the politics of their enemies."[122] At first glance, this seems identical to Mann's statement, but he is talking about how to scrutinize politics post-eventally precisely in order to make a new, pre-evental politics.

Yoshimoto Taka'aki appeared in Kanda Kyōritsu Hall and gave a talk right after the fall of Yasuda Tower (March 13, 1969), in which he emphasized the post-evental "commonality of *politics*" as the "bridgehead of thought" upon which to render the post-evental pre-evental.[123] There was no disavowal of the defeat here; he even accepted—embraced, if you like—the defeat *precisely in order to* retain it as an unembraceable remnant. He also gave a talk at Meiji Gakuin University on July 10, 1970 (just after the automatic renewal of the Anpō security treaty on June 23, 1970). After having confessed that he had known three defeats that "he was aware of"—the defeat in World War II, the defeat of the labor movement,[124] and finally the defeat of the 1960 Anpō protests—he concluded in stride by stating, "I feel a solidarity towards the way those who live on accept *all-out defeat*."[125] It should be interpreted *not* as another truth, in the sense that Heinrich Mann pointed out, but as a remnant of the unembraceable defeat of those who are expected to embrace their own defeat.

120 Andrews, *Dissenting Japan*, 263.

121 Wolfgang Schivelbusch, *The Culture of Defeat: On National Trauma, Mourning, and Recovery*, trans. Jefferson Chase, New York: Picador, 2001, 1.

122 Badiou, "The Fascism of the Potato," 193.

123 Yoshimoto Taka'aki "Jiritsu to hangyaku no kyoten" [Bridgehead for autonomia and revolt] in *Haiboku no kōzō* [Structure of Defeat], Tokyo: Yudachisha, 1972, 402.

124 He is talking about his own individual struggle at the small local companies where he was employed. See "Sengo no Hajimari" [The Beginning of the Postwar], *Gendai shisō* [Modern Thought], December 2007, Tokyo: Seidosha.

125 Yoshimoto Taka'aki "'*Gisei no shūen*' igo jūnen [Ten Years after *An End to Fictions*]" in *Haiboku no Kōzō* [Structure of Defeat], 409–12, my emphasis.

The communist novelist Nakano Shigeharu, in his seminal short piece concerning *tenkō* [recantation or conversion from the left to the right], "The House in the Village," finally writes, in a thin voice, as if forced from his lips, "I understand everything you've said. But I want to keep on writing."[126] Let us call this Beckett's position, but we might also call it the position of Morris, of Lenin, and of ourselves.[127]

126 Nakano Shigeharu, "The House in the Village" (1935), *Three Works by Nakano Shigeharu*, trans. Brett de Bary, *Cornell East Asia Series* 21, August 21, 2011 (1979), 72.

127 Samuel Beckett, *Worstward Ho*, 21–5, 5.

11

Night and Fog in Japan: Toward Another Critique of Violence

Alberto Toscano

> Within that period [the 1960s], the consciousness raised by living with your own agonizing problems was such that it could be possible to transform society or the world through your own struggles and, in that sense, see yourself and society as a single organism. Rather, that was the only way you could see things. It was in no way overly optimistic but rather the common sense shared by so many young people living so vigorously. I don't believe that this was simply a matter of the environment or atmosphere of the times. Isn't it the case that no one expects the current generation to see this age in a similar way, to experience a similar way of being or way of life?
>
> Masao Adachi[1]

Film, Factionalism and the Japanese '68

A few years ago, at the presentation of a French translation of my book *Fanaticism*, I had the opportunity to talk to an activist from the Popular Front for the Liberation of Palestine who, some years before, had been tasked with organizing the group's foreign archives in Gaza—before they were pulverized by an Israeli air strike. He joked about the inconsistency of their Italian fellow travelers and the unpredictability of their German ones, only to then note the unwavering dependability of the

1 Harry Harootunian and Sabu Kohso, "Messages in a Bottle: An Interview with Filmmaker Masao Adachi," *boundary 2*, 35: 3, 2008, 97.

Japanese fighters who'd joined the PFLP.[2] Global perception of the Japanese '68 and its afterlives, briefly turned to the mass student occupations of universities and the beguilingly theatrical confrontation of riot police against a forest of helmets and long fighting staffs, settled in the early seventies precisely on those intransigent militants, now styled "international terrorists," who had taken their fight onto the global stage—figures like Fusaku Shigenobu, leader of the Japanese Red Army, and Kōzō Okamoto, sole survivor from the group responsible for the bloody attack on Lod Airport. In the phantasmagorias of enmity that have marked our long Restoration (to borrow an apt periodizing notion from Alain Badiou), these "left-wing fanatics" played their supporting role.

Where globalized media briefly feasted on these one-dimensional icons of terror, the Japanese left had already provided an incisive political aesthetic to accompany its complex, contradictory, and often tragic history, especially in its student elements. The films of Oshima Nagisa and Wakamatsu Koji, notwithstanding their considerable differences, can be usefully approached in terms of such a political aesthetic, one that doubles as (psycho)analysis. They have the Japanese '68 as their fulcrum, anticipating its intensity and limits, tracing its ambivalent aftermath. Oshima's *Night and Fog in Japan* (1960) and Wakamatsu's films of the late 1960s and early 1970s—rogue, extremist "pink films" such as *Season of Terror* (1969) or *Ecstasy of the Angels* (1972)—succeeded in dramatizing that key site of left-wing "fanatical" subjectivity, *factionalism*, generating filmic languages to grasp the rhetorical, erotic, and spatial coordinates of militancy's involution—the isolation of the cell, the melancholia of defeat, the sexual micropolitics of the sect, the tragic efforts to pierce through the frozen landscapes of power into a sense of historical action.[3] In this respect, the radical Japanese film of the 1960s and 1970s provides a cinematic critique of violence without parallels in its European or American counterparts, in many ways foreshadowing the descent of the Japanese left into internecine strife or *uchi geba* (in Wakamatsu's epically grueling *United Red Army*,

2 This text is an expanded version of "The Empty Subject of Fanaticism," the preface to the Japanese edition of my *Fanaticism*, Tokyo: Koshisha, forthcoming.

3 For the place of landscape in a post-1968 Japanese political aesthetic, and its contemporary relevance, see the discussion of *fukeiron* [landscape theory] in my *Cartographies of the Absolute* (co-authored with Jeff Kinkle), Winchester: Zero, 2015; and Yuriko Furuhata, *Cinema of Actuality: Japanese Avant-Garde Filmmaking in the Season of Image Politics*, Durham: Duke University Press, 2013.

we can see Japan becoming, in a different vein, and for Western audiences, an allegorical country for the critique of fanaticism).[4] Particularly striking, across markedly different filmic styles and sensibilities, is the way in which both Oshima and Wakamatsu generated, on either side of '68, a cinematic aesthetic of social confinement and militant impasse. The very scenography of *Night and Fog in Japan*—which marks a kind of negative beginning of the Japanese sixties in the defeat of the movement against the United States–Japan Security Treaty (Anpō)—underscores the predicament of a militancy trapped in mimesis (and the misery of student life); the dormitory room is graffitied with disconnected watchwords: *cogito ergo sum, l'être et le néant, pendre la bourgeoisie* (these three grimly framing the suicided body of Takao, the supposed "traitor"), K. Marx, Lenin (in Cyrillic). When one of the communist students pontificates to his reading-group comrades about ancient materialism being "cut off from reality," the performative contradiction is almost too blunt. The spaces of study, like those of the meetings, are caught in a kind of loop with the domestic interiors, still charged with a collective hope but also presaging the traps of stability and involution. The interior of the group and the interior of the home, oscillating between claustro- and agoraphobia, hatred of the outside and inner disgust, echo one another. The commonality, the Sartrean *fusion*, comes with the group singing (though this is an object of the activists' own later skepticism and scorn), but, more profoundly and despairingly, in the affirmation of a common pain (or in the attempt to draw authenticity and intensity from the foregone defeat of the anti-Anpō demonstrations). Oshima suggested that the film is, in a sense, redeemed by its one genuine moment of emotion (more precisely, we could add, of an emotion not in the register of anxiety): the mournful singing at the death of a student, brought to a dramatic pitch by the silhouetting of the grieving faces of the protesters against the night (this is paired with the passing by Nozawa of the red flag to the lone Trotskyist student, who has decided to hold the line, in spite of the party and the odds). The collective is both fused and wrecked in defeat. Arranged around this moment of militancy and mourning, the film proceeds as a melodrama

4 I have tried to explore some of these issues in two articles, from which I borrow here: "For a Left with No Exit (*Night and Fog in Japan*)," *La Furia Umana* 3, 2013, 228–31 (originally published in Japanese); and (with Hirasawa Go) "Walls of Flesh: The Film of Koji Wakamatsu (1965–1972)," *Film Quarterly* 66: 4, 2013. I also take this opportunity to thank Sabu Kohso for sharing with me his unpublished translation of Toru Kishida's "Internal Strife aka *Uchigeba*—Another History of Japan's New Left Movement."

of factional struggle, in which the fragmenting of the collective is not the occasion for a revanchist individualism or a liberated subjectivity, but the prelude to two dead ends: the authentic suicide and the reintegration through bad faith into family and party. This is the politics—or, rather, the political impasse—of factional discord, devolving into what Sartre called "seriality" (the mute, anxious looks of the erstwhile comrades at the wedding serving as a kind of chorus of defeat, with the searing image of a parade of torches as its aesthetic transfiguration). The theatricality of the *tableau vivant* is riven with the tension, with the instability accorded to it by the nervous, dissonant melodies of the music and the camera's slow impatience. Artistic and political form are both affected by the movement of what Oshima, at the time, called *self-negation* ("a production must not be an explanation of the script; it must be a reality-based negation of the images expressed in the script and a discovery of new images using that negation as an opportunity").[5]

Rather than teasing out the psycho-political fault lines of Japanese communism from within, Wakamatsu, perhaps aided in this by his plebeian background and distance from student and intellectual milieus, laces his hatred for state authoritarianism and critical militant politics with a celebration of individual and anarchistic activity, especially as carried out by "lumpen" types. The production speed of Wakamatsu's politicized "pink films"—which themselves had marginal and unemployed men as one of their principal audiences—was such that his own footage of student protests and riots in Tokyo neighborhoods could be inserted into the films to give them added immediacy. This is most effective in *Sex Jack* (1970), whose credits run over three minutes of wide-angle shots of helmeted demonstrators moving in snake formation through the streets of Tokyo, squaring the poles of their banners against the police like so many phalanxes, and rioting. (*Season of Terror* starts with a comparably captivating montage of high-contrast photos showing such clashes.) A haunting wide shot of sodden, ripped pamphlets and placards on the empty streets of the city functions as a kind of allegory for the sense of impasse and defeat that haunts how politics appears in these films. What follows the mass clash, the open conflict, is the doubling back onto itself of the cell—to be understood here both as a group and as a space. Persecuted by the police, the militants enter secluded clandestineness, nominally to prepare an action

5 "The Laws of Self-Negation" (1961), in *Cinema, Censorship and the State: The Writings of Nagisa Oshima*, Annette Michelson, ed., Cambridge, MA: MIT, 1992, 52.

(the sex jack of the title alludes to the Japanese Red Army's successful 1970 hijacking of a Japanese airliner, diverting it to North Korea), but in effect to spiral into internal strife, taking turns having grueling sex with their one female member (who shouts slogans during the act while the others slouch about in dejected boredom), their doctrinaire declarations growing ever more disjointed. The young thief who helps them out, first undergoing torture as a possible spy, then welcoming them into another tiny apartment in the shanty outskirts of the city, stands, in his innocence and fervor, as a reminder of the utter incapacity of the militants to connect their action to the world of the dispossessed. It is disputable whether the explosive violence that closes *Sex Jack*, *Season of Terror*, and *Ecstasy of the Angels* is in any way liberating, although it shows the predilection for a passage to the individual antiauthoritarian act that very much mirrors Wakamatsu's anarchic self-image. For all of his partisanship with the students, his shared hatred of society, and desire for extremity, Wakamatsu dwells on the cruel blockages of revolutionary politics, the real and virtual walls rendering wholesale transformation seemingly impossible. Even the moments of violence that close *Ecstasy of the Angels* and *Season of Terror* could seem like explosions of impotence—they ultimately leave the landscape of power unscathed—rather than indications of utopia, although they also function as criticisms of, or at least counterpoints to, the self-destruction of the revolutionary cells. Whether revolt is an antecedent of revolution or the sign of its present impossibility in these films is unclear. What is fairly evident is that in these films, sex is a site of ecstasy, escape, brutality, and evasion, but not of liberation.

The figures of factionalism and the intransigent militant cell as impasses of the political, which the aforementioned films so memorably convey with direct reference to the politics of the Japanese far left in the 1960s, can also be approached in the *longue durée*, perhaps excavating some of the sources of the violent blockages dramatized by Oshima and Wakamatsu. In the rest of this chapter, I hope to do this by exploring the place of Japan in the discourse of fanaticism, a discourse to which the political subjectivity of the faction, the cell, and the uncompromising militant have long been central.

Japan and Fanaticism

Fanaticism has—to borrow an illuminating expression from Italian communist critic and poet Franco Fortini—its "allegorical countries,"[6] nations (or less well-defined ethnic and religious collectives) whose histories provide figurations of distinctive kinds of intransigent subjectivity, the refusal of compromise, or, to use Badiou's formula for the twentieth century, the passion for the real. In my *Fanaticism*, one can find a sampling of such allegories, chief among them the France of Jacobin Terror; the "Germany" of the Radical Reformation, post-Kantian philosophy and the Nazi seizure of power; the USSR of communism as a "political religion"—but also the Islamic "Arabia" that Hegel dubbed "the Kingdom of Fanaticism," or the India that countered British imperial administration with its peasant insurgencies. The European history of this discourse is peculiarly split into a *philosophical-political* history of fanaticism as a name for an excess of universalizing subjectivity, on the one hand, and a *colonial-administrative* history of fanaticism as a name for an intractable negation of modern rationality, on the other. This splitting is transmuted, with illuminating retroactive effects, into a short circuit, or even fused into a kind of identity, in the long wave of decolonization from the period between the two world wars into the 1970s—a temporal vantage from which it became possible, for instance, to see Haiti's "Black Jacobins" as collapsing the distinction between the uncontainable pretensions of the human subject to sovereign knowledge and the urge of the subjugated to free themselves from the simulacra of progress, Enlightenment or modernity foisted upon them by the imperial avatars of a rapacious capitalism.

What kind of allegorical function can "Japan" be seen to play in the long and uneven history of the discourse on, and of, fanaticism? Needless to say, I speak here in the first instance about "distant observers" and not of any autochthonous debate on fanaticism, or analogues thereof—and cognizant that, as Edward Said noted (in the period of the country's global economic ascendancy), "Japan"—like "Islam," "Communism" and "the West"—is a "gigantic caricatural essentialization," though one possessing "styles of polemic, batteries of discourse, and an unsettling profusion of opportunities for dissemination."[7] From a

6 Franco Fortini, *Questioni di frontiera. Scritti di politica e di letteratura, 1965–1977* [Border Questions: Writings on Politics and Literature, 1965–1977], Turin: Einaudi, 1977.

7 Edward Said, *Culture and Imperialism*, New York: Vintage, 1993, 306–7.

European, Euro-American, or Atlantic vantage point, Japan is neither internal to the history of Reason's speculative *hubris* (as in Kant or, in a historicizing vein, Hegel) nor easily relegated to the series of subaltern "fanatics" resisting the West's enlightened domination. It is striking to note in this respect that before the instrumental and racialized emergence of the martial figure of the Japanese "fanatic" during the Asia-Pacific War (itself a partial prolongation of the nineteenth-century racial-moral panic of supremacy known as "the yellow peril"),[8] Japan's most potent allegorical role, both among oppressed populations in the West and throughout the colonized world, was as a singular challenger to white Euro-American domination. Pioneering critic, historian, and sociologist of the racial order W.E.B. Du Bois, welcomed the Russian defeat at the hands of the Japanese Navy in 1905 as a world-historical event:

> Since 732, when Charles Martel beat back the Saracens at Tours, white races have had the hegemony of civilization [but now] the Russo-Japanese war has marked an epoch. The magic of the word "white" is already broken . . . The awakening of the yellow races is certain. That the awakening of the brown and black races will follow in time, no unprejudiced student of history can doubt.[9]

In his recent essay exploring the intellectual history of decolonization in Asia, Pankaj Mishra includes Du Bois among a remarkable host of budding anticolonial critics, thinkers, militants, and future statesmen—among them Sun Yat-Sen, Tagore, Gandhi, Ataturk, Nehru, and Mao—for whom 1905 marked a watershed. As he remarks, "it is the Battle of Tsushima that seems to have struck the opening chords of the recessional of the West . . . Japan's victory over Russia accelerated an irreversible process of intellectual, if not yet political,

8 See Beatrice Trefalt, "Fanaticism, Japanese Soldiers and The Pacific War, 1937–45," in *Fanaticism and Conflict in the Modern Age*, eds. Matthew Hughes and Gaynor Johnson, Abindgon: Frank Cass, 2005.

9 W.E.B. Du Bois, "The Color Line Belts the World" (1906), in *Writings by W.E B. Du Bois in Periodicals Edited by Others*, ed. Herbert Aptheker, Millwood: Kraus-Thomson, 1982, cited in Gerald Horne, *Race War!: White Supremacy and the Japanese Attack on the British Empire*, New York: New York University Press, 2004, 45. For a judicious exploration of the political ambiguities inherent to Du Bois's abiding sympathy for Japan's world-historical role in the struggle against white supremacy—not least his apologias for its colonial efforts in China—see Reginald Kearney, "The Pro-Japanese Utterances of W.E.B. Du Bois," *Contributions in Black Studies* 13: 7, 1995: scholarworks.umass.edu/cibs/vol13/iss1/7.

decolonization."[10] If the critique of the trope of the fanatic as a crucial ingredient in the "prose of counterinsurgency" is a necessary component of any process of intellectual decolonization, then we could say that—irrespective of its place in the Japanese state's own history of colonialism and imperialism—in a purely "allegorical vein," the Battle of Tsushima (though preceded by the less equivocal defeat of Italian imperialism in 1896 at the Battle of Adwa in Ethiopia) could be seen as an episode in the *practical* critique of fanaticism, scuppering the repeated efforts by Western imperial intellectuals to view resistance from beyond the "color line" as fundamentally irrational in kind.

Japanization and the End of History

If the allegorical place of "Japan" in the colonial-administrative history of fanaticism's uses is either a *sui generis* figure of the racialized enemy (the self-annihilating martial subject of the emperor) or as a challenge to colonialism's categories (in the imaginations of Du Bois, Nehru, and sundry anticolonial intellectuals), then its place in a more specifically philosophical discourse on fanaticism, though arguably marginal, is rather different. The philosophical problem of fanaticism is a problem of historical action, of exceptional, extreme forms of subjectivity, often seen to emerge in conjunctures of crisis or transition. Now, Japan has served a notable allegorical function in at least two important treatments of the aporias of the modern Western figure of the historical subject. Both Alexandre Kojève's note to the second edition of his famously influential lectures on Hegel's *Phenomenology of Spirit* and Roland Barthes' *Empire of Signs* are postwar epigones of that crucial genre in the Western philosophical apprehension of otherness, the travel narrative, which from Montaigne's "On Cannibals" onward could be seen to hinge on the creation of "anti-types" to given models of subjectivity or agency, through a "technique of ostensive self-definition by negation" (we are what they are not).[11] Though, unlike the classic secondhand philosophical use of the travel narrative, these are first-person observations, they are also ones shaped—in Barthes' case, reflexively so—by the lack of access to the Japanese language, which is

10 Pankaj Mishra, *From the Ruins of Empire: The Intellectuals Who Remade Asia*, New York: Farrar, Strauss and Giroux, 2012, 6.

11 On the anti-type, see Hayden White, "The Forms of Wildness: Archaeology of an Idea," in *Tropics of Discourse: Essays in Cultural Criticism*, Baltimore: Johns Hopkins, 1978.

parlayed into an emphatic focus on (aesthetic) form, not so much to the detriment but to the disappearance of (historical, political, social) content. Kojève turns to his experience of Japan in 1959 to qualify his earlier observations, which, based on a theoretical reflection on the homogenizing hegemony of "Americanism," outlined the passage from historical Man to "post-historical animals of the species *Homo sapiens*." From our angle, the end of history would seem to denote an end of the very conditions for fanaticism properly so-called. In a Hegelian frame, such as Kojève's, fanaticism is a kind of *ultra-historical* subjectivity—as evident in the example of the Jacobin Terror, it misses historical mediation and institutionalization not by deficit but by *excess* (it is *too* universal), while also serving as a negative ferment for further historical development, or, indeed, culmination, as in the relay from Robespierre to Napoleon. However, whether it is egalitarian or monotheistic (the French Revolution or the "Revolution of the East"), Hegelian fanaticism is deeply bound to conflict, to the negativity manifest phenomenologically in the (master-slave) dialectic of recognition and the reality of labor, and collectively in war and revolution. But with the end of history, what "disappears is Man properly so-called—that is, Action negating the given, and Error, or in general, the Subject *opposed* to the Object."[12] What Kojève's Japanese epiphany suggests to him is the thereto unimagined possibility of a kind of posthistorical subjectivity that wouldn't devolve into "animality." In this Japanese "fringe of ultrahistory,"[13] even the kind of violence that, from a Western standpoint, bears witness to that extreme identity of the subject with itself, which takes on the name of fanaticism, is revealed as a game of forms. As Kojève declares:

> in spite of persistent economic and political inequalities, all Japanese without exception are currently in a position to live according to totally formalized values—that is, values completely empty of all "human" content in the "historical" sense. Thus, in the extreme, every Japanese is in principle capable of committing, from pure snobbery, a perfectly "gratuitous" suicide (the classical épée of the samurai can be replaced by an airplane or a torpedo), which has nothing to do with the *risk* of life in a Fight waged for the sake of "historical" values that have social or political content. This seems to allow

12 Alexandre Kojève, *Introduction to the Reading of Hegel: Lectures on the Phenomenology of Spirit*, eds. Raymond Queneau and Allan Bloom, trans. James H. Nichols, Jr., Ithaca: Cornell University Press, 1980, 158–9.

13 Giorgio Agamben, *The Open: Man and Animal*, trans. Kevin Attell, Stanford: Stanford University Press, 2004, 12.

> one to believe that the recently begun interaction between Japan and the Western World will finally lead not to a rebarbarization of the Japanese but to a "Japanization" of the Westemers (including the Russians).[14]

"Japanization" as the possibility of a posthistorical humanity is based on the continual detachment of *form* from *content*. Kojève sees it emblematized in the "peaks" of Japanese "snobbery"—Noh theatre, tea ceremonies, flower arranging—activities that replace those quintessential Hegelian domains of historical action—martial or revolutionary struggles and the necessities of labor. In snobbery as a kind of *agonistic formalization of life* we can see the separation of form from content (or the voiding of the latter) as a surrogate for or displacement of the subject-object dialectic that makes for the specifically human in the Hegelian frame.[15] In other words, "Japan" stands in Kojève as the name

14 Kojève, *Introduction to the Reading of Hegel*, 162. As Kojin Karatani observes: "Seen as a theory of Japanese culture, of course, this observation would be nothing but a superficial stereotype. However, what Kojève refers to under the names of 'America' and 'Japan' is not an actual existence but a form resulting from philosophical reflection. In this sense, the Japanese snobbism means a way of life in which one risks one's life on a game of an empty form without historical ideals or intellectual, moral contents. It is not a tradition-directed or inner-directed mode, but an extreme mode of other-directed society, in which there is no internality or the other." Karatani, *Nation and Aesthetics: On Kant and Freud*, trans. Jonathan E. Abel, Darwin H. Tsen, and Hiroki Yoshikuni, New York: Oxford University Press, 2017, 132. Though I can't explore it further here, it is important to note that, in Karatani's Marxist-inflected psychoanalytic reading, "Japanization" is not a posthistorical process, but the generalization of a power based on *foreclosure*, tending to replace the traditional form of "Western" power based on subjective *repression*. The title of the chapter that features his discussion of Kojève is "Geopolitics of the Character: Japan-Psycho-Analysis." Crucially, Karatani distances himself from any position that "assumes the essence of so-called mind, idea, or culture, and also identity, by abstracting Japan from its relations to other countries" (126), noting in particular the significance of Korea to the geopolitics of the Japanese character (118).

15 Commenting on Kojève's note, Fukuyama mentions the tea ceremony as "an arena for *megalothymia* [the passionate desire to have one's superiority recognized by another, as opposed to *isothymia*, the passion for equality] in the form of pure snobbery: there are contending schools for tea ceremony and flower arrangement, with their own masters, novices, traditions, and canons of better and worse. It was the very formalism of this activity—the creation of new rules and values divorced from any utilitarian purpose, as in sports—that suggested to Kojève the possibility of specifically human activity even after the end of history." Francis Fukuyama, *The End of History and the Last Man*, New York: Free Press, 1992, 320. It is interesting to note that in his own effort at imagining what action and conflict would like in a society beyond class struggle, Leon Trotsky, in *Literature and Revolution*, imagined the domain of the aesthetic, of artistic productions, schools, and struggles of taste as the one to which the energizing passion for conflict would be displaced after the completed revolution. In and against Fukuyama's terminology, this is the utopia of a wholly new articulation of *megalothymia* and *isothymia*.

for a kind of *negativity without history* (and perhaps also of fanaticisms without substance).

Barthes and the Zengakuren

The singularity of "Japan" qua limit or liminal allegory of subjectivity in European philosophy seems to be further corroborated by the return of the leitmotif of formalization in an exquisitely non-Hegelian guise in the writings of Roland Barthes. Even more than in Kojève, where it serves to contrast America's world-*anti*historical role, "Japan" is in Barthes an anti-type, one whose fictive, polemical, and utopian role the French semiotician happily avows.[16] Unsurprisingly for a travel narrative that deliberately evades the historical density of the signified, Barthes, though not employing the language of "snobbery," revisits many of Kojève's "peaks," while also noting their more contemporary and everyday variants, from packaging to *pachinko*, and across arenas of a formalism that he characteristically envisions as *writing*, from gastronomy to topography. In a sense, *Empire of Signs* can be seen to intensify or exacerbate the tendency at work in Kojève: it is not formalism as such that characterizes the Japanese challenge to the Western model of historical action, but a formalization that always lets an emptiness shine through—not *negation* but *absence*. Though linguistic content is happily foreign to him (the section of the book is pointedly entitled "The Unknown Language"), Barthes does anchor his reflection on the place of *grammatical* subjecthood in Japanese, making the following speculative remark (a variation of his essay's key refrain):

> in Japanese, the proliferation of functional suffixes and the complexity of enclitics suppose that the subject advances into utterance through certain precautions, repetitions, delays, and insistences whose final volume . . . turns the subject, precisely, into a great envelope empty of speech, and not that dense kernel which is supposed to direct our sentences, from outside and from above, so that what seems to us an excess of

16 Though this doesn't thereby exempt Barthes from accusations of exoticism. For an insightful treatment of this question, which homes in on the Barthesian parallax of Japan and Morocco, see Diana Knight, "Barthes and Orientalism," *New Literary History* 24: 3, 1993, 617–33.

> subjectivity . . . is much more a way of diluting, of haemorrhaging the subject in a fragmented, particled language diffracted to emptiness.[17]

Analogously, writing about the hollow imperial center of Tokyo's topography, Barthes notes how "the system of the imaginary is spread circularly, by detours and returns the length of an empty subject."[18] These are travels in a nonmetaphysical country (*antimetaphysical* would suggest a negativity that doesn't accord with Barthes' treatment), the site or surface of (as he says of the haiku) "a repetition without origin, an event without cause, a memory without person, a language without moorings."[19] Yet Barthes' effort to write the exemption of meaning from and into Japan, to draw from the surface of its ritualized forms and everyday life an "ethic of the empty sign,"[20] was also obliged to confront the fact of Japanese political radicalism (his travels to the country took place between 1966 and 1968). Japan's historical present irrupts into Barthes' own cabinet of signs in a remarkable section on the Zengakuren. Here it is as though all that remained of Barthes' Marxism was an exquisite formalism (and it is worth noting that Brecht is the only Marxist whose name appears in the book, as though the whole country were an elaborate "alienation effect");[21] more, it is only as a formalism (in the *sui generis* guise of "writing") that Barthes can encounter a Marxist or communist politics. Japan as anti-type to the political metaphysics of the West, and as the oblique surface of a very peculiar utopia, is particularly present in this section, which strives to imagine something like a

17 Roland Barthes, *Empire of Signs*, trans. Richard Howard, New York: Hill and Wang, 1982, 7. From Barthes' vantage, the quest for "subjectivity" among postwar Japanese intellectuals would appear to be a quintessentially misguided pursuit. See Masao Miyoshi, "Who Decides and Who Speaks? *Shutaisei* and the West in Postwar Japan," in *Trespasses*, ed. Eric Cazdyn, Durham: Duke University Press, 2009. Jacques Lacan tried to provide his own psychoanalytic basis for Barthes' grammatical absenting of the Japanese subject: "the [Japanese] subject is divided as everywhere by language (*langage*), but one of its registers can be satisfied by reference to writing [Chinese characters] and the other by speech. This is without doubt what has given Roland Barthes the giddy feeling (*sentiment enivré*) that of all its manners the Japanese subject does not cover anything. *The Empire of Signs*, he titles his essay, meaning: empire of *semblants*." Jacques Lacan, *Autres Écrits*, Paris: Seuil, 2001, 19; quoted in Karatani, *Nation and Aesthetics*, 128.

18 Barthes, *Empire of Signs*, 32.

19 Ibid., 79.

20 Roland Barthes, "On S/Z and Empire of Signs" (interview with Raymond Bellour), in *The Grain of the Voice: Interviews 1962–1980*, trans. Linda Coverdale, New York: Hill & Wang, 1985, 83.

21 Barthes, *Empire of Signs*, 54–5.

politics without a subject—in Kojève's Hegelian terms, we could say the enigma or utopia of a *posthistorical political action*. In the clashes and demonstrations of radical Japanese students (captured in one of the book's "non-illustrative" photographs), Barthes identifies:

> a writing of actions which expurgates violence from its Occidental being: spontaneity. In our mythology, violence is caught up in the same prejudice as literature or art: we can attribute to it no other function than that of expressing a content, an inwardness, a nature, of which it is the primary, savage, asystematic language; we certainly conceive, no doubt, that violence can be shunted toward deliberated goals, turned into an instrument of thought, but this is never anything but a question of domesticating an *anterior*, sovereignly original force. The violence of the Zengakuren does not precede its own regulation, but is born simultaneously with it: it is immediately a sign: *expressing* nothing (neither hatred nor indignation nor any moral idea), it does away with itself all the more surely in a transitive goal (to besiege and capture a town hall, to open a barbed-wire barrier): yet effectiveness is not its only measurement . . . the features of this writing . . . are indeed discontinuous, arranged, regulated, not in order to signify something but as if to do away (to our eyes) with the myth of the improvised riot, the plenitude of "spontaneous" symbols.[22]

In this remarkable passage, the actions (we could also say the *appearance*, the *form*, the *performance*) of the Zengakuren provide Barthes with the occasion for his own critique of violence. Where for Walter Benjamin it is the termination of the instrumental dialectic of means and ends that makes for the interruptive force of divine violence, in Barthes it is the severing of the *expressive* dialectic between the *forms* of political violence and its supposed subjective content and center (the "sovereignly original force") that marks the utopian valence (for the Western observer) of the politics of the Zengakuren—a practical critique of the *mythology* of spontaneity, though one not founded on the primacy of mediation but on a different kind of immediacy, that of a violence that is "immediately a sign." The Zengakuren's practical critique of violence is also a break with the Western articulation of language and politics, where the former serves as the legitimating instance for the latter. Rather, we get the image (the fantasy?) of a kind of *politique pour la politique* in which language itself becomes a kind of pure means:

22 Ibid., 103–6.

> All this combines to produce a mass writing, not a group writing (the gestures are completed, the persons do not assist each other); finally, the extreme risk of the sign, it is sometimes acknowledged that the slogans chanted by the combatants should utter not the Cause, the Subject of action (what one is fighting for or against)—this would be once again to make language the expression of a reason, the assurance of a good Cause—but only this action itself (*The Zengakuren are going to fight*), which is thereby no longer covered, directed, justified, made innocent by language—that external divinity superior to the combat, like a Marseillaise in her Phrygian bonnet—but doubled by a pure vocal exercise which simply adds to the volume of violence, a gesture, one muscle more.[23]

No doubt this is "aestheticization of politics" of a kind, but it is one that strives to distinguish the anti-expressive formalization of action from its hyper-expressive and fascistic spectacularization. Yet we could also argue that it falters in this effort, not by its refusal to look for a sovereign political subject or a structured social substance "behind" the writing of violence, but because it is unwilling to connect political form with the forms of capital (and state) in their specific Japanese articulations. This is the criticism that transpires from Harry Harootunian's commentary on Noël Burch's pioneering "Barthesian" theory of Japanese cinema, *To the Distant Observer*. As Harootunian writes:

> We must understand that Barthes had undertaken the assignment to construct a fictive "Japan" in order to display how a move to the outside immediately discloses the spurious claims of Western subject-centered universalism, once other non-centered or non-centering positions occupying space are considered. Barthes's little book provided both a practical illustration of the semiological method of reading Japan as a text, much to the unknowing outrage and howling of professional scholars of Japan, and a set of themes enabled by his interpretative strategy . . . What the Barthesian program left out was not merely history but rather what motored it—capitalism itself—even as a modest, vanishing mediator.[24]

23 Ibid., 106.

24 Harry Harootunian, "'Detour to the East': Noel Burch and the Task of Japanese Film," in Noël Burch, *To the Distant Observer: Form and Meaning in Japanese Cinema*, rev. and ed. Annette Michelson, Berkeley, University of California Press, 1979; new digital reprint, Ann Arbor: MPublishing, University of Michigan Library, 2004, 3; available at: quod.lib.umich.edu/c/cjfs/distant-observer.html.

More specifically, what it neglected, thereby occluding the conditions for the genesis and reproduction of the formalizations it drew its writerly pleasures from, is what Harootunian called the "immense sense of unevenness" coursing through Japanese modernity and everyday life.[25]

Fascism, Fanaticism, and Noncontemporaneity

It is perhaps on the basis of such unevenness—which is no mere retardation, anomaly, and exception, but a particular form of inscription into a global capitalism that both generates and exploits "noncontemporaneity" and difference—that one could pose anew the question of fanaticism and Japan. In particular, it may be possible to draw from a consideration of Japanese political and intellectual history a figure of fanaticism as the *forced synchronization of unevenness*, whether by way of partisan acceleration or archaic arrest. Theorizations of a specifically Japanese fascism appear to point in this direction. What, if not a catastrophic fantasy of the end of unevenness, is "overcoming modernity" as a project of ethnonational self-coincidence and imperial expansion—following Ernst Bloch's model of a fascism that would both cunningly instrumentalize and spectacularly disavow the noncontemporaneous? As Harootunian notes:

> Fascism in Japan, and elsewhere, appeared under the guise of what might be called gemeinschaft capitalism and the claims of a social order free from the uncertainties and indeterminacies of an alienated civil society, where an eternalized and unchanging cultural or communal order was put into the service of the capitalist mode of production to establish a "capitalism without capitalism."[26]

Najita and Harootunian's intellectual history of the reactionary efforts in the interwar period to establish a renaissance and reconstruction of Japan that would vanquish and sublate Western modernity also point in this direction, especially when they identify within this "revolt against the West" a kind of reactive passion for the real. The revanchist

25 Harootunian, "'Detour to the East,'" 7. Harootunian has brilliantly analyzed the critical nexus between capital's unevenness, modernity, and everyday life. See, especially, his *Overcome by Modernity: History, Culture and Community in Interwar Japan*, Princeton: Princeton University Press, 2000.

26 Harootunian, *Overcome by Modernity*, xxx.

goal of rebirth and hegemony demanded a violence of another kind than the one "rewritten" by Barthes. For the intellectuals of this revolt:

> violence was a necessity because of its "cleansing" propensities. It was not simply expelling the Western presence from Japan and Asia but purging the spirit of putrefaction and pollution. Absolution of the personal soul (*watakushi no tamashii*) paved the way for the realization of the national spirit (*kokka no seishin*). The implicit Pan-Asianism that Okawa [Shumei] and other contemporaries advocated provided an ideological mapping for the construction of large-scale strategies to eliminate Western power from Asia in an ultimate encounter or, as it was increasingly expressed, "the war to end wars."[27]

How do we read the violence of this nationalist passion for purification? Are the intellectual visions that accompanied "emperor-system fascism" to be understood, contra Barthes' "writing of violence," as an apotheosis of fanatical subjectivity? Kojin Karatani's speculative effort to delineate a political psychoanalysis of Japan suggests the answers to such questions are by no means straightforward. This is particularly evident in his engagement with Maruyama Masao's analyses of Japanese fascism, read here through a partly Lacanian lens. In Maruyama, Karatani identifies a distinction between German and Japanese fascism on the grounds of subjectivity. In Karatani's gloss:

> Nazism at least assumes the articulate will and subject, which makes responsibility possible, but in Japanese fascism there is no distinct political subject that could take on responsibility, and, therefore, no sense of responsibility. In Japan, the action was certainly performed, but it seems as if no one was its subject and what would happen happened. Maruyama called this structure the "system of irresponsibility" or 'structure of the Emperor system."[28]

27 Tetsuo Najita and H.D. Harootunian, "Japan's Revolt Against the West," in *Modern Japanese Thought*, ed. Bob T. Wakabayashi, Cambridge: Cambridge University Press, 1998, 230. Consider also Miyoshi's acerbic comment, according to which "Japan's xenophobic ultranationalism was merely the mirror image of . . . West-worship, which alone can explain the amazingly smooth transition in 1945 from the resolve to fight to the last soldier to the determination to build a peaceful nation." Miyoshi, "Who Decides and Who Speaks?," 99.

28 Karatani, *Nation and Aesthetics*, 119. See also page 129, where Maruyama's thesis is revisited via Lacan. The "absence of self or principle" could later be framed in the postwar period as "the secret of Japan's 'development'" (115). Karatani also brings attention to

But it is in his book *History and Repetition* that Karatani draws from Maruyama a formulation that I believe can further help to advance a critique of fanaticism understood both as an ideology-critique of the pejorative discourse on fanaticism that is constitutive of modern liberalism *and* as a critique of the limits, pitfalls, and perversions of the political mobilization of the refusal to compromise. From Maruyama, Karatani draws the figure of a fascism that is not merely a "system of irresponsibility" in the sense famously argued by landmark texts like Arendt's *Eichmann in Jerusalem* or Bauman's *Modernity and the Holocaust*, but one in which the charismatic figure of the subject of decision is itself displaced. For Maruyama,

> Japanese fascism lacks the single, charismatic subject who possesses a unified will. Instead, like the portable shrine carried at a festival, it is carried forward by someone until a certain stage, then passed on to someone else at the next stage. However, if we understand fascism within its "process," we can view this process of multiple, differing subjects substituting for one another to achieve a single goal as being equivalent to the process of a single subject continually changing over time. For the purpose of achieving the counterrevolution, it does not matter who the subject is.[29]

Fanaticism without unified will or charisma, fascism as a process without a subject or, rather, a process relatively indifferent to its "bearers" (Marx's *Träger*)—this lesson from a Japanese history of violence does not just serve as a necessary corrective to Barthes' problematic contention that the writerly dispersal or absenting of subjectivity can free us from the ravages of the West's sovereign, expressive, legitimating violence; it also provides us with some of the historical and conceptual tools to approach the planetary emergence of "late fascisms,"[30] offspring of the unevenness of today's capital that will not be captured, critiqued, or undone if we rest content with facile analogies from the past.

Maruyama's striking claim that only Marxism could provide the "coordinate axis" that Japan lacked, that only it could "[form] the subject by its unmatchable force" (130).

29 Kojin Karatani, *History and Repetition*, ed. Seiji M. Lippit, New York: Columbia University Press, 2012, 36.

30 Alberto Toscano, "Notes on Late Fascism," Historical Materialism (website), April 2, 2017, historicalmaterialism.org/blog/notes-late-fascism.

12

The Post-'68 Conjuncture

Gavin Walker

"Contrary to what Hegel, Engels, and Stalin thought, there are no laws of history," wrote Louis Althusser, in a late unpublished note, "yet there are *lessons* of history, but these lessons are themselves aleatory, for the same situation, the same conjuncture, the same 'case' never reproduces itself."[1] This book is a testament to the aleatory lessons of history, many still to be gained, from the Japanese '68, lessons that can be derived precisely from the fact that no laws made them *necessary* developments. But those lessons themselves are shrouded in obscurity. We might even say that the lessons that can be given by the Japanese '68 are *themselves* obscure: obscure lessons, whose teaching is neither obvious nor easy to grasp. In a sense, and as I mentioned in the introduction to this volume, we are by now excessively informed about what took place at the level of archival history, and yet we are no more aware of *what happened* than ever. Why did '68—the long '68—manage to take hold in history, to mark a point of divergence, when '55 did not? Why do we trace so many of our cultural-political developments on the left to this moment? What does it *mean* that we continue to do so today, that the generation of '68 has also been placed in such a starring role as opposed to other generations?

Concretely, this book *answers* none of these questions because they cannot be answered. They cannot be answered but only responded to, made actual in our moment. What we have inherited is a received

1 Althusser, *Écrits sur l'histoire (1963–1986)*, Paris: Presses Universitaires de France, 2018, 279.

history, an accomplished fact, of '68—at least, what we believe to be the "reality" of '68—but what we rarely have available to us is the educational encyclopedia that '68 is and was, a living historical entity that breathes and that can speak to us, if we choose to arrange ourselves in such a way as to make it one part of our own lives.

From Melancholy to Politics

In some sense, the greatest danger to the contemporary potential of '68 as thought comes not from its enemies, who have always hated an emancipatory politics, but from the center-liberal *faux amis* of the global '60s. These "false friends" remind us: what a glorious time it was, we thought we could change the world, ah, we were so young and naïve. It is this melancholic disposition and affective structure of selective nostalgia that is the real enemy of the emancipatory aims of '68 as a still-existing figure of thought. Psychoanalytically speaking, we might situate melancholy in terms of "the ego's warring over the object of loss, such that the loss itself becomes the dominant feature and not the lost object."[2] In other words, to have lost '68 becomes itself the testament, it becomes a meta-commemoration of the very fact of having something to commemorate, of sharing this discursive space of *enjoyment*—and I think we can only see it as a kind of enjoyment—generated by collectively re-remembering the loss of another possible historical outcome. Importantly, therefore, what that emancipatory drive actually aimed at has been completely erased; in its place, all that is left is a vague yearning that only serves to complement the resignation within which it is situated.

If the post-'68 liberal has negatively inherited the lessons of '68 and conveniently sealed them away into the dungeon of youth and audacity, the post-'68 post-radicals have often inherited only the worst aspects of that grand, participatory culture that they created out of their drive for rebellion and emancipation from all enclosure, hierarchy, and authority. But as the late Mark Fisher presciently put it in 2013:

> If you want to consider the most telling drawback of horizontalism, though, think about how it looks from the perspective of the enemy.

2 Juliana Schiesari, *The Gendering of Melancholia*, Ithaca: Cornell University Press, 1992, 11.

> Capital must be delighted by the popularity of horizontalist discourses in the anti-capitalist movement. Would you rather face a carefully co-ordinated enemy, or one that takes decisions via nine-hour "assemblies"? . . . The danger is not any more, nor has it been for some time, excessive dogmatic fervor on our side. Instead, the post-68 left has tended to overvalue the negative capability of remaining in doubt, scepticism and uncertainties—this may be an aesthetic virtue, but it is a political vice. The self-doubt that has been endemic on the left since the 60s is little in evidence on the right—one reason that the right has been so successful in imposing its programme.[3]

As Nagasaki Hiroshi teaches us in this volume apropos of the Zenkyōtō drive for "self-negation," it is not sufficient simply to repeat the demands of '68 again—the results of '68 also contain elements of what would become our neoliberal culture of today. We have to think, as Nagasaki teaches us, "in the ruins" of '68 in order to be able to inherit its spirit of rebellion in our own time.

Today, the memory of '68 is recuperated precisely in order to be emptied out, divested of all content, and transformed into an "encyclopedic" element to be arrayed on the shelf of history alongside other trivia. In a sense, the danger that 1968 will be simply transformed into that most reactionary concept—*archival data*—is already too late to reverse. Today, the dominant mode of historical scholarship, even in the realm of intellectual history, is limited to what Foucault dismissively called "the history of ideas," leaving open the possibility that such a historian works *without any idea whatsoever*, merely cataloguing a series of ideas (political statements, fashion choices, who slept with whom) as if they existed on one planar surface, all the better to ensure that periods of radical transformation are re-remembered and conjured up, only to be sealed forever into the domain of trivia. What Foucault posed against this sad conception, surely now the dominant mode of historical inquiry, is what he called "the history of thought," in which the historical nature (the past in the present) of thought itself would be harnessed as a key to *our thought*, restored to the realm of the concept and entered into for its danger and immediacy.

The "sad passions," in the Spinozist sense, are best exemplified by the fascinated liberal: the respectable and "decent" intellectual who outsources

---

3 Mark Fisher, "How to Kill a Zombie: Strategizing the End of Neoliberalism," *openDemocracy*, July 2013.

their enjoyment to the excesses of '68, but who equally ensures that we never attempt to critically and affirmatively *inherit* '68 as our own problem. Thus, 1968 in Japan, or even the entire period of 1955 to 1973, characterized by a New Left determined to make a revolution in their time, is a global story, and it is also our story. As Marx reminded the German reader of *Capital*, who dismissed it as a book concerned only with "English" problems, "*De te fabula narratur*—it is *of you* that the story is told." The Japanese '68 ought to be rescued from its "interpreters," who make of it a trivial religious fable about the inevitable demoralization of excess, the passion and regret of the "fanatic," or the centrist fear of audacity. In Japan and elsewhere, 1968 is not just some historical data, or a fashionable aesthetic phenomenon; it is a living reminder that politics is possible, and that the overturning of the existing order is the only task of politics as such. A politics of commitment alone leads nowhere but to the eventual aestheticization of politics, in the Heideggerean style or Jünger's fascist solution. But, equally, a politics that sees behind every commitment against the status quo the premature sign of downfall can never call itself emancipatory. If there is a post-'68 condition, one that has come to dominate, it is encapsulated by a phrase of Paul Virilio, who once remarked that "the globalization of liberalism is a deterrence of politics." What he meant by this is not simply that liberalism—having been globalized since the oil crisis of the 1970s and the global revenge of market-based solutions to the social sphere—had become the dominant form of politics; rather, he meant something much more terrifying, that we have gradually come to realize: that liberalism in its contemporary global form is the *elimination of politics as such*. Today, politics—and we could do well to simply take the definition here of Jacques Rancière—is not everywhere, but *nowhere*. What we have instead are small, market-type transactions of *doxa* undertaken within the liberal consensus. Any attempts to suspend or puncture this consensus meet with responses of terrifying ferocity.

The sheer domination of liberalism is evident not only at the economic level—in its pursuit of free markets—but also at the cultural level, where resistance to the dominant order has largely been replaced with a primarily gestural politics, in which one is encouraged to say anything, or affirm any identity within the social order, so long as there is a tacit agreement that nothing structural ever changes, eliminating the space of politics in favor of an enclosed game of affect and sentiment, to which the force of capital is utterly indifferent. Alain Badiou has frequently invoked the formulation *il vaut mieux un désastre qu'un "désêtre"*—better a disaster than "non-being." Given the abyss of contemporary liberal identity politics and their full appropriation by capital and the state, it is surely better today to risk even disaster than the form of "non-being" represented by the liberal, census-driven, parliamentary consensus for the eternalization of the status quo—a form of life, politics, and thought bereft of everything, even an idea.

Marx once wrote that "petit-bourgeois socialists either become eclectics or adepts of existing doctrines,"[4] a point that might easily describe the post-'68 post-radicals and the post-'68 liberals, both positions whose "use" of '68 serves only to ensure its inaccessibility to our own thought, and certainly to render it useless as a tool for rebellion again in our time. After all, as Lenin once proclaimed, "Let anyone name even one eclectic in the republic of thought who has proved worthy of the name rebel!"[5]

The Remains of the Day

On March 31, 1970, nine members of the Communist League–Red Army Faction hijacked a domestic flight (Japan Airlines Flight 351) from Tokyo, taking the 129 passengers hostage and demanding passage to North Korea, which they hoped to use as an "international base" for revolutionary work. Five of the members, along with some of their partners, have lived in North Korea, under unclear conditions, since then.

The group, whose primary members continue to reside in North Korea, surfaced and returned to the public eye in 2017, when a website calling itself the Yodogō Nihonjin-mura or [Yodogō Japanese village] emerged. Lately, there has been some interest in Europe and North America for the aftermath of the Yodogō incident and its main protagonists, principally due to the emergence of the website of their small commune in North Korea. Ostensibly, it is a simple self-advertisement for a number of older people, stuck in the Cold War world, who would like to go home to Japan in their twilight years, and who hope, therefore, for diplomatic normalization between Japan and North Korea. In this limited sense, it is not a particularly edifying or even interesting phenomenon.

4 Marx, *The Class Struggles in France, 1848–1850*, in *Marx/Engels Collected Works*, Vol. 10, New York: International Publishers, 1978, 126.

5 Lenin, "Book Review: Karl Kautsky. *Bernstein und das sozialdemokratische Programm. Eine Antikritik*," in *Collected Works of V.I. Lenin*, Vol. 4, Moscow: Progress, 1964, 200. I owe knowledge of this exceptional formulation of Lenin to Ken Kawashima.

But what appeared to surprise people most, when this site was circulated in the media, was the fact that the website was not full of apologies or gestures of repentance for their participation in the struggle. Editorial commentary mostly noticed that the members gave concise political histories of themselves, with simple explanations and nonchalant factual overviews:

> Influenced by the Haneda struggle and the deaths of activists at the hands of police.
> Joined Red Army Faction.
> Participated in hijack action.
> Presently in North Korea.

At this point, there is little outcry against them, but perhaps more telling with regard to our current moment is the curiosity generated by their mere existence and especially by their seeming lack of repentance. In general, it seems that the main interest in such histories is simply to give us the right to say, with proud detachment: what weird people, they really believed in what they were doing!

Clearly, the militants in the Yodogō incident mistakenly believed that individual acts of armed force could simply and directly spark world revolution. They had a tremendously naïve conception of geopolitics. They had a substitutionist understanding of their own relative importance and political acumen.

But that is not what causes such unease today. What causes unease in relation to them is the fact they are not from another world, but from ours. Even after all this time, all this failure and defeat, there they are, on our same Earth, reading, thinking, writing, living, wondering about what is to be done in this world we all inhabit.

Perhaps we can say that it was a strange choice they made, a terrible choice, a mistake. Definitively, it was at least a failure, and although not a particularly bloody episode for the time, it amounted to quite little. But what truly fascinates and makes them an object of curiosity is something else: the fact that, seemingly, they did not give up. Today, not to give up on a politics—even "not to give up" in general—is something totally pathologized by the generalized liberal consensus of all of our societies. The person who does not give up, who refuses to accept the new and "decent" status quo, who refuses to use the alibi of history to invalidate their youth or their commitment, is a criminal, a lunatic, a fanatic.

Instead, it is betrayal that is now normal. Our culture of capitalist triumph and liberal consensus tells us that you should betray your ideas and you should betray justice itself for the sake of "development" and "maturity." You should betray your friends in the name of "professionalism." Above all else, you shouldn't do anything "extreme." If you do something "extreme," you should adopt a new standpoint later: a standpoint of melancholy and inverted nostalgia for your ideas, all coupled to an overriding new notion that you were always already wrong, because you were young.

I think it is just the opposite, and we should uphold in broad terms the struggles of these "Red Years" not as a pyrrhic victory but as *a defeat that must structure a new politics*, because there is functionally no difference between the world they rejected—of imperialism, racism, the rapacious and murderous logic of capital, of oppression, against the liberation of peoples and nations—and our world. In fact, although we make every possible cultural gesture to convince ourselves that it is not true, we actually live in the same world as them. This moment—its history, its sacrifices, its failures—should produce for us, in Yutaka Nagahara's terms, the exigency to "deliver politics to this defeat." And to be able to make such a "delivery," we must first refuse to exoticize these years of struggle as some simple cultism or collective delusion. Instead we must stick to an old adage from the long global '60s: *There is no guilt in revolution—to rebel is correct.*

Contributors

Gavin Walker is Associate Professor of History at McGill University. He is the author of *The Sublime Perversion of Capital* (Duke University Press, 2016), the editor of *The End of Area: Biopolitics, Geopolitics, History* (Duke, 2019, with Naoki Sakai), the editor and translator of Kojin Karatani's *Marx: Towards the Centre of Possibility* (Verso, 2020), and a member of the editorial collective of *positions: asia critique*. His new book, *Marx et la politique du dehors*, is forthcoming from Lux Éditeur.

Hiroshi Nagasaki is a critic and theorist of politics, one of the foremost thinkers of the 1968 generation, and was a leading participant in the Zenkyōtō movement, following the 1960 Anpō struggle. He is the author of dozens of works in Japanese, including the legendary *Hanranron* [Theory of Rebellion] (1969), *The Phenomenology of Politics, or the Pilgrimage of the Agitator* (1977), *The 1960s Generation of Rebellion* (2010), *Philosophy of Revolution: Towards the 1968 Rebellion* (2012), and many more.

Yoshihiko Ichida is Professor in the Graduate School of Intercultural Studies at Kobe University. He is the author of numerous books and articles in French and Japanese, including *Althusser: Philosophy of Conjunction* (2010) and *Contemporary Thought and Politics: Capitalism, Psychoanalysis, Philosophy* (co-edited with Kenta Ohji, 2016).

Setsu Shigematsu is Associate Professor in the Media and Cultural Studies Department at the University of California, Riverside. She is the author of *Scream from the Shadows: The Women's Liberation Movement in Japan* (University of Minnesota Press, 2012) and the co-editor of *Militarized Currents: Towards a Decolonized Future in Asia and the Pacific* (University of Minnesota Press, 2010). She is also the director of *Visions of Abolition* (2011), a documentary about the prison industrial complex and women's activism in the prison abolition movement.

Hidemi Suga is a literary critic and the author of dozens of books in Japanese, including, most recently, *Revolutionary, All Too Revolutionary: On the History of the 1968 Revolutions* (2003), *1968* (2006), *An Anti-Nuclear Intellectual History: From the Cold War to Fukushima* (2012), and *The Jargon of the Emperor System* (2015).

Koizumi Yoshiyuki is Professor in the Graduate School of Core Ethics and Frontier Sciences at Ritsumeikan University, the author or editor of dozens of works in Japanese in the domain of philosophy, and the translator of major works by Deleuze and others. Recent books include *The Philosophy of Life and Illness* (2010), *Deleuze and Madness* (2014), and *A New History of Madness* (2018).

Chelsea Szendi Schieder is Associate Professor in the Faculty of Economics at Aoyama Gakuin University in Tokyo, Japan. She writes about protest, women, violence, and Japan for academic and general audiences, with articles in *Dissent, World Policy Journal,* and the *Funambulist.* Her book on the gender dynamics in the campus-based New Left in Japan, entitled *Co-Ed Revolution: The Female Student in the Japanese New Left*, is forthcoming from Duke University Press. She is also engaged in the radical practice of raising a kid.

Yoshiko Shimada is a lecturer on 1960s and '70s Japanese art and politics at the University of Tokyo's College of Arts and Sciences. She has been called "Japan's premier feminist and antiwar artist." Shimada's works are held by the New York Public Library, Tokyo Metropolitan Museum of Photography, Keio University Art Center, Kyoto Seika University, and City University of New York. She has had solo exhibitions in Japan, Hong Kong, the Philippines, Canada, and the United States, and her work was included in the 2002 Gwangju Biennale in South Korea. Shimada curated the Bigakkō portion of the Anti-Academy exhibit at the John Hansard Gallery in 2013–14.

William Marotti is Associate Professor in the Department of History at UCLA and chair of the East Asian Studies MA Interdepartmental Degree Program. He teaches modern Japanese history with an emphasis on everyday life and cultural-historical issues. Marotti's *Money, Trains, and Guillotines: Art and Revolution in 1960s Japan* (Duke University Press, 2013) addresses politics in Japan in the 1960s through a focus on avant-garde artistic production and performance. His current book project, "The Art of Revolution: Politics and Aesthetic Dissent in Japan's 1968," analyzes cultural politics and oppositional practices in Japan, with particular emphasis on 1968 as a global event.

Yutaka Nagahara is Professor of Economic History at Hōsei University. He is the author of *The Emperor System and Peasants* (1989), *We, the Defective Commodities* (2008), *The Rabble on the Streets: Introduction to the Political Economy of Damaged Life* (2015), and *Defeat and Reminiscence* (all in Japanese). He is one of the principal translators into Japanese of Slavoj Žižek, Alain Badiou, Fredric Jameson, and others. He is also a regular contributor to many leftist journals as well as literature and poetry journals in Japan, and is currently working on the reassessment of Marx's *Grundrisse* and *Capital*, seen from the viewpoint of the theoretical contrast between Deleuze, Negri, and Badiou, forthcoming under the title *The Strategraphy of Capitalism*. He is also working on the reconstruction of *The Debate on Japanese Capitalism* with Gavin Walker and others.

Alberto Toscano is Reader in critical theory and Co-Director of the Centre for Philosophy and Critical Theory at Goldsmiths, University of London. He is the author of *The Theatre of Production: Philosophy and Individuation Between Kant and Deleuze* (2006), *Fanaticism: On the Uses of an Idea* (2010), and (with Jeff Kinkle) Car*tographies of the Absolute* (2010). He has sat on the editorial board of the journal *Historical Materialism: Research in Critical Marxist Theory* since 2004 and is series editor of the Italian List for Seagull Books.

Bibliography

Adorno, Theodor. "Sociology and Psychology—II." *New Left Review* 1: 47, 1968, 79–97.

Akasegawa, Genpei. *Tsuihōsareta yajiuma*. Tokyo: Gendai Hyōronsha, 1972.

———. *Zenmen jikyō!* [Total Confession!]. Tokyo: Shōbunsha, 2001.

Akatsuka, Yukio. *Geba an goten* [Gewalt/Underground Dictionary]. Tōkyō: Jiyū Kokuminsha, 1970.

Akiyama, Yōko. "Yan to ani" in *Ribu shi shi nōto*, 15–24. Tokyo: Inpakuto Shuppankai, 1993.

Althusser, Louis. "Le Courant souterrain du matérialisme de la rencontre," in *Écrits philosophiques et politiques*, Vol. 1, ed. François Matheron, 539–79. Paris: Stock/IMEC, 1994.

———. *Réponse à John Lewis*. Paris: F. Maspero, 1973.

———. *Être marxiste en philosophie*. Paris: PUF, 2015.

———. *Écrits sur l'histoire (1963–1986)*. Paris: Presses Universitaires de France, 2018.

Andrews, William. *Dissenting Japan: A History of Japanese Radicalism and Counterculture from 1945 to Fukushima*. London: Hurst & Company, 2016.

Apter, David and Nagayo Sawa. *Against the State: Politics and Social Protest in Japan*. Cambridge: Harvard University Press, 1984.

Avenell, Simon Andrew. *Making Japanese Citizens: Civil Society and the Mythology of the Shimin in Postwar Japan*. Berkeley: University of California Press, 2010.

Badiou, Alain. *Peut-on penser la politique?* Paris: Seuil, 1985.

———. *Manifesto for Philosophy*, trans., ed. Norman Madarasz, Albany: SUNY Press, 1999.

———. *Ethics: An Essay on the Understanding of Evil*, trans. and intro. Peter Hallward. London: Verso, 2001.

———. *Theory of the Subject*, trans. and intro. Bruno Bosteels. New York: Continuum, 2009.

———. *The Communist Hypothesis*, trans. David Macey and Steve Corcoran. New York: Verso, 2010.

Balibar, Étienne. "Ich, das Wir, und Wir, das Ich ist: Le Mot de l'esprit" in *Citoyen sujet et autres essais d'anthropologie philosophique*, 209–41. Paris: PUF, 2011.

Bensaïd, Daniel. "Alain Badiou and the Miracle of the Event" in *Think Again: Alain Badiou and the Future of Philosophy*, ed. Peter Hallward. London: Continuum, 2004.

Bidet, Jacques. "Kōzō Uno and His School: A Pure Theory of Capitalism" in *Critical Companion to Contemporary Marxism*, eds. Jacques Bidet and Stathis Kouvelakis, HM Books Series. Leiden: Brill, 2007.

Boltanski, Luc and Eve Chiapello. *Le nouvel esprit du capitalisme*. Paris: Gallimard, 1999.

Carr, E.H. *The Russian Revolution: From Lenin to Stalin, 1917–1929*. London: Palgrave Macmillan, 1979.

Davis, Angela. "Rape, Racism and the Myth of the Black Rapist" in *Women, Race and Class*, 172–201. New York: Vintage, 1983.

Deleuze, Gilles. *Desert Island and Other Texts 1953–1974*, ed. David Lapoujade, trans. Michael Taormina. Los Angeles: Semiotext(e), 2004.

———. (with Félix Guattari). "May. '68 Didn't Happen" in *Two Regimes of Madness: Texts and Interviews 1975–1995*, ed. David Lapoujade, trans. Ames Hodges and Mike Taormina. New York: Semiotext(e), 2006.

Deutscher, Tamara. "E.H. Carr—A Personal Memoir." *New Left Review* I: 137, 1983, 78–86.

Dowsey, Stuart, ed. *Zengakuren: Japan's Revolutionary Students*. California: Ishi Press, 1970.

Evans, Sara. *Personal Politics: The Roots of Women's Liberation in the Civil Rights Movement and the New Left*. New York: Vintage, 1980.

Freeman, Jo. *The Politics of Women's Liberation: A Case Study of an Emerging Social Movement and its Relation to the Policy Process*. New York: McKay, 1975.

Frölich, Paul. *Rosa Luxemburg: Ideas in Action*. London: Pluto Press, 1972.

Fujii, Kazuyuki. *Minshu shūchūsei to tōnai minshushugi*. Tokyo: Aoki Shoten, 1978.

———. *Shakai shugi to jiyu*. Tokyo: Aoki Shoten, 1976.

Fuwa, Tetsuzō. "Kagaku-teki shakai shugi ka'tagen shugi'ka—'Takguchi riron' no hihanteki kenkyū." *Zenei*, January 1979.

Havens, Thomas. *Fire Across the Sea: The Vietnam War and Japan, 1965–1975*. Princeton: Princeton University Press, 1987.

Hiraoka, Masaaki. *Jazz yori hoka ni kami wa nashi* [There is no God but Jazz]. Tokyo: San'ichi shobo, 1971.

Hirokazu, Mizunuma, Matsuoka Takeshi, and Iwao Yoshinobu, eds., *Akasegawa Genpei no geijutsu genronten: 1960 nendai kara genzai made* [*The Principles of Art* by Genpei Akasegawa: From 1960s to the present]. Chiba: Chiba National Museum of Art, Japan, 2014. Exhibition catalog.

Hirotani, Shunji. *Gakusei undō nyumon*. Tokyo: Nippon Seinen Shuppansha, 1971.

Honda, Nobuyoshi. "Haneda tōsō no igi to tatakai no tenbō." *Zenshin* 337, October 30, 1967. Reprinted in Honda, *Honda Nobuyoshi Chosakusen I*, 341–2. Tokyo: Zenshinsho, 1975.

Ichihiro, Itari (Isato, Kazutomo). *Kibun wa komyunisuto—Miyamoto gichō no taijin wo motometa Tōdaiinsei no hanron*. Tokyo: Nitchū Shuppan, 1986.

Iijima Aiko. "From Personal Experience to Political Activism in the 1970s: My view of Feminism" in *Gender, Nation and the State in Modern Japan*, eds. Andrea Germer, Vera Mackie, and Ulrike Wöhr; trans., annotated, and intro. Germer, 290–306. New York: Routledge, 2014.

——. "Onna ni totte sabetsu wa nini ka" in *Shiryō Nihon ūman ribu shi*, Vol. 1, eds. Mizoguchi, Saeki, and Miki. Kyoto: Shōkadō, 1992.

——. *"Shinryaku = sabetsu" no kanata e: aru feminisuto no hansei*. Tokyo: Inpakuto Shuppankai, 2006.

Imai Yasuko. "Bunto to feminizum" [Bund and feminism] in *60-nen Anpō to Bunto o yomu* [Reading 1960 Anpō and the Bund], Vol. 2, ed. Shima shigeo kinen bunshū kankō-kai, 74–9. Tokyo: Jōkyō Shuppan, 2002.

Imaizumi Yoshihiko. "Daini no teigen" [The second proposal]. Reprinted in *Kikan* 11, 1980, 43–4.

——. "Karera no sore wa shiso dentatsu no gu ni narieruka?" [Can Theirs Be a Tool for Communication?] *Keisho* 8 (1963).

Ishii Kyoji. Editor's note, *Minshushugi no Shinwa*, new ed., eds. Tanigawa Gan, Yoshimoto Takaaki, and Haniya Yūkō. Tokyo: Gendai Shichōsha, 1966.

Jones, Jason Christopher. "The Black Panther Party and the Japanese Press." *Journal of African American Studies* 21: 1, 2017, 42–70.

Kanō Akihiro and Kanō Kenta. *Omae no 1960-nendai o, shinu mae ni shabettoke!* [Tell Me Your 1960s Before You Die!]. Tokyo: Potto shuppan, 2010.

Kanō Mikiyo, ed. *Ribu to iu kakumei: kindai no yami o hiraku* [The Revolution Called Ribu: Uncovering the Darkness of Modernity]. Tokyo: Inpakuto Shuppankai, 2003.

Kara Jūrō. *Karagumi: Jōkyō Gekijō zenkiroku: shashinshū*. Tokyo: PARCO Shuppan, 1982.

Kashiwazaki Chieko. *Taiyō to arashi to jiyū o: Gebaruto Rōza tōsō no shuki* [Sun and Storm and Liberty: Notes from Gewalt Rosa's struggle]. Tokyo: Nōberu Shobō, 1969.

Katō Michinori. *Rengō Sekigun Shōnen A* [The United Red Army: Boy A]. Tokyo: Shinchōsha, 2003.

Katō Mitsuko. "Tōdai zenkyōtō no naka de" [In the University of Tokyo Zenkyōtō] in *Joshi zengakuren gonin no shuki* [Notes from Five Female Zengakuren], eds. Yamasaki Yoshiko, Katō Mitsuko, Kuwabara Yōko, Yoshiwara Isami, and Aoyama Michiko. Tokyo: Jiyū kokumin-sha, 1970.

Kawakami Tōru and Ōkubo Kazushi. *Sobyō: 1960-nendai*. Tokyo: Dōjidaisha, 2007.

Kawani Hiroshi. "*Keisho* ni yosete" [About *Keisho*]. *Bijutsu techo nenkan* 347, October 1971.

Kazuko Tanaka. "The New Feminist Movement in Japan, 1970–1990" in *Japanese Women: Feminist Perspectives on the Past, Present and Future*, ed. Kumiko Fujimura-Fanselow and Atsuko Kameda, 342–52. New York: Feminist Press at the City University of New York, 1995.

Kim, Hong N. "Deradicalization of the Japanese Communist Party Under Kenji Miyamoto." *World Politics* 28: 2, 1976, 273–99.

Kobayashi Tetsuo, *Kōkō Funsō 1969–1970* [High School Strife 1969–1970], Chūkōshinsho, 2012.

Koizumi Hiroshi. *Fukushi to hinkon no keizairon*. Tokyo: Shin Nihon Shubbansha, 1973.

Koizumi Yoshiyuki. "Seishin eisei no taisei no seishin shi—1969 wo megutte" in *Taisei no rekishi—Jidai no sen wo hikinaosu*, eds. Amada Jōsuke, Yōhei Kadosaki, and Satoshi Sakurai, 205–32. Kyoto: Rakuhoku Shuppan, 2013.

———. "The Theory and History of the Subject's Domination of the Self and Others: From Althusser to Foucault." *Zinbun* 47, 2017, 81–9.

Lazarus, Sylvain. *Anthropology of the Name*, trans. Gila Walker. London: Seagull Books, 2015.

Lenin, V.I. *Letters on Tactics*. Moscow: Progress Publishers, 1970.

Maro Akaji. *Kaidanji Maro Akaji ga yuku: ukiyo tawamurete sōrō*. Tokyo: Asahi Shimbun Shuppan, 2011.

Marotti, William. "The Art of the Everyday, as Crisis: *Objets*, Installations, Weapons, and the Origin of Politics." *boundary* 2: 42: 3, 2015, 79–96.

———. "Challenge to Music: The Music Group's Sonic Politics" in *Tomorrow Is the Question: New Directions in Experimental Music Studies*, ed. Benjamin Piekut, 109–38. Ann Arbor: University of Michigan Press, 2014.

———. "Japan 1968: The Performance of Violence and the Theater of Protest." *American Historical Review* 114: 1, 2009, 97–135.

———. *Money, Trains, and Guillotines: Art and Revolution in 1960s Japan*. Durham: Duke University Press, 2013.

Maude-Roxby, Alice. *Anti-Academy*, ed. Joan Giroux. Manchester: John Hansard Gallery, 2013.

Mihashi Toshiaki. *Rojō no Zenkyōtō 1968* [Zenkyōtō 1968 on the Streets]. Tokyo: Kawade Shobō Shinsha, 2010.

Miki Sōko. "Kugitsukerareta nichijo—kaji" [Housework—the daily pounding of the nail] in *Onna no Shisō* [Women's Thought], ed. Saeki Yōko, 198–230. Tokyo: Sanpō, 1972.

Miyahara Yasuharu, ed. *Akai fūsen arui wa mesu okami no yoru*. Tokyo: Akaifūsen, 1963.

Miyaoka Maki. "Zengakuren dai 30 kai teiki zenkoku taikai deno sei no sabetsu = haigaishugi to tatakau ketsuihyōmei" in *Onna no shisō*, ed. Saeki Yōko. Tokyo: Sanpō Books, 1972.

Miyazaki Manabu. *Toppasha—Sengoshi no kage wo kake nuketa 50 nen*, Vol. 1. Tokyo: Gentōsha, 1998.

Mizoguchi Akiyo, Saeki Yōko, and Miki Sōko, eds. *Shiryō Nihon ūman ribu-shi, 1969–1972* [Documents of Japan's History of Women's Lib], Vol. 1. Kyoto: Shōkadō Shoten, 1992.

———. eds. *Shiryō Nihon ūman ribu-shi, 1972–1975*, Vol. 2. Kyoto: Shōkadō Shoten, 1994.

———. eds. *Shiryō Nihon ūman ribu-shi, 1975–1982*, Vol. 3. Kyoto: Shōkadō Shoten, 1995.

Moore, Joe. *Japanese Workers and the Struggle for Power 1945–1947*. Madison: University of Wisconsin Press, 1983.

Mori Setsuko. "Shisō shūdan esu.ii.ekkusu soshikiron? Josetsu" [An Organizational Theory for Thought Group SEX? Introduction] in *Shiryō Nihon ūman ribu shi*, Vol. 1, eds. Mizoguchi, Saeki, and Miki. Tokyo: Shōkadō, 1992.

Nagahara Yutaka. "The Corporeal Principle of the National Polity: The Rhetoric of the National Polity, or, the Nation as Memory Machine," trans. Gavin Walker, in *Perversion in Modern Japan: Experiments in Psychoanalysis and Literature*, eds. Nina Cornyetz and Keith Vincent. New York: Routledge, 2009.

———. "We, the Defective Commodity-Beings." *Journal of International Economic Studies* 26, 2012.

Nagasaki Hiroshi. *Hanranron*. Tokyo: Sairyūsha, 1991.

———. "Gimanteki de jiyūna gerira" [The deceptive and free guerrilla] in *Kessha to Gijutsu* [Association and Techne]. Tokyo: Jōkyō Shuppan, 1971.

———. *Seiji no genshōgaku aruiha ajiteta no henrekishi*. Tokyo: Tabata Shoten, 1977.

Nagata Hiroko. *Jūroku no bōhyō: hono to shi no seishun* [Sixteen Graves: The Spring of Fire and Death]. Tokyo: Sairyūsha, 1982.

Nakajima Yoshio Syndrome Committee, ed. *Nakajima Yoshio Syndrome: Art is Always the Next Possibility*. Tokyo: Nakajima Yoshio Syndrome Committee, 2015.

Nakamura Takafusa. *The Postwar Japanese Economy: Its Development and Structure, 1937–1994*, 2nd ed. Tokyo: University of Tokyo Press, 1995.

Nakanishi Natsuyuki. "Chokusetukodo-sha no hokoku" [Report of direct action]. *Keisho* 8, 1963.

Nakano Masao. *Gebaruto jidai since 1967–1973* [The Days of Gewalt since 1967–1973], City: Chikuma Bunko, 2011.

Nakano Tetsuzō, Takaoka Kenjirō, and Fujii Kazuyuki, eds. *Sutarin mondai kenkyū jyosetsu*. Tokyo: Ōtsuki shoten, 1977.

Nanako Kurihara. *Ripples of Change*. New York: Women Make Movies, 2010.

Negri, Antonio. "Une ouverture vers le deleuzisme: Conversation avec Antonio Negri" in Aloocha Wald Lasowski, *Althusser et nous*. Paris: PUF, 2016.

Nihon Kyōsantō Chuō I'inkai Shuppan-kyoku. *Seinen gakusei undō to Nihon Kyōsantō*. Tokyo: Nihon Kyōsantō Chuō I'inkai Shuppan-kyoku, 1973.

———. *Shin hiyorimi shugi hihan*. Tokyo: Nihon Kyōsantō Chuō I'inkai Shuppan-kyoku, 1973.

Ochiai Emiko. *The Japanese Family System in Transition: A Sociological Analysis of Family Change in Postwar Japan*. Tokyo: LTCB International Library Foundation, 1997.

Oda Makoto, Kazumi Takahashi, and Nobuhiko Matsugi, eds. *Henkaku no shisō wo tou*. Tokyo: Chikuma Shobō, 1969.

Oguma Eiji. *1968*, 2 Vols. Tokyo: Shin'yōsha, 2009.

Ōhara Kimiko. *Tokeidai wa takakatta* [The Clock Tower Was Tall]. Tokyo: San'ichi Shobō, 1969.

Okada Takahiko. "Bigakkō—waza no shutoku ni gendaibijutsu no ariyo o saguru" [Bigakkō—Search for the existence of contemporary art through mastering skills]. *Bijutsu techo nenkan* 343, 1971.

Onna-tachi no ima o tō kai, ed. *Zenkyōtō kara ribu e* [From Zenkyōtō to Lib]. Tokyo: Inpakuto Shuppankai, 1996.

Ōta Motoko. "Onna-tachi no zenkyōtō undō" [Women's Zenkyōtō Movement] in *Zenkyōtō kara ribu e*, ed. Onna-tachi no ima o tō kai, 71–9. Tokyo: Inpakuto shuppankai, 1996.

Ozawa Yōko. "Ūman ribu no hachijyū nendai." *Gendai no me* 17: 1, 1976, 136–43.

Panagia, Davide. *Ten Theses for an Aesthetics of Politics*. Minneapolis: University of Minnesota Press, 2016.

Postone, Moishe. *Time, Labor, and Social Domination: A Reinterpretation of Marx's Critical Theory*. Cambridge: Cambridge University Press, 1993.

Rancière, Jacques. *Disagreement: Politics and Philosophy*. Minneapolis: University of Minnesota Press, 1999.

———. "Ten Theses on Politics" in *Dissensus: On Politics and Aesthetics*, ed. and trans. Steve Corcoran, 27–44. London: Continuum, 2010.

Rawls, John. *A Theory of Justice*. Cambridge: Harvard University Press, 1971.

Ribu Shinjuku Sentā shiryō Hozon kai, ed. *Ribu Nyūsu, kono michi hitosuji—Ribu Shinjuku Sentā shiryō shūsei* [Ribu News—Collected Documents of the Ribu Shinjuku Center]. Tokyo: Impakuto Shuppankai, 2008.

Rōdōsha Kyōiku Kyōkai, ed. *Kimi no Okinawa*. Tokyo: Gakushū no Tomo Sha, 1971.

Ross, Kristin. *May '68 and Its Afterlives*. Chicago: University of Chicago Press, 2002.

Saeki Yōko. "Oto naki ko o umu—mikon no haha" in *Onna no shisō*, ed. Saeki, 166–96. Tokyo: Sanpō Books, 1972.

Sakaguchi Hiroshi. *Sakaguchi Hiroshi Kakō* [Sakaguchi Hiroshi Poems], Tokyo: Asahi Shinbunsha, 1993.

Satoshi Sakata. *Ie to Mura Shakai no Seiritsu* [The Formation of Family and Village Society]. Tokyo: Kōshi Shoin, 2011.

Sawara Yukiko. "The University Struggles" in *Zengakuren: Japan's Revolutionary Students*, ed. Stuart Dowsey, 136–92. Berkeley: Ishi Press, 1970.

Sekihara Riichirō (Sakaki Toshio and Ueda Koichirō). "Zeneitō no soshiki gensoku no seimei—Taguchi Fukuji-shi no 'Minshuchūsei-ron' no ma daiten." *Akahata hyōron tokushū-ban*, November 1977.

Shibata Hiromi and Akane Saburō. *Zenkyōtō*. Tokyo: Kawade shobō shinsha, 2003.

Shima, Hiroko. "Onigiri nyōbō" [Rice Ball Wife] n *Bunto shinshi* [A Personal History of the Bund], eds. Shima Shigeo and Shima Hiroko, 222–62. Tokyo: Hihyōsha, 2010.

Shimada, Yoshiko, ed. *From Nirvana to Catastrophe: Matsuzawa Yutaka and his "Commune in Imaginary Space."* Tokyo: Ota Fine Arts Tokyo, 2017. Exhibition catalog.

Shigematsu, Setsu. "The Japanese Women's Liberation Movement and the United Red Army: A Radical Feminist Response to Political Violence." *Feminist Media Studies* 12: 2, 2012, 163–79.

———. "Rethinking Japanese Feminism and the Lessons of Ūman Ribu: Toward a Praxis of Critical Transnational Feminism" in *Rethinking Japanese Feminisms*, eds. Julia C. Bullock, Ayako Kano, and James Welker, 205–29. Honolulu: University of Hawaii Press, 2017.

———. *Scream from the Shadows: The Women's Liberation Movement in Japan.* Minneapolis: University of Minnesota, 2012.

———. "Tanaka Mitsu and the Women's Liberation Movement in Japan: Towards a Radical Feminist Ontology." PhD diss., Cornell University, 2003.

———. "The Women's Liberation Movement and Sexuality in Japan" in *Routledge Handbook of Sexuality Studies in East Asia,* eds. Mark McLelland and Vera Mackie, 174–87. New York: Routledge, 2014.

Steinhoff, Patricia. "Death by Defeatism and Other Fables: The Psychodynamics of the Rengo Sekigun Purge" in *Japanese Social Organization,* ed. Takie Sugiyama Lebra. Honolulu: University of Hawaii Press, 1992.

Suga Hidemi. *68-nen.* Tokyo: Chikuma Shobō, 2006.

Sunenaga Tamio. *Ikinobiru tame no komyūn* [Commune for Survival]. Tokyo: San'ichi Shobō, 1973.

Suwa Kanenori, Iwama Yūki, Kageura Junko, Kojima Ryō, Takekawa Shingo, and Taguchi Fukuji. *Garan ga akakatta toki—1970 nendai wo kangaeru.* Kasugai: Chūbu Daigaku, 2012.

Taguchi Fukuji. *Senshinkoku kakumei to tagenteki shakai shugi.* Tokyo: Ōtsuki Shoten, 1978.

———. "Senshinkoku kakumei to zeneitō soshikiron—'Minshuchūsei' no soshiki gensoku wo chūshin ni." *Gendai Shisō* 29, 1977.

Takahashi Hiroshi. *Tuwamono-domo ga yume no saki* [The Rank and File Has Surpassed the Dream]. Tokyo: Ueitsu, 2010.

Takeda, Haruhito. *Kōdo seichō* [High Economic Growth], Shirīzu Nihon kingendaishi 8 [Japanese Contemporary History Series 8]. Tokyo: Iwanami Shoten, 2008.

Takei Teruo. *Sō toshite no gakusei undō* [The Movement of the Student as Stratum]. Tokyo: Supēsu Kaya, 2005.

Tanaka, Kakuei. *Nihon Rettō kaizōron.* Tokyo: Nikkan Kōgyō Shinbunsha, 1972.

Tanaka, Mitsu. "Benjo kara no kaihō (kaisei ban)" [Liberation from the Toilet (rev.)] in *Doko ni iyou to riburian: Tanaka Mitsu hyōgenshū,* 265–80. Tokyo: Shakai Hyōron Sha, 1983.

———. "Benjo kara no kaihō (kaisei ban)" in *Inochi no onna-tachi e: torimidashi ūman ribu ron* [To Women with Spirit: Toward a Disorderly Theory of Women's Liberation], 333–47. Tokyo: Pandora, 2001.

———. "Declaration of the Liberation of Eros," Appendix I in "Tanaka Mitsu and the Women's Liberation Movement in Japan," Setsu Shigematsu. trans. Shigematsu. PhD diss., Cornell University, 2003.

———. "Erosu kaihō sengen" [Declaration of the Liberation of Eros] in *Ribu Shinjuku Sentā shiryō shūsei,* ed. Ribu Shinjuku Sentā Shiryō Hozonkai, 7–8. Tokyo: Inpakuto Shuppankai, 2008.

———. "Naze 'sei no kaihō' ka: josei kaihō e no mondai teiki" [Why "Sex Liberation"—Raising the Problem of Women's Liberation], Appendix II to Shigematsu "Tanaka Mitsu and the Women's Liberation Movement in Japan," trans. Shigematsu. PhD diss., Cornell University, 2003.

———. "The New Left and *ribu*" Appendix III to, "Tanaka Mitsu and the Women's

Liberation Movement in Japan," Setsu Shigematsu trans. Shigematsu, PhD diss., Cornell University, 2003.

———. "Shinsayoku to ribu" [The New Left and ribu] in *Inochi no onna tachi e: torimidashi ūman ribu ron* [To Women with Spirit: A Disorderly Theory of Women's Liberation]. Tokyo: Pandora, 2001.

———. "Tanaka Mitsu, *1968* o warau." *Shūkan kinyōbi* 781, December 25, 2009, 22–30.

Tanigawa Gan. "Eikyu bakannsushugi" [Permanent vacation-ism]. *Katen* 7, 1963, 25.6. *Kō-hō no Kai.*

———. *Tanigawa Gan no shigoto* [Works of Tanigawa Gan], 2 vols. Tokyo: Kawade Shobō, 1996.

Tanner, Leslie B. *Voices from Women's Liberation*. New York: Mentor, 1970.

Tatakau Onna. "Okinawa to shofu" [Okinawa and Prostitutes] in *Tatakau Onna Metoroparichen kikanshi* 5, 1971. Reprinted in *Shiryō Nihon ūman ribu shi*, Vol. 1, ed. Mizoguchi, Saeki, and Miki, 159–60. Kyoto: Shōkadō, 1992.

Thompson, Edward P., *William Morris: Romantic to Revolutionary*, rev. ed. Stanford: Stanford University Press, 1955.

Tōdai Tōsō Zengaku Kyōtō Kaigi, ed. *Kishi no ue ni wareware no sekai wo*. Tokyo: Aki Shobō, 1969.

———. ed., *Toride no ue ni ware ware no sekai*. Tokyo: Aki Shobō, 1969.

Tokoro Mitsuko (Mimie Tomano). "Yokan sareru soshiki ni yosete" [The Organization to Come] in *Waga ai to hangyaku*, 149–59. Tokyo: Shinmu Shobō, 1969.

Tokuyama Haruko. "Watashi ga ugokeba yo no naka ga hitori bun ugoku to iu jikkan" [The feeling that if I move one more person in the world is moving] in *Zenkyōtō kara ribu e*, ed. Onna-tachi no ima o tō kai. Tokyo: Inpakuto Shuppankai, 1996.

Tokyo Daigaku Zengaku Daigakuinsei Kyōgikai—Tōdai Tōsō Kiroku Kankō I'inkai, ed. *Tōdai henkaku e no tatakai*. Tokyo: Rōdō junpōsha, 1969.

Toscano, Alberto. "The Sensuous Religion of the Multitude: Art and Abstraction in Negri." *Third Text* 23: 4, 2009.

Tozuka Hideo et al. *Nihon niokeru 'Shin-Sayoku' no Rōdō Undō* ["New Left" Labour Movements in Japan], 2 vols. Tokyo: Tokyo Daigaku Shuppankai [University of Tokyo Press], 1976.

Tronti, Mario. *Operai e Capitale*. Torino: G. Einaudi, 1966.

———. *La Politique au crépuscule*, trans. Michel Valensi. Paris: Éditions de l'Éclat, 2000.

Tsubouchi Yūzō. *1972—"Hajimari no Owari" to "Owari no Hajimari"* [1972: "The End of the Beginning" and "the Beginning of the End"]. Tokyo: Bunshun bunko, 2006.

Uehara Yoshihiro. *Roji no ko*. Tokyo: Shinchōsha, 2017.

Ueno Chizuko. "Nihon no ribu: sono shisō to haikei" [Japan's *ribu*, its thought and background] in *Femininzumu riron*, ed. Inoue Teruko, Ueno Chizuko, Ehara Yumiko, and Amano Masako, Vol. 1 of *Nihon no feminizumu*. Tokyo: Iwanami Shoten, 1994.

Uno, Kathleen. "Death of 'Good Wife, Wise Mother'?" in *Postwar Japan as History*, ed. Andrew Gordon, 307–22. Berkeley: University of California Press, 1993.

Vaneigem, Raoul. *The Revolution of Everyday Life*. Oakland: PM Pres, 2012.

Walker, Gavin. "Tanigawa Gan and the Poetics of the Origin." *Positions* 25: 2, 2017, 351–87.

———. *The Sublime Perversion of Capital: Marxist Theory and the Politics of History in Modern Japan*. Durham: Duke University Press, 2016.

Watanabe Hitomi. *1968 Shinjuku*. Tokyo: Machikarasha, 2014.

Yamada Kaiya (Pon). *Ai amu hippī: nihon no hippī mūbumento '60–'90*. Tokyo: Morito shuppan, 2013.

Yamamoto Yoshitaka. "Barikeedo fūsa no shisō" [Thoughts on the Barricade Blockades] in *Chisei no hanran* [Rebellion of the Intellect]. Tokyo: Zeneisha, 1969.

———. *Watashi no 1960 nendai* [My 1960s]. Tokyo: Kin'yōbi, 2015.

Yanase Norihisa, ed. *Senretsunaru taiken—Shuppan no jiyū to Nihon Kyōsantō*. Tokyo: Nitchū Shuppan, 1984.

Yonezu Tomoko. "Barikêdo wo kugutte" [Passing through the barricades] in *Zenkyōtō kara ribu e*, ed. Onna-tachi no ima o tō kai, 120–3. Tokyo: Inpakuto Shuppankai, 1996.

Yoshida Yoshikiyo. *Gensuikyō de nani ga okotta ka*. Tokyo: Nitchū Shuppan, 1984.

Yoshimoto Takaaki. "Nihon shihonshugi ni sakarau 'dokuritsu-sayoku'" ["Independent Left" against Japanese Capitalism] in *60-nen Anpo / Miike Tosō: 1957–1960*, ed. Nishii Kazuo. Tokyo: Mainichi Shinbunsha, 2000.

Zenkyōtō Hakusho henshū iinkai. *Zenkyōtō hakusho* [White Paper on the Zenkyōtō]. Tokyo: Shinchōsha, 1994.

Documents

Action Memorandum, President's Question about Visit of Nuclear Carrier Enterprise to Sasebo, Japan, Philip J. Farley and Samuel D. Berger to Undersecretary of State Nicholas Katzenbach, January 22, 1968, 2, Secret, DNSA, doc. JU00877.

Airgram A-309, "The Japanese Student Protest Movement," American Embassy Tokyo to Department of State, April 10, 1969, 19, Limited Official Use, CF 1967–1969, Def 7 Japan-US, 3, Confidential, in Confidential Files: Japan, reel 10, 0248–0278.

Airgram A-1098, "The Enterprise Visit," February 23, 1968, 15, Secret, in Confidential U.S. State Department Central Files: Japan 1967–1969, reel 3, 0318–0334.

East Asia Interdepartmental Group, NSSM 5: Japan Policy, undated, 25, attachment to Jeanne W. Davis, NSC Memorandum, April 28, 1969, Top Secret, DNSA, doc. JU01061.

Imaizumi Yoshihiko. Personal diary of 22 November 1962. Imaizumi archive, Tokyo.

Nonpori hansen shūdan. "Nonpori no gakuyū ni uttaeru" [Appeal to Nonpolitical School Friends], July 2, 1968. Tōdai tōsō shiryo shū. National Diet Library, Tokyo.

"Notes of the President's Meeting with Senator Dirksen and Congressman Ford," January 30, 1968. Top Secret. LBJ Library, Austin, TX.

"A Statement on the Current Difficulties at the University of California Study Center, Mitaka-Tokyo, Japan," November 10, 1969. Hans H. Baerwald papers, 1945–1991. UCLA Library Special Collections, Box 22, Folder 22.

Telegram 4763, "Enterprise Visit to Sasebo," January 17, 1968, 3, Secret, DNSA, doc. JU00876.

Index